About the Book:

"The timesharing system field has matured to the point where one can recognize many common design goals and common design and implementation concepts and mechanisms being used in a wide variety of systems. My goal in this book is to present a selection of these common concepts and techniques which seem to me to have become central to timesharing system design. My approach is to present the selected concepts through illustrative examples, both to show the motivation for their development and to introduce basic implementation mechanisms.... Each example discussed is covered only in the detail necessary to understand the concept under consideration and the problem it solves or raises."

From the Preface

With the above purposes in mind, the author has divided the book into three distinct sections. Part One consists chiefly of introductory material; Part Two discusses the motivation for the development of hardware concepts such as memory addressing and allocating techniques; and Part Three introduces software concepts for the organization, allocation, and protection of user and system resources. It is important to note that the author has emphasized the close interconnection between hardware and software oriented parts throughout the book.

Special features include: the detailed coverage of principal aspects of operating system design; the use of examples from two computer systems, XDS-940 and GE-645 Multics, for the bulk of its illustrations; and a cogent discussion of the difficult, and often misunderstood, concept of segmentation.

TIMESHARING SYSTEM DESIGN CONCEPTS

McGRAW-HILL COMPUTER SCIENCE SERIES

RICHARD W. HAMMING
Bell Telephone Laboratories

EDWARD A. FEIGENBAUM
Stanford University

Timesharing System Design Concepts

Richard W. Watson
Shell Development Co.
and
Department of Electrical Engineering
  and Computer Science
University of California, Berkeley

McGraw-Hill Book Company

New York   St. Louis   San Francisco   Düsseldorf
London   Mexico   Panama   Sydney   Toronto

Timesharing System Design Concepts

Library of Congress Catalog Card Number 74-119831
68465

1 2 3 4 5 6 7 8 9 0   M A M M   7 9 8 7 6 5 4 3 2 1 0

This book was set in News Gothic by The Maple Press Company, and printed on permanent paper and bound by The Maple Press Company. The designer was Edward Zytko; the drawings were done by John Cordes, J. & R. Technical Services, Inc. The editors were Richard F. Dojny and Cynthia Newby. Stuart Levine supervised the production.

TO THE ILLUSION AND ITS SUSTAINER

Preface

The timesharing system field has matured to the point where one can recognize many common design goals and common design and implementation concepts and mechanisms being used in a wide variety of systems. My goal in this book is to present a selection of these common concepts and techniques which seem to me to have become central to timesharing system design. My approach is to present the selected concepts through illustrative examples, both to show the motivation for their development and to introduce basic implementation mechanisms. This approach was taken because it has been my experience, in observing my own reasoning process and that of others, that once an idea is understood in a particular context, it can easily be recognized in other variations, generalized and extended. This is generally the approach used to learn programming; one learns about basic ideas such as identifiers, subroutines, loops, and conditional statements in the context of one language, and then he can easily learn and criticize how these ideas are handled in another language.

To help the reader remain focused on the concept, rather than getting bogged down in the details of its several possible implementations, I have taken many of the illustrations from two systems, the XDS-940 timesharing system developed at the University of California, Berkeley,* and the GE-645 Multics timesharing system developed at MIT.† Illustrations are also taken from other systems when they are felt to be useful. Each example discussed is covered only in the detail necessary to understand the concept under consideration and the problem it solves or raises.

* W. W. Lichtenberger and M. W. Pirtle, A Facility for Experimentation in Man-Machine Interaction, *AFIPS Conf. Proc. Full Joint Computer Conf.*, vol. 27, pp. 589–598, 1965.
† F. J. Corbato and V. A. Vyssotsky, Introduction and Overview of the Multics System, *AFIPS Conf. Proc. Full Joint Computer Conf.*, vol. 27: pp. 185–196, 1965.

The XDS-940 and Multics systems were chosen because (1) they encompass much of the experience gained on earlier systems, (2) they have had a major influence on the development of concepts in this field, and (3) they reflect important differences in design philosophy.   Another reason for choosing the XDS-940 is that this is the system with which I have worked closely.   It is a medium-scale system.   The goal of XDS-940's research designers was to develop a very flexible system which would support, in a highly interactive manner, a limited number of users.   Most user programs are less than 16,000 words in size.   The system concepts as developed at the University of California have lead, with further development, to commercial success of the XDS-940 in industrial and government laboratories and, possibly more important, to wide use by firms marketing timesharing services.   The Multics system is a large-scale system.   The goal of its research designers was to develop a system which would serve the computing needs of a large community of users working on a broad spectrum of problems.   Two of the specific goals are to provide the user with a large machine-independent virtual memory and to allow single copies of procedures and data to be shared with great generality.   This project has been very fertile in conceptual developments.   Concepts developed in the Multics effort appear in the XDS-940 and have strongly influenced other systems such as the IBM 360/67 system.   Other important work such as the System Development Corporation timesharing system,* MIT CTSS system,† or Dartmouth system‡ is not discussed here because many of the concepts developed there can, for our purposes, be illustrated by examples from the XDS-940 and Multics systems.

Again, my goal is to cover basic concepts and mechanisms, and I feel that after understanding the material presented here, the student can easily gain access to the literature for further details or implementation variations.   Similarly the professional in the field can, after studying the material in this book, more easily understand the literature, the reference manuals for the system in his installation, or the systems possibly being proposed for his installation.

This book is intended primarily for two groups:

1   those people who as part of their responsibilities or out of curiosity desire to understand developments and underlying principles in time-shared systems but are not likely to have to design, implement, or directly maintain such systems and,

* J. Schwartz, E. G. Coffman, and L. Weissman, A General Purpose Time-sharing System, *AFIPS Conf. Proc. Spring Joint Computer Conf.*, vol. 25, pp. 397–411, 1964.
† F. J. Corbato et al., An Experimental Time-sharing System, *AFIPS Conf. Proc. Spring Joint Computer Conf.*, vol. 21, pp. 335–344, 1962.
‡ R. F. Hargraves, Jr., and A. G. Stephenson, Design Considerations for an Educational Time-sharing System, *AFIPS Conf. Proc. Spring Joint Computer Conf.*, vol. 34, pp. 657–664, 1969.

2   those people who are or expect to be involved in the design, implementation, or maintenance of timeshared systems.

The strategy and background required for reading this text are different for
these two groups.   The background required of the first group is some
limited programming experience and some general knowledge of the structure of a digital computer.   The strategy for reading the book for this group
is probably to skip the more detailed examples, although the book has been
written to be self-contained.

The background required of the second group is more extensive.
This group must be able to take the concepts presented here and visualize
or recognize the detailed programming mechanisms by which they would
be implemented.   This requirement implies some familiarity with hardware
logic and register operations and some familiarity with common data-struc-
turing techniques such as elementary list processing, table construction and
lookup, and last in, first out lists.   The strategy for this group is probably
to read through the material once fairly rapidly, skipping over detailed
examples, then to return for further careful reading.   Using the analogy of
learning a foreign language, the first group is like those requiring a reading
knowledge of the language and the second like those who must be able
to read, write, and speak it.

Looked at another way, this text is intended to be read at the following levels:

1   As a primary text for an undergraduate course in software system
design and as a supplementary text for an advanced programming
course which introduces system design concepts.   The background
expected would probably be completion of an advanced programming
course.   As exercises, the student would be expected to program
mechanisms required in an operating system such as queue-handling
disciplines or table-manipulation routines.

2   As a supplementary text for an undergraduate course in machine
organization.   When used for such a course, the student should have
had programming experience.   The book can be used at this level not
only in colleges and universities but at technical institutes and in
industrial training courses.

3   As a primary text for a graduate course in system design and programming.   When used at this level, the material would be supplemented with additional reading from the published literature or documentation of a specific system to give more familiarity with problems
in the design of implementation details.   The students would also be
expected to produce detailed system or system-module designs as term
projects, in order to develop facility at extending, modifying, and
criticizing the concepts presented.

4   As a primary or supplementary text for a graduate course in machine
organization.   In this context, this book is particularly useful in introducing software concepts.   It clearly shows the need for hardware de-

signers to be familiar with software concepts if they are going to design effective systems.

5 As a self-study text for professional programmers, installation and EDP managers, and hardware designers who wish to solidify their experience and sharpen their ability to read the published literature. At this level the book can be easily read thoroughly if the reader has some system-programming or hardware experience. The book is still highly valuable to less experienced professionals who can skip some of the more detailed examples. At this level it is useful to those professionals, particularly managers, who want to understand the basic concepts being used in the systems they work with or manage.

The text has three parts and seven chapters which are organized as follows. Part One consists of introductory material organized in one chapter. Chapter 1 briefly reviews the motivation for the development of timesharing systems, outlines the major design goals and problems of such systems, and introduces a few basic concepts required throughout the book.

Part Two introduces hardware concepts found to be important in machines to be used for timesharing. This part is organized in three chapters. Chapter 2 discusses in some detail the motivation for the development of concepts of memory addressing and allocation, such as base registers, paging, and segmentation, and presents examples. Chapter 3 discusses communication concepts in the design of memory-bus and control organizations, in handling input/output, and in handling communication with remote terminals. Chapter 4 considers hardware memory and control protection, the interrupt system, and microprogramming as an approach to control-unit design.

Part Three introduces software concepts for the organization, allocation, and protection of user and system resources and considers other important design topics. This part is organized into three chapters. Chapter 5 discusses problems of scheduling and allocation of the hardware processors and memory. Protection mechanisms implemented in software are also discussed. Chapter 6 discusses the goals of file-system design, such as easy access, sharing, and protection, and the concepts evolved to meet these goals. The handling of input/output operations is discussed in further detail, and the interface to the user is also briefly presented. Chapter 7 discusses the importance of considering measurement, evaluation, reliability, recoverability, and maintenance from the early design stages. The concepts evolving in these areas are presented.

There is a comprehensive bibliography on timesharing at the end of the book.

In courses on system programming, the material in Part Two would probably be used unsupplemented by additional reading or exercises. The material in Part Three would be used with additional examples from the system available to the students and with programming or design exercises. In graduate courses, the material would be supplemented with additional reading from the literature.

In courses on machine organization, the material in Part Three would probably be used unsupplemented by additional reading. The material of Part Two might be supplemented by carrying the illustrations into more hardware detail and would be supplemented with material for those other important topics not covered in this text such as data-path and register organization, arithmetic algorithms, control design, and so forth.

The material in this book is very closely related to two of the courses recommended by the ACM curriculum committee in the report Curriculum 68, published in the March 1968 issue of the *Communications of the ACM*. These related courses are I4, Systems Programming, and A2, Advanced Computer Organization. The book also is related to course I3, Computer Organization, and contains important material considered in course I1, Data Structures. Courses giving background useful in reading this book are B1, Introduction to Computing, and B2, Computers and Programming. This book is also related to course I11, System Design, in Arden's suggested Ph.D. programming curriculum.*

Although the book consists of hardware-oriented and software-oriented parts, the close interconnection of the two is emphasized throughout. In fact, this close connection makes it useful to introduce some important software concepts in the hardware discussions and vice versa. As technology changes and understanding grows, the line between hardware and software will shift, but the underlying concepts and problems will remain.

The concepts and mechanisms presented in this book have in general not been developed by the author. All credit for these timesharing developments belongs to those whose works are referenced. In instances where my development closely parallels that of a particular author, I have given explicit reference by name. In other areas the original material which is the source of a local group of ideas is referenced by number. The set of references presented at the end of each chapter are, to the best of my knowledge, the sources of the material for that chapter. While all credit for the concepts presented belongs to others, I accept full responsibility for any misinterpretations or lack of clarity which may exist in the presentation.

I would like to express my appreciation to the many people who have contributed to the development of this book. My debt to workers in the timesharing and operating system field, as mentioned above, is evident throughout, particularly to the ideas of researchers formerly at the University of California and now with the Berkeley Computer Corporation, L. P. Deutsch,

---

* B. W. Arden, The Role of Programming in a Ph.D. Computer Science Program, *Commun. ACM*, vol. 12, no. 1, pp. 31–37, January, 1969.

B. W. Lampson, W. W. Lichtenberger, M. W. Pirtle, and their associates, and at
MIT, F. J. Corbato, R. C. Daley, P. J. Denning, J. B. Dennis, J. H. Saltzer, and
their associates.   I also thank M. D. Kudlick, E. A. Feigenbaum, J. H. Saltzer,
M. W. Pirtle, B. W. Lampson, and K. Siberz for their useful suggestions on
reading the manuscript.   I have had many valuable conversations with my
coworkers at Shell Development, particularly Dr. M. D. Kudlick.   Special
appreciation is extended to the management of Shell Development Company,
particularly Dr. Robert S. Miller and Mr. F. G. Stockton, who first recognized
the need for a work like this.   Some of the material in this manuscript first
appeared in a Shell Development technical progress report.   Appreciation is
extended to Shell Development for release of this material for publication.
Sharon Overton deserves special gratitude for being able to read my hand-
writing and for her careful typing of the manuscript.   Finally, I would like
to thank my wife and daughter for their patience during the writing of this
book.

                                                    RICHARD W. WATSON

Contents

Part TWO   HARDWARE CONCEPTS

Chapter 2
MEMORY, ADDRESSING, AND ALLOCATION   37

part ONE

Introduction

chapter ONE

Introduction to general purpose timesharing systems

1.1 MOTIVATIONS FOR TIMESHARING SYSTEMS

1.1.1 Introduction The designer of a system should have a clear understanding of the function his system is to perform and its probable impact
on the environment in which it operates. For this reason it is useful to
review the motivations which have led to the development of general purpose
timesharing systems and some of the characteristics of their impact on
their environment.

   Stored-program digital-computer systems have matured from giant
calculators to general purpose information-processing systems.[28]* The
capabilities of these systems have evolved from the simple storing, retrieving,
and transformation of numbers to the storing, retrieving, and transformation
of the most general types of symbol systems and structures. Some of
the implications of this evolution are reviewed in the sections to follow.

1.1.2 Early Batch Systems Early systems allowed the current user to
sit at the computer console during program debugging and running. As
these systems became more complex and as the number of applications
for their services grew, it became apparent that the speed mismatch between
the machine and the user made it uneconomical to operate with users sitting
at the operator's console. These systems could be more effectively utilized

---

* Numbered references appear at the end of each chapter. A comprehensive bibliography
is included at the end of the book.

if users prepared their programs away from the computer, punched them on some input media such as cards, and then submitted them to an operator for execution. The operator would *batch* together card decks for many users and load the batch in the card reader; then a program in the computer written to aid the operator, called an *operating system*, would read one program at a time into the machine and execute it, writing out the results on a printer.[29]   The operator would retrieve the printed output and return it along with the input card deck to the user.   The user's only contact with the machine was through a slot in the computer center where he deposited his cards and retrieved his output.

These *batch operating systems* have been continually refined to offer more services to the user and utilize expensive system resources more effectively.   The prime orientation of the design of these systems, however, has usually been toward effective utilization of computer resources rather than toward effective utilization of the user resource.   In the above mode of operation, there is a time lag between the input of a card deck to the computer center and the retrieval of the output.   This time lag, or *turnaround time*, in early systems could be anywhere from a couple of hours to several days, depending on the user's distance from the computer center, the program load mix of the computer center, and the computer-center system characteristics.

The batch mode of operation is suitable for many types of *production runs*, i.e., processing data against written and debugged programs that are used again and again.   A large amount of computing fits into this category. During program writing and debugging, this mode of operation has often proved unsatisfactory.[1]   A misplaced semicolon can cost several hours' or days' delay in program preparation.   Before the program can run, there are several delays of this kind.   Once the program is running, additional effort and more runs are required to remove logical errors.   This constant frustration in writing and debugging programs led to the initial motivation for timesharing.

1.1.3   The Timesharing Concept   The original researchers in the timesharing field reasoned that because human thinking processes and responses are slow relative to the logical and arithmetic capabilities of the computer, it should be possible to switch the computing resources from one user to another in such a way that each user could interact from a terminal online to the computer and think he had sole access.   The idea was to commute, or multiplex,* computer resources in time (timesharing) from one

---

* The term *multiplex* has been borrowed from the communications industry, where it is used to denote a line used to transmit multiple messages simultaneously.   The term multiplex, as used here, denotes the sharing of a computer-system resource in such a way as to create the effect of simultaneous use by several processes.

user to another. In contrast, a batch mode of operation forces a user to commute from one intellectual activity to another between computer runs. Early systems demonstrated the feasibility of the timesharing mode of operation. Powerful online editing and debugging facilities were written to satisfy the programmer's original goals of being able to correct programming errors as soon as they were discovered and to help discover them.[1,2]

1.1.4 Timesharing as an Aid to Problem Solving

The major benefit of timesharing, however, is not the reduction of programmer frustration but a new mode of machine-aided problem solving.[3] A user can sit down at a console and in one or more continuous sessions write, debug, and run his programs interactively. In this way, he usually can maintain better contact with his problem, be more imaginative in his trial solutions, and make more such trials because the risk in terms of time lost for unsuccessful efforts has been significantly decreased. Further, using the system's file-storage facilities, information can be updated and retrieved on demand and shared with others. These capabilities have modified the way existing problems are attacked and have opened up whole new areas to computer assistance. The timeshared mode of computer operation is not just an extension of previous batch-oriented computer aids to problem solving and decision making but a qualitative departure when used to full advantage. This qualitative change seems to result because human mental processes appear to be of two fundamentally different types, *intellectual* and *intuitive*. Intellectual processes are largely conscious and seem to proceed sequentially in an orderly fashion. These processes are modeled by conventional logical systems, e.g., completed mathematical proof. Intuitive processes, on the other hand, are largely unconscious, seem to proceed in parallel, and are not orderly but leap from insight to insight. The completed mathematical proof may be conscious, sequential, and orderly, but usually the process by which the mathematician arrives at the insight that the theorem is true and the outline of the proof is not orderly or fully conscious. These insights have the characteristic of appearing suddenly. Insight and intuition can be cultivated, but no procedure with which we are familiar seems able to guarantee their appearance. Intuition and intellect are both required. Intuition leads and suggests, and intellect checks, reviews, corrects, fills in the gaps, and communicates the results to others.

We have found it useful to view the function of the computer as an aid to the intellectual part of the problem-solving and decision-making process. Human intuition proposes a problem solution or decision, and the problem solver writes a computer program to aid his process of checking. With batch computing, the user pays a fairly high price in terms of time and effort to prepare and run each program. Since the problem solver wants to be sure this effort will produce useful results, in batch mode he invests heavily in analysis and checking before deciding how and whether to use the computer. Problem solving in batch mode appears to be biased toward intellect, analysis, and sequential thinking.

With a timesharing system, on the other hand, the user pays much less of a penalty for each hypothesis or trial which does not check out because he is closely coupled in time and may even be able to use graphical consoles for a man-computer dialogue more closely attuned to his information-processing needs. As a result, a timesharing mode of computer usage used to full advantage appears to allow freer reign to intuition. Thus, a timesharing mode of computer use can be qualitatively different from a batch mode of operation.

Some of the response gains achieved by timesharing systems over earlier batch systems have been recovered by newer batch systems. By using many system design techniques similar or identical to those described in this book, newer batch systems are often able to cut turnaround time to tens of minutes instead of hours. These newer batch-oriented systems also place more emphasis on sharing information files. As a result, users of these batch systems can also afford to experiment more freely and build more easily on each other's work.

1.1.5 Studies Comparing Timesharing and Batch Systems. What objective evidence supports these views on timesharing and problem solving? A number of studies have attempted to compare timeshared and batch modes of operation,[4,5] but this type of research is difficult to carry out. The batch mode in the studies was the older mode, with several hours' turnaround time. Our subjective feeling is that batch computing with more rapid turnaround, under 30 minutes, allows a mode of problem solving much closer to that available with timesharing.

Most of the studies were rather narrow in scope and tried only to determine relative costs between approaches to perform moderately difficult programming tasks requiring 40 to 60 hours to complete. The savings in man-hours to perform the tasks using timesharing were about 20 percent, or higher if the programmer was experienced with timesharing. The idea that experience in using a timesharing system is important in achieving maximum effectiveness should not be overlooked. This finding is what one would expect. It takes time and experience to develop new modes of problem solving to fully exploit a given set of tools. Timesharing users generally took more computer time to perform a programming task than required to write and debug the same program under a batch mode. The great variability in individual programmer performance—as much as 10 to 1—found among users of a given mode makes it difficult to set up controlled experiments.

The most interesting study we have seen is that performed by Gold,[5] who was interested not only in cost comparison but also in other factors associated with the problem solution, such as the problem-solving performance and user's feeling about level of problem understanding achieved through the timesharing and batch modes. Gold's experimental problem required students in a graduate course in industrial dynamics to develop a simulation model of the construction industry and its market. The student's task was to learn to operate the model, its parameters, and constraints and to devise new decision rules over those presently used in the construction industry to maximize the profit of a small independent builder in the market simulated. Gold's findings were similar to other studies with respect to man-hours and computer time required to solve the problem. That is, the timesharing users required an average of 16 man-hours to solve the problem versus an average of 19.3 man-hours for the batch users, but timesharing users required an average of 5.74 minutes of central-processing-unit (CPU) time versus an average of 1.25 minutes of CPU time for the batch users. Given fair wage rates for the type of men who would perform the task in a real situation and standard computer charges, the total cost would have been less for timesharing users. The most important findings from our point of view were that the timesharing users achieved a considerably higher profit level than the batch users and were evaluated to have a deeper perception and understanding of the problem. Much more research is required in human problem-solving behavior using various computer facilities before firm objective conclusions can be drawn about the relative merits of different systems, but studies such as Gold's and acceptance of timesharing by many classes of users tend to support the subjective motivations given above.

1.1.6 Sharing of Procedures and Data The concepts of sharing of data and procedures, whether on a timesharing or batch system, should be mentioned here.[6] Computer systems which can be accessed remotely acting as repositories of technology and general information for communities of users is a significant idea. Users have always been able to share procedures or data by obtaining a duplicate card deck, but there is a qualitative difference when the information can be directly accessed from many remote points. Systems which provide such facilities open new ways for groups of people to work together and new ways of increasing the effectiveness of individual efforts. Providing such facilities also adds complexities to the design and environment. Controlled access methods and backup must be developed. Certain levels of confidence must be developed in the shared procedures and data. To achieve this confidence may require review or other extra checking by persons other than the programmer before procedures or data can be widely shared. Technical journals and books which share and store technology are usually reviewed before release, in order to create confidence. Various levels of checking are also required of computer procedures and data to be widely shared. The term *program library* to describe a body of shared procedures has been in common use for some time, but, generally speaking, program libraries have not received the attention and care given to libraries of printed matter.

1.1.7 Summary We have pointed out that the motivation behind timesharing is to allow the user close contact with the machine by allowing him to interact online from a terminal and receive rapid responses to his requests for service.

The idea to be emphasized is that as speeds and scope of functions increase, important qualitative changes seem to take place which deserve careful consideration by the designer. Awareness of these qualitative changes may make the designer realize that he is solving a very different problem from the one he started out to solve. As a result, he must constantly adapt his design goals to the new situation. More rapid response and wider sharing of information made possible by timesharing and newer batch systems have opened up new modes of working and important new areas of computer application.

1.2 TYPES OF TIMESHARING SYSTEMS

1.2.1 Introduction The development of computer-operating systems has been motivated by a desire to achieve more effective utilization of total system resources. *Resource sharing* is the fundamental concept, and different classes of operating systems can be distinguished by looking at the relative importance given to basic computing system resources such as the following:

> arithmetic-logic unit
> main memory
> auxiliary memory (drums, disks, etc.)
> peripheral devices (card readers, printers, etc.)
> communications equipment (communication lines, remote terminals)
> compilers
> data files
> service and application routines
> programming and debugging time
> application user time

Because operating systems share, or multiplex, resources, many of which can be used only by a single process at a time, all operating systems could be called *timesharing* systems. This sharing of resources sequentially in time is the reason that such a wide variety of systems have been called timesharing.   In this book we restrict the term timesharing to those systems in which the user is a prime system resource and which effectively make the user a part of the system by allowing him to interact online (directly connected) from a terminal, receiving in turn rapid response from the system.   Since this definition permits a wide variety of systems to be called timesharing, further definition and classification are required.

1.2.2 Online File-maintenance and Retrieval Systems These systems are highly specialized and are characterized by the limited range of queries or additions which can be made to a common information base.   Most members of this class of system do not allow the users to generate procedures or to generate queries outside a fixed set.   Examples of this class are airline reservation systems, banking and stock information systems, and online inventory and control systems.   A well-known specific example is the American Airlines SABRE system.[7]

1.2.3 Special Purpose Timesharing Systems These systems are characterized by their ability to allow users to prepare and execute programs in a very limited number of languages (usually one).   They require very little file manipulation and simple file structures.   Examples of this class are the JOSS system at The Rand Corporation and the IBM Quiktran system.[8]

1.2.4 General Purpose Timesharing Systems These systems have several distinguishing features:

> 1   Their emphasis on rapid response to many users, usually 20 or more
>
> 2   The concurrent utilization of a wide variety of online software facilities such as text editors, debugging aids, assemblers, a variety of compilers, and a library of special application routines
>
> 3   Their provision of a file system using bulk storage which allows users to store, easily access, and share programs and data
>
> 4   An open-ended ability to add additional facilities

Examples of these systems are the MIT Multics (multiplexed information and computing service) system,[3] System Development Corporation Q-32,[2] and University of California at Berkeley XDS-940 system.[9]

1.2.5 Multiprogramming Batch Systems Allowing Online Access These systems, as mentioned earlier, can have the characteristics of general purpose timesharing systems but are distinguished in that the design goals of the resource-sharing algorithms tend to emphasize maximum rate of completion of programs prepared offline.[10]   As a result of this design emphasis, a given hardware configuration can usually respond adequately to fewer online users than if a different design goal had been chosen.   Other restrictions may also exist on the mode of program preparation and execution and handling of files.   Examples of this class of system are the operating systems supplied by computer manufacturers such as IBM's OS/360, UNIVAC's Exec 8, and GE's GECOS.

A major concept in common between newer batch-oriented systems and general purpose timesharing systems is their use of *multiprogramming*, or the concurrent execution of two or more processes in one computer system.   By concurrent we mean that two or more processes are in partial states of completion and that resources are being allocated among these processes to balance system loads and to meet response or throughput requirements.   In a system which is not muitiprogrammed, one job is completed before the next one begins.   The term multiprogramming is not to be confused with *multiprocessing*, which is used to designate a system having more than one central processing unit (arithmetic-logical unit).

All operating systems in the above classes share many fundamental concepts of design and implementation.   Understanding the detailed design concepts of any one class provides a solid foundation for the study of the others.   This book discusses basic design requirements and concepts of general purpose timesharing systems.   In the remainder of this chapter we define further concepts used throughout the book, give some design rules of thumb, and outline some requirements of timesharing systems which have developed from experience in the timesharing field.   None of the design guidelines or system requirements given in this chapter or in the remainder of the book should be taken as absolute "musts" for future systems but should be recognized as one man's engineering judgment and interpretation of the experience of others.   They can be usefully viewed, however, as one possible base from which to develop one's own design guidelines or to begin the study of a current design problem.

1.3   DESIGN REQUIREMENTS AND PROBLEMS

1.3.1   Intrinsic and Technological Problems

In thinking about design requirements and problems for a timesharing system, or any system, it is useful to classify the requirements and problems into two classes, as suggested by Saltzer,[11] *intrinsic* and *technological*.   Intrinsic requirements and problems are inherent in the problem itself.   Technological requirements and problems are inherent in the technology of a given point in time and arise as one tries to use this technology to meet the intrinsic requirements in some economic fashion.   That is, with appropriate advances in technology, technological problems either disappear or change.

The intrinsic problems associated with the design of a general purpose timesharing system center around communication between people, sharing of algorithms and information, and communication between man and computer. There are many users of a timesharing system. Each has his own store of data and procedures. Two important intrinsic problems are (1) to provide an easy ability to access, transform, and share information in a controlled manner and (2) to provide protection of this information against system and user errors.

The technological problems associated with a general purpose time-sharing system center around providing the above capabilities given a computer system consisting of several processors, main memory, auxiliary storage, and a variety of input/output (I/O) devices. The reason we are interested in sharing one computer system among many users is that this approach is the only way we can solve the intrinsic problems economically now and for the foreseeable future. The hardware and software required to provide users with the capabilities and ease of access desired are extensive. No one user or his computation can utilize all the facilities continuously. Therefore, one of the goals is to balance the utilization of all the resources over many computations. While one computation is performing I/O, another can be computing, and a third computation may be idle while the user at the console is thinking.

The concepts chosen for discussion in this book are either related to intrinsic problems, such as communication and sharing, or are related to technological problems existing now and for the foreseeable future, such as resource allocation among processes in concurrent execution. Many of the concepts presented which are now implemented in software may appear in hardware in future systems or be implemented with additional hardware aids, but the basic problems are expected to remain.

1.3.2 The File System and Information Sharing One of the jobs for the designer is to define the intrinsic goals the system is to meet, and one of the central goals is usually the creation of a file system which serves as the prime means for both private storage of information and sharing of information with others.

The file system is one of the most visible parts of the system to the user and one of the most important resources available to him. A *file* is a collection of related information with a name. Files are stored as strings of elements, characters, bits, computer words, and so forth. The intrinsic problems associated with the file-system design center around transforming, retrieving, protecting, sharing, and storing various kinds of information. The file system, in other words, should meet all the requirements of any good file system with which the reader may be familiar, whether it is implemented by manila envelopes and file cabinets, rotary card files, or other means.

To meet the requirement for flexibility and speed of storing and retrieval, devices are required which allow rapid access to the stored information. There should be sufficient storage space at reasonable cost so that the user does not feel severely restricted in what or how much he stores. To meet this requirement with present and foreseeable technology may require a hierarchy of devices, including removable media, such as disk packs and tape. The technological problems are to provide mechanisms so that little-used information can slowly percolate to slower-speed larger-capacity devices and to make all user functions totally hardware-independent. It is also desirable that the user be able to refer to his files by an alphameric name and without having to know where or how his files are stored.

The intrinsic and technological requirements for privacy and security are as important as those for flexibility and speed. Users should be able to share procedure and data files with each other in order to build on each other's work, but a given user should be able to specify who can access his files and what manner of access (read only, read/write, execute only) is to be allowed each person or group of persons. The latter requirement, of course, includes the ability to have private files which only the owner can access. Since the user or someone allowed access by the user may accidentally delete or otherwise damage a file, it is good practice to provide backup and means of recovery in such situations. The above requirements are intrinsic.

The problem of multiple copies of shared information must be considered. When one copy of a file is updated, it may not be easy to find all the other copies for similar updating. The obvious example is a procedure file which has had a logical error removed or has been improved in some other respect. There are also technological reasons, associated with saving main-memory and auxiliary storage space, for wanting to minimize the number of copies of shared information in the system. However, since sharing single copies of procedures and data with full generality may create technological problems, some compromise on how sharing is to be handled may be required at a given level of technology.

Because the files of all users are maintained on one collection of equipment, which should be assumed unreliable, there must be adequate means to ensure that users cannot access each other's files accidentally and that backup is provided in case the system software or hardware causes damage to a file. These problems are technological. The file system and other I/O are discussed in Chap. 6.

1.3.3 Communication with the System

The second set of intrinsic goals involves communication with the system and requires the designer's consideration of terminal design, transmission of information to locations remote from the computer, communication between terminals, and language design for communication with the system.

The latter requirement leads to the design of (1) a command language and interpreter for communicating with the system, (2) programming languages and translators in which to write procedures for controlling the processors, and (3) a library of other procedures to aid the above. The command language is used for communication with the file system, gaining access to the system and to such subsystems as text editors, debugging aids, language translators, and other system resources. The command language should be as carefully designed as any other language (see Chap. 6).

The design of terminals is a special subject in itself, and only the most general considerations are discussed in this book. Provision should be made in the design for attachment of a wide variety of terminals, e.g., typewriters, graphic terminals, remote computers, remote card readers, and remote printers, because the number of types of terminals available will continue to increase. Each terminal may require a different rate of information transmission. The transmission of information to remote locations is also a large subject, and only those logical concepts which appear to be of use to the digital and software system designer are introduced in Chap. 3. Software problems associated with terminal communication are discussed in Chap. 6.

1.3.4 Reliability and Recoverability A prime intrinsic goal is reliable operation. The user expects the system to operate correctly during its scheduled available times. If a failure should occur, the user expects recovery to be as smooth and fast as possible. That is, recovery should leave the system as close as possible to the state it was in at the time of the failure. The system designer must assume that hardware and software malfunctions will occur in spite of all the care taken in design and implementation. Therefore, it is obviously good design practice to build error-detection, error-location, and recovery procedures into both hardware and software from the earliest design stages. This important subject is discussed in Chap. 7.

1.3.5 Resource Allocation After the intrinsic goals have been clearly defined, the designer can determine how to achieve them with existing technology. The central technological problem is to share one hardware complex among many users, preferably keeping the sharing invisible to the users. A useful way of looking at the problem of sharing one hardware complex among many users has been described by Saltzer,[11] upon whom the following discussion and figure draw. To accomplish this sharing of resources, the timesharing-system designer can view the solution to his problem as taking one hardware system and by using software mechanisms creating an arbitrary number of independent *virtual*, i.e., pseudo or apparent, *processors* for assignment to the users of the system.   Each virtual processor has:

   1 An instruction set, consisting of the hardware processor instructions or a subset of them, and additional capabilities implemented in software

   2 Its own address space, which can be shared with other virtual processors

   3 Means of communicating with other virtual processors in the system

   4 Access to a large information-storage system called the *file system*

   5 The ability to communicate with a variety of I/O devices including remote terminals

   6 The capability of terminating itself

These virtual processors are hardware-independent in the sense that the user does not have to be aware of the system configuration given by number, kind, and speed of devices.   The virtual processors have all the characteristics of independent computer systems which can be coupled together. These processors have the advantage, however, that they are highly organized for easy use by the man at the console.   In its most general form, the above concept could allow each user to think he was working with a processor with characteristics oriented toward his problem.   In other words, each user would think he had his own set of hardware and his own operating system. The IBM CP/CMS system, implemented on a 360/67, illustrates one approach to the concept of virtual processors.[30]   Each user can specify his own System 360 configuration in terms of memory size and complement of I/O devices.   The control program creates such a virtual configuration for each user, by means of tables, and simulates I/O for the different devices by use of the disk.   The instruction set of all virtual machines is that of System 360.   Each user has his own operating system, which can run on a stand-alone 360, or he can develop his own operating system, although several users may share a given operating system.   This concept of the virtual processor is illustrated in Fig. 1.1.

After the virtual processors have been created, they must be allocated to the users and the system and total system usage must be accounted for.   Because not all the virtual processors can control the limited physical hardware modules simultaneously, techniques must be developed for scheduling or allocating physical hardware modules to them.   Some of the common design goals of the allocation routines are that they should allow each user to receive rapid response to his service requests, they should not in themselves be a serious drain on system resources, and they should assure that virtual processors which are temporarily idle do not contribute significantly to scheduling time or expend more critical resources, such as main memory, than necessary.   A virtual processor may require some memory

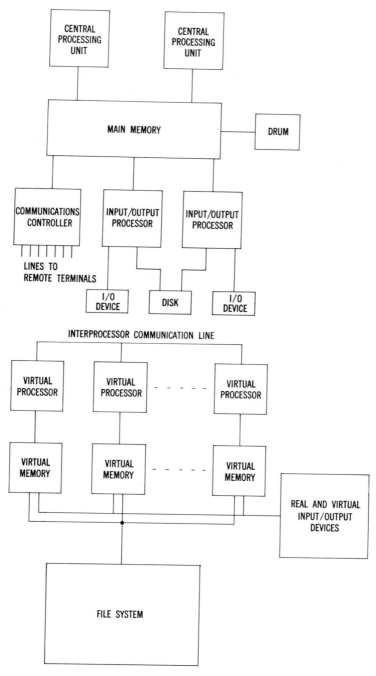

FIG. 1.1 (*a*) Typical hardware complex; (*b*) virtual-system complex.

for I/O buffers if it is idle waiting for an I/O operation to complete. Another important problem is to provide protection of one virtual processor from malfunction of other virtual processors and to protect the system against malfunctioning virtual processors. The creation and allocation of virtual processors is discussed further in Sec. 1.5 and Chap. 5.

1.3.6   System Overhead, Utilization, and Response Time   Time spent performing system functions, such as scheduling or protection, is commonly referred to as *overhead*. The term is very imprecise and is generally used in a way that implies that overhead is bad. We can use the distinction made earlier between intrinsic problems and technological problems to gain more insight into the idea of overhead. System functions performed to solve intrinsic problems increase the total effectiveness of the user. System functions performed to solve technological problems enable one user to share the cost of an expensive system with others. Thus, the user is able to have access to a much more powerful facility than he could afford on his own. System functions from either point of view are of value to the user.

The measure of time spent in system functions has no absolute meaning. One cannot say a 20 percent overhead is good or bad without examining the services provided and the given state of the technology. Overhead, however, can be a useful indicator for the designer when he attempts to assess the cost of his solutions to intrinsic and technological problems and to spot potential problem areas. One certainly wants to minimize, relative to a given level of service performed by the system, the time the machine spends on system functions, but one must recognize the usefulness of system functions in the total work of the user.

In a system in which there is much use of shared information, the time spent by the system in protection functions may have to be increased, but it is hoped that the use of shared information increases the user's productivity significantly. Similarly, using large virtual-memory spaces will increase the time spent in system routines but possibly to the total advantage of designers of large application systems. The determination of tolerable overhead is possible only with a sound weighing of all the costs associated with a computer operation, which must include the user. Different figures will be acceptable by different installations, depending on the nature of their workload.

A more meaningful measure of system utilization than overhead is system idle time. The amount of idle time is a direct indication of the total design balance of hardware-component performance characteristics with each other and with the resource-allocation algorithms. Nielsen's[12,13] simulations of early versions of the IBM 360/67 system showed clearly the idle time resulting from a poorly balanced system.

Besides overhead and equipment utilization, another parameter discussed frequently in conjunction with timesharing systems is *response time*. This is the time measured from some indication made by the user at a terminal requesting service, e.g., hitting the carriage-return key, to a reply by the system completing the request. The general mode of operation in a timesharing system finds a user thinking for several seconds, requesting service, waiting for a response, receiving the response, and then starting the cycle over again. The basic cycle of thinking, waiting for a response, and receiving a response is called a *transaction*. The statistic of main interest is the real work accomplished by man and machine together over a period of time. This statistic involves many subjective factors and is thus impossible to determine precisely. Response time is of interest because it is assumed that a given unit of useful work is made up of many transactions. Response time is thus assumed to be a measure related to total useful work during a console session.

Response time is a function of the number of users of the system, the nature of their requirements, the nature of the specific request, and the design of the system. The user generally expects very fast response for transactions requiring trivial processing and is more tolerant of slower response for transactions he knows to require more time.

Response time, like overhead, is a rather meaningless figure unless it is backed up with information about the circumstances under which it was measured. Average response time is more meaningful and is based on statistics gathered over a period of time. To be of much use the average response-time figure requires additional statistical information on the number of users and their requirements over the time of measurement.

Measurement of system component utilization (hardware-software) and time parameters is an engineering discipline which has recently been growing.[14-22] Only with the help of data that clearly show the information-flow bottlenecks can more economical and responsive timesharing systems be developed. Unless provision is made for measurement and evaluation of the design from the earliest design stages, many aspects of the design will prove difficult or impossible to evaluate at the point of completion. The designer wants to utilize all the potential information to make his design the best possible. Further, the designer wants to utilize the full experience attainable in the current design in future systems. This important subject is discussed in Chap. 7.

1.3.7 Interaction of Hardware and Software Another important job of the system designer is to determine what base hardware to provide for use by the virtual processors and what hardware functions to provide to aid the software in the creation, allocation, and protection of independent virtual processors, file systems, and other I/O. The close interaction of hardware and software cannot be overemphasized.   In the past, the design cycle consisted of hardware design followed by software design.   The hardware design was often performed by men who did not fully understand software and vice versa.   Such an approach no longer seems reasonable. General purpose timesharing and other modern computer systems can surely be more effectively designed by men familiar with both hardware and software.

Our experience indicates that it is better if the hardware-software design can proceed together for as long as possible, before the hardware design is firmly set.   This can be done by having the men responsible for the hardware and software designs settle on a preliminary set of hardware and software functional specifications.   The software designer can feed back information on what additional features may prove useful or what features appear to be bottlenecks.   The hardware designers in turn can determine which desired hardware features may not be economically or technically feasible with current technology or what additional features may be easy to provide.   These studies can utilize simulations or other measurement and evaluation tools.   Hardware features which have been found to be useful in timesharing systems are discussed in Chaps. 2 to 4.

1.4   SYSTEMATIC DESIGN GUIDELINES

1.4.1   Introduction   A timesharing system is a complex entity requiring the cooperation of many people both in its design and in its implementation. The design and implementation of complex hardware-software systems have often been less than satisfactory in the past, in terms of meeting performance goals and estimated completion dates.   From this past experience, a few guidelines and suggestions can be made for the design and implementation of future systems.[23-25]   Two principles seem to emerge as of particular importance:

1   The design should be functionally modular at several levels.
2   The design should use a few basic mechanisms to perform most of the work.

1.4.2   Modularity   Hardware designers have frequently been much better at following these two principles than software designers.   Consider the central processing unit (CPU), for example.   The major function of the CPU is to take information from memory, perform an arithmetic or other logical transformation on this information, and return the result to memory. One could theoretically construct the CPU from some minimal number of single storage cells and logical gates using theories of combinatorial (logic circuits without memory) and sequential (logic circuits with memory) circuit design.   Such a design would probably create a bewildering array of elements individually interconnected and would be difficult to understand. Instead, designers use a modular approach. The CPU is designed using a fixed number of registers, decoding modules, arithmetic-logic modules, and control modules. These modules are interconnected with a few well-defined data-transfer paths and control-signal paths. With such a modular approach, the flow of information and control is easily grasped. The modules are in turn constructed of nested submodules until one arrives at a small number of basic logical elements, such as AND gates, OR gates, and storage cells (flip-flops). Besides the high degree of modularity, one should recognize in CPU design the small number of basic control and data-transfer mechanisms used.

A system formed from the interconnection of clearly defined modules is usually easier to understand, modify, maintain, and evaluate. Experience indicates that each module should perform some function having a conceptual integrity.[25,26] Each module should have a small well-defined set of input and output signals or parameters. A module may in turn consist of submodules. The goal is to produce modules of such a size that one man can program and test the module in a specified time period. The concept of levels of modularity follows naturally because the user interacts with a virtual system, which in turn is created from a complex of physical devices. For example, consider the file-system design. Several functional levels translate the intrinsic goals into a particular technological implementation.[26] They are:

1 The level of the logical file system, where files are addressed by symbolic name and consist of logical records

2 The level of the physical file system, consisting of physical device addresses and physical records

3 The level for determining among the many requests for access the best schedule of accesses to utilize device and file characteristics and position

4 The level for addressing and performing transfers between individual devices

Each level consists of several functional tasks which must be performed to communicate with next higher and lower levels. If the designer can define the entire design in such terms, he has a much better chance of allocating tasks to others for further refinement and ultimately for implementation.

1.4.3 Small Number of Mechanisms Using as few mechanisms as possible to perform most of the work of the system is important both for design and for maintenance. For example, queues of requests for use of resources will exist in several places in the system: these queues can be handled with a uniform mechanism. Many tables exist in the system for recording the status of processes and devices: these tables can be handled in a uniform manner, in terms of access, error checking, and so forth.

1.4.4 Understanding the Design Ensuring that the design is going to be modular and utilize a minimum number of basic mechanisms seems easiest when there are a small number of key designers.[23] In fact, if the system is so complex that one man cannot understand the general functioning and interconnection of the major modules and submodules, there is danger that the design will slip out of control.

Experience also indicates that it is good practice not to begin implementation until the design has been criticized and documented.[23] Managers and designers are often impatient to produce working programs, but usually the best way to speed up the total system development is to go slow in the critical design stages.

There are usually several ways to perform a given function. A good designer must consider these different possibilities and be able to defend the particular choice made. If a designer cannot think of alternatives and clearly defend the design decision he has made, he may not fully understand the problem. It is easy to pass over tough problems or be unaware that lack of understanding exists, unless the discipline of design review and documentation before implementation is adhered to. The documentation must be clearly understandable by people with the level of technical skill of those who are going to maintain the system. Many levels of people need to use the specification—from designer, to implementer, to maintainer, to user. If a design cannot be clearly explained, it is probably not understood.

1.4.5 The Specification Process In describing the approach to the specification process in more detail, which we have found useful, we closely parallel the approach and discussion documented by Trapnell.[25] The design and specification process, in our view, are identical. The process is iterative and proceeds from general requirements to detailed specifications of individual modules. As one works at a higher-level function specification, many new sublevel problems become apparent. At each step one may have to go to more detailed levels of design to determine feasibility of a higher-level function, but one must be careful to remain at the detailed levels only temporarily. The sublevel problems should not be solved in detail at this point. We have seen designers go to more detailed levels too soon and get caught there, only to overlook many important general considerations.

The design specification consists of the following general levels:

> **1** External specification. This level clearly specifies the functions available to the user and the communications required between the user and the system.

2 Determination of major internal functional units required to provide the external functions.

3 Specification of interfunction communication conventions and mechanisms. This level specifies linkages, various tables, and so forth, and it is here that the number of mechanisms required can be controlled.

4 Program module specification. This level specifies all inputs required by each program, all outputs generated by each program, and all system-wide facilities, such as tables.

5 Detailed program coding.

Associated with all the above levels are performance and size requirements and a set of test procedures. Design of tests corresponding to each stage is a difficult and demanding job and must be given as high a priority as the actual implementation if all submodules are to be integrated easily into the final system.[25]

The specification should be hierarchical, starting with a general system description of how it works and how it communicates with the world; it should have a description of system facilities and major functional modules. A similar set of general descriptions of facilities and communications should exist for each function and subfunction, right down to the individual routine.

Throughout the design process, the designers must ask themselves whether they have thought of all situations and conditions which must be taken care of. When satisfactory documentation of one level is completed, detailed consideration can be turned to the next level. Parallel efforts may proceed occasionally as a major function is specified, but the overall serial philosophy of proceeding from the general to the particular can still be maintained. Consideration of lower-level functions will uncover changes required in higher-level specifications, thus necessitating an iterative approach through the total system design.

This kind of careful approach appears cumbersome to some programmers, but some discipline seems required if effective designs are to be developed, implemented, and tested.[23] One can provide machine aids to the specification process to print out information about module interconnection, table usage, and so forth. These machine aids can help determine the scope of changes necessary when any module or system facility is modified. Hardware designers use such facilities as part lists, wire-routing lists, and so forth. Software designers can also use such machine aids to good effect.

As the implementation proceeds, performance specification of some modules may not be met. The programmer may be able to see how, by not following system communication conventions, he can improve performance by more direct private communication with associated modules.

Such shortcuts should probably be avoided, and instead the system communication conventions should be reconsidered.

The design and implementation of a large system requires much more than technical skill in design and implementation; just as important are the managerial skills of organization and dealing with people.

1.5   THE PROCESS CONCEPT

1.5.1   The Virtual Processor and Process   Because of its importance throughout the book we examine the concept of a virtual processor and its related concept, the *process*, in more detail at this point.[11,27,31]

Every group of timesharing system designers we are familiar with seems to mean something different by these terms.   For example, one group tends to restrict the term processor to refer to the physical hardware processor but makes extensive use of the concept of a process.[9,27]   Another group uses the concept of virtual processors in discussing the entities created by their control program but rarely uses the term process.[30]   Yet another group uses both terms, often interchangeably.[3,11]   Basically what all the groups are trying to do is to develop a terminology for describing the concepts and mechanisms by which one set of hardware is shared among many uses and users, with each user thinking that he has sole control of the system.

The concepts of a processor and process can be defined rigorously in the context of a specific system.   However, to give such a definition would be to strip the concepts of much of their wider intuitive content. Therefore, in this book we take the approach that the concepts of a virtual processor and process are intuitive and will not be rigorously defined, even though the statements below have the form of rigorous definitions.   We give these definitions only as a starting point.   Further discussion to follow adds to the intuitive understanding of the concepts.

A *processor* is an entity which performs transformations of information.   More simply put, a processor executes commands or instructions.   A processor can (1) be implemented in software, such as an operating system, compiler, or command-language interpreter, or (2) it can be implemented in hardware, such as an arithmetic-logic unit (central processor) or an I/O processor, or (3) in the usage of this book it can be implemented as a combination of hardware and software functions.   A *process* is an entity which can control and define a virtual processor.   In the situation of interest here, the operating system is going to create an arbitrary number of virtual processors.   The entity which can define and control one of these virtual processors is a process.   A *program* is a sequence of instructions for a processor, but a process is an entity made up of one or more programs and contains the additional information which defines the virtual processor on which these programs run. The nature of this extra information is discussed below.

Because there is a one-to-one relationship between virtual processors and the processes which define them, it is understandable how the terms virtual processor and process came to be regarded as interchangeable and why one or the other term is often treated as redundant. We favor the former usage in this book. The terms are discussed further in the sections to follow.

1.5.2 Address Space The concept of address space needs clarification because it is related both to the storage-management problem of the system and to the addressing problem as seen by a programmer. *Addressing* is the means by which a process distinguishes among the storage locations in its address space. We give informal definitions for two address spaces which exist:

> 1 The *physical-address space,* which consists of the set of actual main-memory locations directly addressable
>
> 2 An *abstract, virtual,* or *logical-address space* (often called the *name space*), which consists of the set of abstract or logical locations addressed by processes

The logical-address space may be a one-dimensional array of logical locations, or it may have a more complicated structure. In a logical-address space, the locations can be thought of as numbered in some way. Each logical location is identified by its number, which is its address. To be run on a hardware processor, at least some of the instructions and data of a process must reside in physical main memory. A design problem is to provide a suitable logical space and a mechanism to translate logical-address references into the physical addresses at which the instructions and data reside when in physical memory. If the logical-address space is larger than the physical-address space of main memory, the term *virtual memory* is often used. In this book terms such as virtual memory, virtual-address space, logical memory, and logical-address space have identical meaning.

The logical, or virtual-address, space available to the virtual processor may be larger than, equal to, or smaller than the physical-address space available to hardware processors. The main memory taken together with auxiliary memory (drum or disk) contains the totality of all the virtual-address space for all virtual processors in the system. It is the task of the system to maintain in physical main memory that portion of the total virtual space relevant to a process when it is in control of the processor. The translation or mapping from a logical-address space to physical addresses is handled by both hardware and software techniques. Some common techniques for creating a logical-address space and translating logical addresses to physical addresses are discussed in Chap. 2.

1.5.3   The Context Block   As we saw in Sec. 1.3.5, it is useful to view each virtual processor as having an instruction set, an address space, access to auxiliary storage, the ability to communicate with other processors, the ability to communicate with a variety of I/O devices, and the ability to terminate itself. The information necessary to define a specific virtual processor is contained in a set of tables and data words. This set of information is often collected together as a unit and called the *context block*. A context block and the programs and data which run on the virtual processor defined by the context block constitute a process.

Let us now outline some of the information required in the context block. In order to switch the physical processor from one process to another certain information must be saved when a process is removed from control, and restored again when a process returns to control. The following is the type of information which must be saved and restored.[27]

1   The process must know which instruction to execute next when it resumes control of the physical processor. Therefore, the program counter must be saved and stored.

2   The contents of the physical processor's registers must be saved so that they can be restored before proceeding.

3   The address space of the process must be saved; i.e., the system must know whether the contents of a process's virtual memory are in main memory, are on auxiliary storage, or some combination of the two and where.

4   The state of the real or simulated I/O devices affecting the process or being used by it must be saved.

Additional information may be required to define a virtual processor, e.g., the number and type of I/O devices it can access, the amount of memory it can use, and any other capabilities it will be given. When a process is not in control of a physical processor, the context block can be stored on auxiliary storage, and only a pointer to the context block and minimal additional information required for scheduling purposes need be kept permanently in main memory. In other words, the context block contains a representation of a virtual computer system, including an image of the internal registers of the processor.

That minimal part of the context block which must be placed in the hardware processor and main memory to start execution of a process has been called the *state word* or *state vector*.[32,33] The state vector includes the contents of the operand and address registers, the contents of the registers which assist the translation from logical to physical-address space, and any additional state or protection information to be set into the processor.

One wants to minimize the size of the state vector relative to other requirements for processor registers in order to be able to switch a processor from one process to another as quickly as possible. Additional information in the context block which resides in main memory while a process is running can be brought into main memory along with all or part of the programs and data of the process before the state information is actually switched to start the process, or it can be brought in as needed. The transfer of context-block information from auxiliary storage to main memory can often be overlapped with the running of another process.

In review, then, we have seen that the virtual processor is defined by the context block. To create a process we have only to be able to create a context block. The address space of the virtual processor, called the virtual, logical, abstract, or name space in various publications, is defined by information stored in the context block. Details are discussed in Chaps. 2 and 5.

The instruction set of the virtual processor may contain the same instructions, a subset of the instructions, or a superset of the instructions found in the physical processor. It may contain the same set or a subset depending on how physical-processor instructions, such as I/O instructions, are handled by the system. The instruction set of the virtual processor may be a superset because it may include calls to system procedures which handle I/O, signal other virtual processors, and manipulate the address space and the file system. These calls create a processor easier to use than the physical hardware and one possibly having many more capabilities. The ability to call on these system procedures is an important concept and requires careful design in order to ensure adequate system protection and minimal administrative drain. This topic is discussed in Chaps. 4 and 5.

1.5.4 Users and Jobs We now discuss how processes are allocated and accounted for by the system to entities called *users* or *jobs*. Some of the discussion in this section follows that of Lampson.[32] A user, or job, in its most general form, can have associated with it several processes. The reasons for wanting to associate more than one process with a job are several, three such being: (1) to take advantage of possible multiple hardware processors of the system, (2) to take advantage of the possibility within a job for concurrent processing, and (3) to allow a job to be broken into smaller units to avoid system limitations or to simplify program organization. There is a one-to-one relationship between processes and virtual processors. Thus, concurrently executing or independent processes are possible.

One process may proceed to a point where concurrent effort is possible and call the system to create another process. It is usually convenient both to the programmer and to the system to organize the processes of a job hierarchically as a tree structure. It is convenient to the programmer because a hierarchical organization may simplify and structure the flow of control and other information. It is convenient to the system because the restrictions of information and control flow implied by a tree organization simplify the mechanisms required for interprocess communication.

In a tree structure, processes originating at a given node are said to be parallel to each other and may not communicate directly with each other. All communication must proceed along the branches of the tree. More general types of structure, which allow direct communication between all processes of a job, are possible and can be provided for in the system design. In order to simplify the discussion we restrict ourselves here to considering jobs which organize processes in a tree structure.

The basic feature of a job is its complete independence from other jobs as far as the system is concerned. Processes of a job usually interrelate, communicate, share resources, and interlock with each other. The root of the tree of processes is created by the system and is responsible for recognizing commands to the system, for handling illegal actions by lower-order processes, and for initiating and destroying further processes. A job and its tree of processes is shown in Fig. 1.2, where process 2 is the root of the tree. Processes 21 to 23 were created by process 2 and cannot communicate directly with each other. They can communicate only with the parent process which created them or with the processes which they have created. Similarly, processes 211 and 212 were created by process 21 and are parallel. Each process runs on its own virtual processor. Processes can communicate with each other and share memory. A common example of several processes existing as part of a job is given by the use of a program to aid debugging. In this case, the root process would create a subsidiary process to run the debugging program. The debugging program would in turn create a subsidiary process to run the program being debugged. The use of a more extensive tree of parallel processes depends upon the nature of the facilities for defining parallel operations in programming languages and for interprocess communication. This problem is discussed further in Chap. 5.

The job or user is usually the basic accounting entity in the system, although accounting could in principle be handled for individual processes. A user or job commonly has the following attributes:[32]

1   A name
2   Authority to expend certain resources
3   A collection of permanent and temporary files holding procedures and data and possibly authority to access files of other jobs or users
4   A collection of zero or more processes

Associated with the user are certain protection and access rights. A user is a named accounting entity and thus could be one or more people using this authority to access the system.

It is important to emphasize that if the system has been so designed, a job or user can access the procedures and data of other jobs subject to proper authorization. In this book we often use the term *user* to refer to a person sitting at a terminal, but the concept of a user is an abstraction, and the properties of a user given above should be kept in mind.

In this discussion of user no relationship between users and remote terminals was given. In many systems there is a one-to-one relationship between a job which is active on the system and a person sitting at a console. In its most general form, the concept of a user or job can include jobs which are active but which are not associated with a terminal. For example, a user might *log in* (establish contact with the system), create a program, compile and debug the program, and then put the program on a file. The user could then tell the system to run the program against data in another file and leave the results in still another file in the evening when computer time is less expensive. The user would then *log out* (break

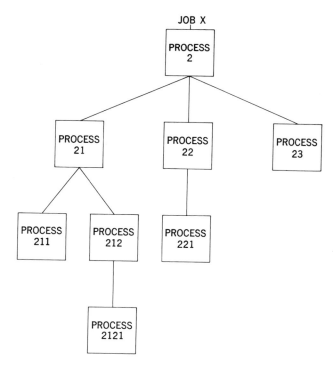

FIG. 1.2   A job and its tree of processes.

contact with the system). In the evening, the system would create a job not connected with a terminal and run it.

Other uses of processes not attached to terminals are to perform system functions. For example, one such process might run when system load is low or run periodically every few seconds or minutes as a form of preventive maintenance and check system tables and data structures for consistency or see that no I/O devices are hung up. Another use of such processes is to perform system functions which are not of top priority and whose need for resources can be scheduled like the needs of a normal user.

1.5.5 Summary This discussion has shown the usefulness throughout the system design of the concept of a virtual processor and its controlling entity, the process. The discussion showed how a processor is created and what the nature of its instruction set, address space, and communication needs may be. Additional concepts were also introduced related to virtual processor allocation, both to users and to physical hardware modules. The process concept and its uses are discussed further in Chap. 5.

1.6 A CONSOLE SESSION

1.6.1 Making Contact with the System The types of system activities required to meet the user's needs can be illustrated by a scenerio for a session at a terminal on a typical system such as the XDS-940. Some additional concepts can be brought out which are discussed in more detail later in the book.

When the user sits down at his terminal and turns it on, if it is directly connected, or dials the system, if it is connected by switched telephone lines, the computer establishes a job for this terminal. The job is established by allocating and initializing certain tables, by assigning a *job number*, which the system uses in administrating this job, and by creating a process to accept input from, and communicate with, the terminal. This process usually is the command interpreter, which we call the *root process* here. The command interpreter requests the user to identify himself by communicating "please log in."

Because the remote terminals are anonymous and anyone with an acceptable terminal and a telephone can make contact with the system, the user must present proper identification. This identification is usually an account code and project or other name. The system checks this identification in a table of legal users and if a match is found tells the user to proceed. At this point, the system knows the access privileges available to the user from information stored in the table. System-resource use is metered during the session for later billing to the user's account.

1.6.2 Writing the Program   The user wants to write, debug, and run a program against some data stored in a coworker's file and therefore commands the system to place him in contact with the text editor.   The system creates a new process for the text editor, subsidiary to the root process, and transfers control to the editor process.   The editor program has its own command language, which allows the user to enter, delete, and modify text and write it on a file.   The file name is requested by the editor, and the name PROG, for example, might be supplied by the user, who uses this name throughout his dealing with this information.   The user can change the name if he wants to.   Unless explicitly stated by other commands, the file is assumed to be *private* by the system, and only someone who logs in with the same identification as this user can access it.

When the file has been created, the user presses a system call button on the console.   The editor process is terminated, and control returns to the root process.   The user can then instruct the system to compile his source program stored in file PROG with the appropriate compiler and store the binary output on another file, which he is asked to name, say, BINARY.   The root process creates another process to control the compiler, passes the file's physical addresses to the compiler, after consulting the file system, and transfers control to the compiler.

1.6.3 Reentrant Programs   Let us digress briefly to bring out an important concept.   There may be several people using the compiler, or editor, at the same time.   Intrinsically this is no problem because separate copies of these programs could be provided each user.   However, main memory is a valuable resource, and therefore one wants to share the code in such a way that only one copy of these programs need be in the system, particularly in main memory.   This requirement illustrates another need for the distinction between a program and a process.   There is only one program being shared, but each job using it does so as part of a separate process. Use of the program as part of a separate process for each job is necessary to keep data and program in a separate address space and to keep track of the program's execution state for each job when the hardware resources are being switched from one process to another under control of some resources-allocation routine.

A single copy of a program which can be used concurrently by several processes is called a *pure procedure* or is said to be *reentrant*.   To be reentrant, a program must meet certain conditions: (1) it must not modify itself during execution and (2) it must not store data local to itself.   The first objective is easily achieved by avoiding the use of instruction-modifying programming techniques in compiler-code generators and by assembly-language programmers.   The second objective is satisfied by providing a separate data and temporary storage area for each use of the program, usually within the address space of each process using the program. Techniques for accomplishing program sharing are discussed in Chap. 2. We return now to our scenario.

1.6.4   Compiling and Debugging the Program   The compiler compiles the program stored on file PROG and reports syntax errors to the user's console or to a designated file for later examination.   The user can recall the editor and correct his program and compile again until a correct binary program is stored in his file named BINARY.

Another mode of program preparation is to use an interactive compiler which has built-in editing functions and compiles each line of source code as it is entered.   This type of system also allows the user to execute line by line and insert new lines.

When the user has created his binary file, he may want to debug the logical errors.   If so, he commands the root process to supply him with the debugging program.   The root process creates a process to run the debugging program and transfers control.   The debugging process creates a subsidiary process to control the users' binary program.   These two processes then communicate control back and forth during the debugging session.   This example illustrates the need for communication between processes.

1.6.5   Running the Program   When debugging is finished, both processes are terminated and the user requests that the program on file BINARY be run with data from his coworker's file named DATA and that results be printed at the terminal.   The file system checks to see if this user is allowed access to file DATA and, if so, reports this fact back to the root process.   The root process then creates yet another process to run the program and data.   The file naming for the input file and output file may have taken place within the user's program, and checking would have taken place at run time.   The application process is run and (depending on how it is written) may ask the user for further input, report results, or idle until receiving a signal to continue from the console.   When the user is finished, he regains contact with the root process and logs out.   Files created during the session are preserved for future sessions.

1.6.6   The System Functions during the Session   Unseen by the user, the system is performing many functions during the session.   File backup procedures may be used periodically to duplicate the user's files on tape or other media; diagnostic routines may run to check the state of the system; resource-management routines are creating, allocating, and destroying processes and switching hardware resources from process to process in order to give good response to each user.   Processes may be created to run jobs in a batch mode with low priority.   Routines are buffering and transfering information between auxiliary storage, I/O devices, and main memory. The system is keeping track of what information belongs to each job and assuring the privacy and protection of one user from another.   Finally, resource use is being accounted for in a fair and adequate manner.

1.7 SUMMARY

This chapter has set the framework and introduced some important basic concepts, requirements, and problems which the chapters to follow discuss in more detail.   The basic ideas introduced here include the idea of a general purpose timesharing system and the distinction between intrinsic and technological problems.   We have seen how the raw hardware resources are organized into virtual processors and a file system for allocation to the users.   We have seen that after the operating system performs this function, it must switch control of the hardware resources from process to process in order to accomplish real work.   The entire operation will probably contain protection and backup mechanisms and is probably being metered both for accounting purposes and for maintenance and evaluation.

Our treatment has been broad for those areas which are to be discussed in the chapters to follow and occasionally has gone into some detail on central concepts used throughout the book.   The material to follow has been organized into two main classifications, hardware concepts and software concepts.   As we have pointed out, these areas have no clean dividing point and will overlap more in time.   Many of the basic problems introduced will probably remain, but the implementation details of particular solutions will change.   Because of the close interconnection between hardware and software, some software concepts are discussed in the hardware chapter in order to provide proper background for what is discussed there, and some hardware concepts seemed more naturally discussed in the software chapters.

REFERENCES

1 **Corbato, F. J., et al.:** An Experimental Time-sharing System, *AFIPS Conf. Proc., Spring Joint Computer Conf.*, vol. 21, pp. 335–344, 1962.

2 **Schwartz, J., E. G. Coffman, and C. Weissman:** A General Purpose Timesharing System, *AFIPS Conf. Proc., Spring Joint Computer Conf.*, vol. 25, pp. 397–411, 1964.

3 **Corbato, F. J., and V. A. Vyssotsky:** Introduction and Overview of the Multics System, *AFIPS Conf. Proc., Fall Joint Computer Conf.*, vol. 27, pp. 185–196, 1965.

4 **Sackman, H.:** Time-sharing versus Batch Processing: The Experimental Evidence, *AFIPS Conf. Proc., Spring Joint Computer Conf.*, vol. 32, pp. 1–10, 1968.

5 Gold, M. M.: Time-sharing and Batch Processing: An Experimental Comparison of Their Values in a Problem Solving Situation, *Commun. ACM*, vol. 12, no. 5, pp. 249–259, May, 1969.

6 Corbato, F. J., and J. H. Saltzer: Some Considerations of Supervisor Program Design for Multiplexed Computer Systems, *IFIP Conf. Proc., Edinburgh, August, 1968*.

7 Evans, G. J., Jr.: Experience Gained from the American Airline SABRE System Control Program, *Proc. ACM Natl. Conf., 1967*, pp. 77–84.

8 Shaw, J. C.: Joss: A Designer's View of an Experimental On-line Computing System, *AFIPS Conf. Proc., Spring Joint Computer Conf.*, vol. 26, p. 455, 1965.

9 Lichtenberger, W. W., and M. W. Pirtle: A Facility for Experimentation in Man-Machine Interaction, *AFIPS Conf. Proc., Fall Joint Computer Conf.*, vol. 27, pp. 589–598, 1965.

10 *IBM Systems J.*, vol. 5, no. 1, 1966 (devoted to a description of OS/360).

11 Saltzer, J. H.: Traffic Control in a Multiplexed Computer System, MAC-TR-30, thesis, Massachusetts Institute of Technology, Cambridge, Mass., July, 1966.

12 Nielsen, N. R.: Computer Simulation of Computer System Performance, *Proc. ACM Natl. Conf., 1967*, pp. 581–590.

13 Nielsen, N. R.: The Simulation of Time-sharing Systems, *Commun. ACM*, vol. 10, no. 7, pp. 397–412, July, 1967.

14 Bryan, G. E.: JOSS 20,000 Hours at the Console: A Statistical Survey, *AFIPS Conf. Proc., Fall Joint Computer Conf.*, vol. 31, pp. 769–778, 1967.

15 Calingaert, Peter: System Performance Evaluation: Survey and Appraisal, *Commun. ACM*, vol. 10, no. 1, pp. 12–18, January, 1967.

16 Campbell, D. J., and W. J. Heffner: Measurement and Analysis of Large Operating Systems during System Development, *AFIPS Conf. Proc., Fall Joint Computer Conf.*, vol. 33, pp. 903–914, 1968.

17 Cantrell, H. N., and A. L. Ellison: Multiprogramming System Performance Measurement and Analysis, *AFIPS Conf. Proc., Spring Joint Computer Conf.*, vol. 32, pp. 213–221, 1968.

18 Estrin, G., et al.: SNUPER COMPUTER: A Computer in Instrumentation Automation, *AFIPS Conf. Proc., Spring Joint Computer Conf.*, vol. 30, pp. 645–656, 1967.

19 Freeman, David N., and Robert R. Pearson: Efficiency vs. Responsiveness in a Multiple-services Computer Facility, *Proc. ACM Natl. Conf. 1968*, pp. 25–34B.

20 Schulman, Franklin D.: Hardware Measurement Device for IBM System/360 Time-sharing Evaluation, *Proc. ACM Natl. Conf. 1967*, pp. 103–109.

21 Sherr, A. L.: An Analysis of Time-shared Computer Systems, Ph.D. thesis, *MIT Project MAC Doc.* MAC-TR-18, June, 1965.

22 Varian, L. C., and E. G. Coffman: An Empirical Study of the Behavior of Programs in a Paging Environment, *Commun. ACM*, vol. 11, no. 5, May, 1968.

23 Corbato, F. J.: Sensitive Issues in the Design of Multi-use Systems, *MIT Project MAC Mem.* MAC-M-383, Dec. 12, 1968.

24 Kay, R. H.: Management and Organization of Large Scale Software Development Projects, *AFIPS Conf. Proc., Spring Joint Computer Conf.*, vol. 34, pp. 425–433, 1969.

25 Trapnell, F. M.: A Systematic Approach to the Development of System

Programs, *AFIPS Conf. Proc., Spring Joint Computer Conf.*, vol. 34, pp. 411–418, 1969.

26   Madnick, S. E.: A Modular Approach to File System Design, *AFIPS Conf. Proc., Spring Joint Computer Conf.*, vol. 34, pp. 1–13, 1969.

27   Lampson, B. W.: A Scheduling Philosophy for Multi-processing Systems, *Commun. ACM*, vol. 11, no. 5, May, 1968.

28   Rosen, Saul: Electronic Computers: A Historical Survey, *ACM Computing Surv.*, vol. 1, no. 1, pp. 7–36, March, 1969.

29   Rosin, Robert F.: Supervisory and Monitor Systems, *ACM Computing Surv.*, vol. 1, no. 1, pp. 37, 54, March, 1969.

30   CP/CMS Program Logic Manual, IBM Cambridge Scientific Center, Cambridge, Mass., 1969.

31   Dennis, J. B., and E. C. Van Horn: Programming Semantics for Multi-programmed Computations, *Commun. ACM*, vol. 9, no. 3, pp. 143–155, March, 1966.

32   Lampson, B. W.: Scheduling and Protection on Interactive Multi-processor Systems, *Univ. Calif. Berkeley Proj. Genie Doc.*, 40.10.150, Jan. 20, 1967.

33   Dennis, J. B.: Segmentation and the Design of Multiprogrammed Computer Systems, *J. ACM*, vol. 12, no. 4, pp. 589–602, October, 1965.

part TWO

Hardware concepts

chapter TWO

Memory, addressing, and allocation

2.1 INTRODUCTION

2.1.1 Hardware Requirements in a Resource-sharing System The types of hardware features required for general purpose timesharing systems are usually also required for the other classes of timesharing systems introduced in Sec. 1.2. The essential characteristic of such systems is the dynamic allocation of system resources. The major hardware features required by such systems are (1) protection mechanisms to help safeguard one process from another and the system from itself and user processes and (2) mechanisms which contribute to efficient dynamic allocation of resources. Both these requirements are interrelated. An additional requirement of such systems is high reliability. Protection and control mechanisms are discussed in Chap. 4, and reliability is discussed in Chap. 7. This chapter discusses mechanisms to aid the allocation of main memory. Chapter 3 discusses the important hardware communication problems involved in a resource-sharing system.

2.1.2 Memory-system Design Problems We view the central resource in current systems as main memory. It is main memory which holds instructions for the arithmetic-logic processors (CPUs) and for the I/O processors (IOPs), is used as a buffer for information passing over communication lines and moving between various I/O and secondary storage devices, and holds the code for the resident operating system. The proper design of the memory system is critical to the success of a large-scale timesharing

37

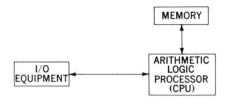

FIG. 2.1 CPU-centered model of a computer system.

system.   Until the past few years the standard computer-system model was that of Fig. 2.1, in which the arithmetic-logic processor is shown in the center and has been called the central processing unit (CPU).   Now another model is required which shows the memory as the central resource, as in Fig. 2.2.

One can recognize five major problem areas in the design of a total memory system:

1 Development of memory-addressing techniques which allow processes to address a logical-address space possibly larger than the physical space of main memory

2 Development of physical-memory allocation techniques and techniques for mapping the logical-address space into the physical-address space

3 Development of memory-protection techniques

4 Development of a memory organization and an address, data, and control-line structure (bus structure) which permits all processors and devices utilizing main memory to operate at full speed with minimal interference

5 Development of techniques to utilize a hierarchy of storage devices in a device-independent manner

The last problem is discussed in Chap. 6.   Problems 1 to 3 are usually solved with interrelated techniques and have been given considerable attention.   Problems 1 and 2 are the subject of this chapter.   Problem 3 is discussed in Chap. 4, and problem 4 has only recently been given the attention it deserves and is discussed in Chap. 3.

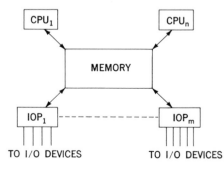

FIG. 2.2 Memory-centered model of a computer system.

2.1.3   Addressing and Allocation Problems   The multiplexing properties of main-memory devices must be fully considered in order to specify an appropriate addressing and allocation scheme for a timeshared computer. In principle, any fraction of main memory can be allocated to a process. This is not true of processors, which can be allocated only as a unit.   Processors, on the other hand, can be multiplexed rapidly, while main memory cannot be, because of the time required to move information between main and auxiliary memory.   Moving processes between main memory and auxiliary storage in order to multiplex main memory is called *swapping*.   One of the requirements in the design of an addressing scheme for a timeshared computer is that it should help emphasize the allocation advantages of memory and minimize the multiplexing disadvantages.

For example, one would prefer to have only one copy of a particular procedure, say a compiler, in main memory used by several processes rather than requiring each process to obtain a separate copy.   The concept of programs designed to be shared by several processes was introduced in Sec. 1.6.3.   These programs are called *reentrant programs* or *pure procedures*.   It will be recalled that a reentrant program has two characteristics: (1) none of its instructions or addresses can be modified during its execution, and (2) temporary storage and data areas are maintained outside the procedure itself, usually in the memory space of the calling programs.   Although programs with the above capability can be written for machines with a wide variety of addressing techniques, some addressing techniques make the writing and protection of such programs simpler.

Another way of utilizing memory more effectively is to achieve flexibility with respect to where processes can be placed in physical memory. This ability to relocate processes dynamically in physical memory can be achieved with a variety of addressing and allocation techniques.

The effect of the addressing and allocation scheme on the user must also be considered.   The cost of designing and implementing application systems—and even the possibility of attacking certain classes of problems—is likely to be affected by the properties of the addressing and allocation scheme.   The various tradeoffs possible in the design of an addressing and allocation system must take into account both user needs and system considerations.

One of the decisions a designer must make is the size of the logical-address space; in particular, is it going to be smaller than, equal to, or larger than the physical-address space?   The structure of the logical-address space must also be determined.   Many structures are possible, e.g., the large linear array commonly used, a set of linkable linear arrays, as found in Multics, or a tree structure.   It must be decided how much of this structuring to perform in hardware and how much in software.   The technique of translating or mapping the logical addresses to physical addresses must be determined.   There are three points at which present systems perform this mapping:[1,2]

> **1** *When the procedure is prepared as an operable computer program;* the result is an *absolute* program, which, in effect, is assigned the same resources each time it is run.
>
> **2** *When the program is loaded;* this is known as *static relocation.*
>
> **3** *When the program is in execution;* this is called *dynamic relocation.*

Memory-protection schemes are easily developed for any of the above approaches, and a discussion of this topic is given in Sec. 4.1.2. In the sections below, some of the factors influencing the choice of a logical-address-space structure and mapping technique are considered. We consider only the linear array or set of linear arrays as forms of hardware memory structures, because more specialized structures, such as trees, lists, or rings, are usually left for implementation by software processors. The sections on relocation which follow describe each technique in common use and discuss the motivation for the development of each technique.

2.2 STATIC RELOCATION

The translation of data references to physical addresses is easily accomplished during program preparation but suffers from the severe problems which arise when one attempts to share or modify programs. For example, if one inserts an instruction into a program, all references to instructions and data beyond the point of insertion must be updated. Similarly when one constructs a program out of routines prepared independently, the address references must be modified to reflect the locations into which the routines are loaded. Further, translation at that time restricts the size of the logical-address space to that of the physical-address space.

The process of static relocation involves a fair amount of computation. In systems using static relocation, programs are usually assembled as if they were to be loaded with the first instruction at location zero, with succeeding instruction and data words being placed in contiguous cells from this point. The location of the first word of the program is called the *base* address. All instructions or data words with address references are marked by the assembler. Then at load time, a program called the *loader* adjusts all address references to reflect the actual base address at which the program was loaded. If several programs assembled independently are to be loaded as a unit, the loader, using information supplied by the assembler, adjusts the interprogram address references to reflect the actual locations of the different programs. This process is called *linking.*

With static relocation, a user can be initially loaded anywhere in memory. However, when the process is removed to auxiliary storage and then returned during swapping, it must be placed in the same locations as before, to avoid the loading process. (Even to go through the loading process again implies that the program must be separable into a pure procedure part and a data part and that the data part must contain no absolute-memory addresses.) The major gain of static relocation is that during the loading process independently written programs and data can be combined into a computation with proper linking of parts. The proper mapping to the physical-address space is performed by the loader. Each program can be written in a logical space of its own, but no duplication of symbolic location names is allowed, although programming techniques can be developed to resolve such duplication.

The ability to load programs anywhere in physical memory is useful in the linking process above but of little value in achieving effective memory utilization in a timeshared system. For example, when a new process is to be started, the system can attempt to find a process which would fit in an available block of cells. If such a process can be found and it can remain in main memory until completion, static relocation is sufficient to enable several processes to share main memory. (The assumption of some sort of memory-protection scheme is implicit; this topic is covered in a separate discussion.) A more usual situation will be that the total number of free cells available is sufficient for the number required by a new process but that these cells are not in a contiguous block.

If swapping is required, then even if a contiguous block were available on initial loading, the same contiguous block will not necessarily be available each time the process is run, without moving some information to another spot in main memory or moving it to secondary storage. For these reasons, systems without dynamic-relocation hardware, when used for timesharing, generally have allowed only one complete process to reside in memory at a given time.[3] Thus, during the swapping operation, the system must remain idle. It is this situation which motivated the development of dynamic-relocation methods.

2.3 DYNAMIC RELOCATION USING BASE REGISTERS

2.3.1 Introduction One of the simplest and most common dynamic-relocation techniques uses *base registers*,[1] which are registers that can have their contents added to the address of each memory operation. By adding the contents of a base register to all addresses, one can load a program anywhere in memory in a block of contiguous cells and then set the appropriate base address of the program into the base register. Using base registers, programs are initially loaded using static-relocation techniques but can be dynamically relocated as a unit later without going through the loading process. This flexibility results because the loading is to logical space not physical space. The base registers form a hardware map which maps logical space to physical space. Further flexibility is gained if there is more than one base register, which facilitates sharing programs and makes it possible to split a program for loading into noncontiguous storage areas.

There are many possible variations of the base-register technique. In fact, techniques such as segmentation (to be discussed) are implemented using some hardware registers called base registers. In this section, we are interested in the concept of base registers in its simplest form as defined above and illustrated in Fig. 2.3. There are two common ways of specifying which base register to use in forming an address. One technique, represented by the IBM System 360, requires the base registers to be directly addressed by the program and allows the program to access the base registers. The second technique, represented by the UNIVAC 1108, does not allow programs to access the base registers and implicitly addresses the base registers depending on the type of memory operation being executed. For example, all instruction fetches use one base register and all data fetches and stores use another base register. Dynamic relocation can be achieved using either approach, although, as pointed out by Corbato, the programming conventions required to achieve dynamic relocation in systems allowing program access to the base registers may be difficult to enforce.[24]

Program sharing is performed in a system using base registers by writing the reentrant programs to make memory references to themselves through one base register and to make memory references to data in the calling process through a second base register.

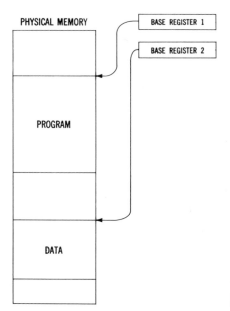

FIG. 2.3   Two base registers used for dynamic relocation of program and data.

2.3.2   Size of Logical Space   The size of the logical-address space using static relocation or dynamic relocation with base registers is usually equal to or less than the size of the physical-address space.   A larger physical space can be simulated by the user by explicitly overwriting a portion of his computation not immediately required with another part brought in from auxiliary storage.   This process is called *overlaying*.   Overlaying is closely related to the concept of swapping except that overlaying is a user responsibility whereas swapping is a system responsibility.   Overlaying is used by an individual to overcome limitations on main-memory size, and swapping is used by the system to overcome limitations on main-memory size.   Overlaying requires careful organization by the programmer of the physical-memory requirements of his computation.   Careful planning is required to assure that no two procedures or data structures which are to be used concurrently occupy the same positions in logical or physical space. Whether or not overlay planning should be looked upon as a chore or as an opportunity for programming discipline is open to discussion.   Certainly one can provide the programmer with system aids to facilitate overlay planning and implementation.

2.3.3   Memory Utilization   One of the problems uncovered by static relocation is the fact that, once loaded, a process's address references are *bound* to a certain contiguous area of memory and that during swapping the process must be returned to the same area of main memory each time it is given control of the physical processor.   When base registers are used, this restriction no longer holds.   When the processor is to be switched to a process not in main memory, a free contiguous block of main memory must be found for it to reside in.   If such a block exists, no information need be saved on auxiliary memory in order to make room for the incoming process.   The more usual situation results when although enough free cells are available in main memory for the process, they are not in a large enough contiguous block.   In this case, a system designed to use base registers can do three things: (1) search for a process which will fit into one of the available contiguous blocks, (2) swap out part of some process presently in main memory bordering on a free area in order to make a large enough contiguous area, or (3) perform a compacting operation on main memory. Systems giving good user response can be designed using one or more of these approaches.[4]   Figure 2.4 illustrates the last two ideas.

Figure 2.4a shows memory at a given point in time.   There are two programs entirely residing in memory and three free-space areas (holes). It is desired to bring into memory a third program C which is larger than individual holes but smaller than total space available in holes 1 and 2. Figure 2.4b shows one approach to making enough space available to fit in program C.   Program A is moved entirely to start at the beginning of memory, thus creating enough free space for program C.   Figure 2.4*c* shows another way of making enough space available to fit in program C.   Enough of program A bordering on hole 1 is removed to auxiliary storage to make room for program C.

One solution to the problem of finding a large enough contiguous area might be to use multiple base registers so that smaller pieces of the process could be loaded into existing free spaces.   This approach seems to be impractical because the instructions of a given piece must refer to the correct base register.   Thus, the programmer or compiler must decide how to split up the process and which base registers to assign which pieces. Binding instructions to base-register addresses at load time means binding the process to a portion of logical space.   The problem we are attempting to solve arises at run time and not load time.

The system could not easily perform this base-register assignment function dynamically because it would be very time-consuming and complicated to determine which instructions to modify.   When a process is started up, the proper numbers must be established so that the system knows which base register a given program piece is using.   All instructions referring to a given piece must also use the proper base-register address. Conventions would also be required so that shared programs could use different base registers from those of the calling process or other shared processes being used concurrently.   Even with all this complexity, the prob-

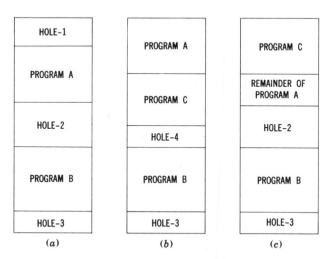

FIG. 2.4   Memory allocation using base registers: (*a*) typical memory snapshot at a point in time; (*b*) making room for program C by compaction; (*c*) making room for program C by partial removal of program A.

lem would not be solved because further pieces of free space smaller than the program pieces would result after the system had been running. To get around these problems of memory fragmentation one could break up processes and physical memory into uniform-sized pieces. Such a step leads us to the concept of paging introduced in Sec. 2.4.

The problem of memory fragmentation occurs in many areas of computing, whenever memory is being allocated dynamically and areas of memory no longer in use are being reassigned to new uses. Usually the problem is solved by assigning memory in multiples of fixed-sized blocks, using list processing, or moving information in memory to assemble a free block large enough for a given requirement. The reader is referred to Knuth's excellent book for further discussion of this important topic.[21]

2.3.4 Summary We have seen how base registers allow programs and data to be dynamically relocated anywhere in main memory at run time. Using two base registers allows a straightforward sharing of programs. The difficulties with the base-register approach pointed out in the previous discussion are two: (1) Even with use of base registers memory may not be fully utilized because contiguous free areas smaller than needed by many processes will develop during operation. The inability to achieve full memory utilization may lead to compacting or swapping which theoretically could be avoided if the free areas could be fully utilized. (2) Logical-address space using presently available mechanisms is limited in size by the size of physical-address space. Overlay techniques can give some of the effect of a larger space.

It has been asked whether the added hardware and software complexity and expense to overcome the problems mentioned introduced by more sophisticated dynamic-relocation techniques really result in a corresponding increase in system efficiency, improved response, and programming ease. We discuss some of the arguments pro and con after introducing further dynamic-relocation concepts.

2.4 DYNAMIC RELOCATION USING PAGING

2.4.1 Introduction Dynamic relocation using base registers, which requires programs to be located in contiguous areas of main memory, leads to difficulties in fully utilizing main memory because free areas develop which are not large enough to be used. If, however, programs and main memory could be broken into small units and the program pieces could be located in corresponding sized blocks anywhere in main memory, then the possibility exists of utilizing main memory more effectively. *Paging* is the name given to a set of techniques which enable such a uniform memory fragmentation to be implemented. Paging techniques can also allow economic implementation of a logical-memory space larger than the physical-memory space.[5]

In a paged system, physical memory is considered to be broken up into *blocks* of a fixed size, usually 512, 1,024, or 2,048 words. The term *page* refers to units of logical space, while equal-sized units of physical space are called blocks. The programs are also considered to be split into *pages* of a size equal to the block size of physical memory. Thus, the address in such a system is considered to be represented by two numbers: (1) a page address or number and (2) a line-within-page address. For a machine with an n-bit address field, the high-order p bits are considered the page address and the remaining $n - p$ bits are the line address. The operating system may occupy less memory than a multiple of a larger page size. In newer systems the page size can be changed dynamically by the system. The memory can be more fully utilized by the system if smaller page sizes are available (64, 128, or 256 words). More effective utilization of memory results from using smaller page sizes for the following reason. Since a given process is not usually going to require an amount of memory space which is an even multiple of a page size, the last page of a process will not utilize all the block assigned to it. It seems reasonable to assume that on the average the last page of a process will use half of its assigned block. The larger the page size, the more potential waste space there is going to be. As the reader will see in the following discussion, a paging mechanism requires a table, called a *page table*, or map with one entry for each page in order to perform address translation from logical to physical space. The smaller the page size, the larger the table required for a given logical-address space. Thus, there is a tradeoff between waste space related to page size and resources used to store and manipulate larger page tables. The total amount of waste space due to unused block locations depends on the number of processes expected to reside in main memory.

The paged addressing scheme on the XDS-940 illustrates the basic concepts of paging.

2.4.2 Paging on the XDS-940 The address space of a process in the XDS-940 can be as large as 16K* words. Physical memory in the XDS-940 can be as large as 64K, and thus the logical-address space is smaller than the physical-address space. The more general case of a paged system yielding a virtual memory larger than the physical-address space is discussed in Sec. 2.4.4. A process in the XDS-940 is broken up into 2K word pages, and memory is similarly broken into 2K word blocks. There are 14 bits in the address field of a 940-instruction word. The address field is considered

---

* K stands for 1,024. Thus 16K means 16 × 1,024.

to contain two parts, a 3-bit page number and an 11-bit line-within-page number. The relocation mechanism (Fig. 2.5) uses eight 6-bit bytes called a *memory map*. The memory map in the XDS-940 is organized as two 24-bit registers. Each register contains four map bytes. These registers are called the *real relabeling registers,* because they relabel (map) the page number into a physical-memory block number. These map bytes are considered by the hardware numbered 0 to 7 and correspond to logical pages. A given map byte is addressed by the page number contained in the memory address. Within a given map byte is a number for the actual physical block containing the code for the logical page. For example, in Fig. 2.5 logical page 0 is in physical block 32, logical page 1 is in physical block 3, and so forth. The numbers in the physical blocks of the figure indicate which logical pages they contain.

The logical address is converted to a physical address as shown in Fig. 2.6.

The 3-bit page number indicates which map register contains the physical-block number where the page actually resides. The map register is 6 bits long and is shown in Fig. 2.7; 5 bits contain the physical-block number, and 1 bit is for memory protection (see Sec. 4.1.2). The physical address is simply formed by concatenating the physical-block number with the line number to form a 16-bit address. With 16 bits, 64K of memory can be addressed.

This hardware mechanism is quite simple, but to work as part of the total system it requires additional software tables, which keep track

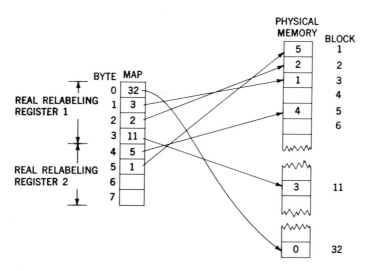

FIG. 2.5 Paging in the XDS-940.

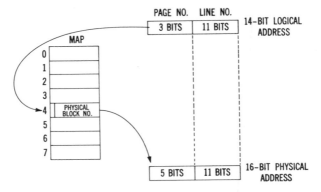

FIG. 2.6 Mapping from logical to physical address in the XDS-940.

of the memory space of each process (see Sec. 5.3.2). The basic idea is that when a process is to be brought into main storage, the software monitor examines the state of main storage and swaps out only as many pages as are required in conjunction with free pages to meet the needs of the incoming process. The monitor then assigns the available physical blocks to the logical pages of the incoming process and swaps its pages into these blocks. The memory map is updated. Then after restoring the processor registers and program counter to the values they had when the process was last executing, the process is restarted.

2.4.3 The Memory Map The most important general concept introduced above is that of a *memory map*. A map translates the logical-address space into the physical-address space. In the dynamic-relocation techniques, the map is a set of tables in memory or a set of hardware registers. In the static-relocation technique the map is a program. In the dynamic-relocation method using base registers, the base registers are the map. In the dynamic-relocation method using paging, the page map can be looked at as a way of efficiently implementing multiple base registers. The paging process is completely invisible to the users and to the compilers, which function as if they were working with one contiguous logical chunk. The ability to fragment memory uniformly, made possible by splitting main memory into blocks, means that all blocks of main memory can be used, although

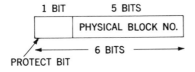

FIG. 2.7   Map byte in the XDS-940.

some blocks may only be partially filled. Therefore it may be possible to decrease the time lost through swapping by being able to maintain more processes or process fragments in memory at a given time. The concept of a memory map which dynamically converts logical addresses to physical addresses has been an important innovation in machine organization.

2.4.4 A More General Approach to Paging The XDS-940 paging mechanism does not allow a straightforward implementation of a logical-address space larger than the physical-address space. A more general approach to paging is shown in Fig. 2.8., where the map is a *page table* in main memory. One page table exists for each process. The physical-block number corresponding to a given page is found by a table lookup in this page table using the page number as an index. The control bits in each table entry (page descriptor) can be used to indicate whether the page represented by that entry resides in memory or on an auxiliary storage device. The page-table base register points to the base of the page table for the process

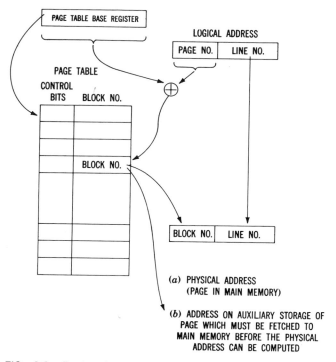

FIG. 2.8 Paging in a more general form allowing a large logical-memory space.

currently in control of the machine. The page number from the logical address when added to the contents of the page-table base register indicates which word in the page table contains the block number where the page resides. The figure in the block number portion of the table can indicate an actual starting address for the page in main memory or a location on auxiliary storage where the page can be found. If the control bits indicate that the latter case holds, a call to the system, often referred to as a *page fault,* can be generated to fetch the page to memory before resuming computation. With this approach, the logical-address space can be larger than the physical-address space. The main factors limiting the size of the virtual memory are (1) the number of available address-field bits which can be generated and (2) an economical limit for a page-table size.

A difficulty with the approach just outlined is that all memory references require an additional access time to get the block number from the page table. One solution would be to implement the page table used by the currently running process in hardware, as is done on the XDS-940. However, it would probably be too expensive to implement the page table (map) required for a virtual memory of large size directly in hardware. It would also take too much time to change this hardware table (map) each time the processor is switched from one process to another.

To eliminate the extra memory reference most of the time, a special hardware map using an associative lookup can be implemented[5] (Fig. 2.9). The map is called an *associative map* because it is addressed by association or content rather than explicit address. Using the associative map, the page number of the logical address is simultaneously compared against

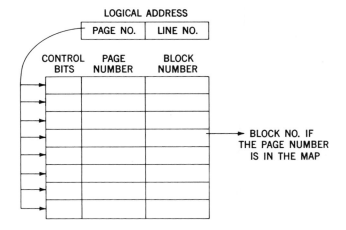

FIG. 2.9   An associative map.

all the page numbers in the map. If the page number is found, the block number is output and the physical address is formed by concatenating the line number with the block number. If no match is found between the page number of the logical address and the page numbers of the map, reference must be made to the page table in main memory. The new page number–block number pair is inserted into the map, replacing one of the entries there. The associative-map size and the strategy for replacing entries already in the map are design problems of such a paged system. In studying these problems, one must consider such factors as hardware cost and the page-reference characteristics of processes. The simulation techniques like those discussed by Conti[22] and others for a related problem seem to be useful in studying alternative designs.

With a paging scheme like that outlined above, the entire process would not have to be loaded into main memory at the time computation began. Only those pages initially required could be loaded, and as reference was made to pages not in main memory, the page table would indicate the fact by generating a call to the supervisor, which would then bring in the page. The pros and cons of this *demand-paging* approach are discussed in Sec. 5.3.3.

2.4.5 Sharing of Programs and Data The sharing of programs and data is a desirable feature for a timesharing system, as mentioned earlier. Sharing can be implemented in many ways. One way requires each job to obtain a separate copy of the procedure or data structure to be shared. Obtaining separate copies increases the memory requirement and may lead to increased swapping activity. Therefore, it is desirable to share frequently used procedures and data in such a way that only one copy is required in memory. Figure 2.10 illustrates how such sharing is accomplished in a paged system. In Fig. 2.10a, two source programs A and B share a compiler C. The compiler's pages are labeled C_1, C_2, and C_3. Note that entries for the compiler's pages must be placed in the map of each job which uses it, although only one copy of the compiler exists in physical memory. Note further that the compiler's entries must be in the same relative positions in each map. Similarly the source programs SA and SB must have consecutive entries starting at the same relative position in the two maps. This use of consecutive entries is required because when the compiler is initially loaded into the system its memory references are bound to fixed areas of the logical-address space. This binding to logical space takes place because the address field contains a page number and a line-within-page number, each of which is given a value at load time. The page number is the index to the entry in the map which contains the base location of the block of memory containing the page. Every time the compiler is executing, it is referencing the same relative location in a map. Therefore, every process using the compiler must contain entries in its map for the compiler and in the correct positions which were determined at the time the compiler was loaded into the system. The initial loading could place the compiler anywhere in logical space. This concept of loading as a *binding process* to positions in physical space in the case of static relocation and to positions in logical space in the case of systems using base registers or paging is a very important concept which should be understood before proceeding.

An alternative to placing the compiler's pages in the same relative location in each user's logical space is to have a separate map for the compiler. This map is invoked when the compiler is called. If the compiler is shared, the difficulty arises of how to handle the logical placement of the user's source code in the compiler's map. Because each source-code program being compiled must be stored starting in the same position in the compiler's logical space, the compiler's map would have to be modified each time control is switched to a different job. Another alternative is to have some way of indicating that certain memory references are to be made through the compiler's map and that others (those referring to the source code) are to be made through the user's map. These alternatives introduce extra complexity and seem to offer no useful advantage.

Let us now consider the problem of two procedures P_A and P_B sharing data, as shown in Fig. 2.10b. To share data the logical page D, representing the data, can be in different locations in each map. This situation is true as long as the data themselves contain no addresses. For example, if indirect addressing through D back to P_A and P_B could take place, then P_A and P_B would have to reside in the same relative locations in logical space. This location would be determined at the time the data were created. If indirect references through D to itself were to be allowed, P_A and P_B could occupy different relative locations but D would have to be placed in the same relative location in each map.

2.4.6 Summary and Conclusions We have seen how paging allows memory to be uniformly fragmented and gives the potential for more effective memory utilization. The important concept of a memory map was introduced. A memory map can be implemented in hardware, software, or both.

This discussion showed how programs and data can be shared if certain conventions are followed. What are the implications of these conventions? (1) More space must be taken in the page table of each process using a shared data structure or a shared program and (2) no process can simultaneously use two or more shared routines or data structures which occupy the same position in logical space. The second problem can be avoided if the logical space is large enough and the bookkeeping of the installation careful enough to ensure that all shared programs and their data which could be used concurrently are loaded into the system in different positions in logical space. This solution could require large page tables (maps). The page tables discussed in Sec. 2.4.4 used the page number as an index to the entry containing the corresponding block address. This technique is simply implemented, but it requires one word of table entry for each page of logical space. If the table is structured and addressed by the page number as a simulated associative memory, hash table (see Sec. 5.3.2), then only one table entry is required per logical page used. Another way around the problem is to use hardware base registers as part of the address-formation process before going through the paging schemes above, but this seems impractical because it would require multiple base

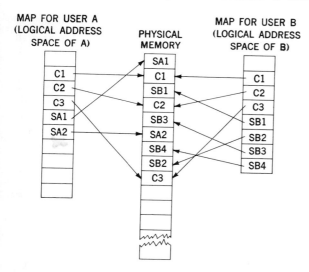

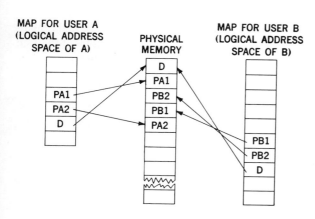

FIG. 2.10 (*a*) A compiler being shared in a paged memory; (*b*) sharing data in a paged memory.

registers, very careful bookkeeping, and the establishment of possibly un-enforceable conventions on base-register use.

Besides restricting the full generality of program and data sharing, paging techniques offer no help to the programmer in dealing with memory allocation for data bases, such as lists, symbol tables, and pushdown stacks, which can grow and contract during execution. The programmer must ex-plicitly plan for such situations so that the map can be set properly. In the XDS-940 system this problem is reduced somewhat through system calls, which allow the process to interact with the system to change its map. Thus, the process has considerable power to control the contents of its logical-address space. This latter ability, however, is more in the line of facilitating overlays than in fundamentally altering the structure of the logical space obtainable with paging.

The structure of the logical space obtained with paging is identical to that obtained using base registers. The structure in either case is that of a large contiguous array which is dynamically relocatable. To the user there is no difference in the way he would program using either approach. What is gained in using paging over base registers is a method which possibly may yield more effective memory utilization through memory fragmentation. One also obtains a practical method for the implementation of a large virtual memory. More flexibility may also be given the system programmer in his design of program- and data-sharing conventions because one need not establish conventions on base-register use.

The apparent disadvantages of paging over the use of base registers are that (1) paging requires a hardware memory map to be efficient, (2) the software implementation may be more complex if the full advantage of paging is to be utilized, and (3) the resident software system will probably be larger, thus requiring more main memory. Given the trend toward de-creasing hardware costs, the extra cost of a hardware map is a very small part of the cost of the total system. The software complexity and system memory required to utilize paging is not great (Sec. 5.3.2). Better utiliza-tion of memory enables more processes to reside concurrently in main mem-ory, which increases the possibility of performing useful computation in one process while the swapping of another takes place. Faster auxiliary storage devices can minimize this advantage, however. In our view, the small extra cost of paging hardware seems worthwhile considering the extra flexibility offered the system programmer to experiment with CPU and memory-allocation, and swapping algorithms.

2.5 DYNAMIC RELOCATION USING SEGMENTATION

2.5.1 Motivation for Segmentation   The concept of segmentation does not seem to be widely understood, for several reasons:

1   The motivations for its development may not be completely clear.

2   Different versions of the concept exist in different machines; e.g., segmentation as it exists in the IBM 360/67 system has important differences from segmentation as it exists in the GE-645 system.

3   The distinctions between a logical-address space and a physical-address space are not always understood.

4   Because many of the implementation mechanisms are similar between paging systems and segmentation systems, these two distinctly different concepts tend to be blurred together.

In this section, we try to give a clear explanation of segmentation as we understand its most general form, indicate some of the differences between various versions of the concept, reemphasize the difference between logical- and physical-address space, make clear the distinction between paging and segmentation, and review the motivation for the development of segmentation. Segmentation is looked at from a slightly different point of view in the discussion of file systems in Chap. 6.

The discussion of dynamic relocation so far has showed that certain problems of *physical-memory* allocation are inherent in systems using base registers; solutions to these physical-memory-allocation problems were offered by the introduction of paging. Paged systems in turn have problems with *logical-memory* allocation if programs and data are to be shared with full generality and if data structures are to be allowed to grow and contract at will without explicit allocation planning by the programmer. Segmentation offers solutions to these problems.

These problems could be solved in a paged system if a very large logical-memory space could be created. Then all shared procedures could occupy a unique position in this space, and data structures could occupy positions far enough apart from each other and from procedures so that they could grow at will. This solution could be achieved in a paged system by having enough address bits and a large logical-to-physical-memory map (page table) for each job. Such a solution has certain practical difficulties because the map for each job, to assure that there would be no conflicts of positioning in logical space, would have to be very large if the map were the indexed type discussed in Sec. 2.4.4. It would contain large gaps if one wanted to allow data structures to grow at will because in such a paged system one must preassign logical space even though physical space can be allocated as needed. Gaps would also arise because concurrently shared procedures could occupy widely separate positions in logical space. These gaps might result because all combinations of shared procedures which could possibly be used concurrently must be loaded into separate areas of logical space. Thus, one could choose a combination of procedures which, to meet the above requirement, had been loaded into widely separated areas of logical space. Further, careful bookkeeping would be required to assure that no two shared procedures which might be used concurrently occupied the same position in logical space. If the page table were organized and addressed as an actual or simulated associative memory, then it could be reduced in size because no gaps need result. The practical problem of implementing in hardware and software such a large associative map for efficient execution may still create difficulties, although further study may be fruitful.

In summary, then, the difficulty of using paging for sharing single copies of procedures and data in full generality and for allowing for data-structure growth results:

> **1** Because of the large number of address bits required to ensure unique page numbers in a large logical space.
>
> **2** Because of the large, possibly sparsely filled, map required using an indexed page table (with an efficient associative map this argument is reduced, although duplicate entries for each page of shared procedures and data must exist in the map of each process using the shared procedures or data).
>
> **3** Because of the careful bookkeeping required by the installation and the system to be certain that procedures used concurrently do not occupy the same position in logical space (i.e., have the same page numbers), and to properly position data which contain address references.

The technique of segmentation was developed to simplify management of a very large *logical* space.[6,11] A large logical space is required to solve the problem discussed above. It is useful to make the following somewhat simplified distinction. Segmentation is a technique for dealing with *logical-space* allocation and should be kept separate in one's mind from paging, which is a concept for dealing with *physical-space* allocation. The fact that some implementations of the segmentation concept also use paging for physical-memory allocation should not be allowed to confuse the distinction between the concepts.

2.5.2 The Segmentation Concept The problems with physical-space allocation using static relocation resulted because address references were bound to positions in *physical* space when procedures and data were loaded into the system. Once loading was accomplished, all addresses were *absolute physical* locations. This restriction was removed in the base-register and paged systems by introducing mechanisms which allowed physical-address references to be made *relative* to either a base register or block number, the contents of which did not have to be set until execution time. However, the particular base register or map entry to be used was bound into the instructions at load time. In other words, once loading was accomplished, all addresses were to *absolute logical* locations.

The problem which segmentation sets out to solve is that of allowing relative addressing within the logical-memory space.   This means that logical space must be broken up into chunks of contiguous locations and all addresses within a given chunk are to be relative to the start of the chunk.   We then need a hardware or software base register which points to the base location for each chunk.   Interchunk references must refer to the proper base register and give a relative address within the referenced chunk.   The trick is to develop an efficient mechanism which allows these base registers to be assigned at execution time.   The chunks of contiguous logical locations are commonly called *segments*.   The basic idea of segmentation is thus quite simple, but the mechanisms for allowing assignment of base registers at execution time are more involved.

A *segment* is an ordered set of data elements (usually computer words) having a name.[6]   A particular data element within a segment is referenced by the symbolic segment name and the symbolic data-element name within the segment, $\langle S \rangle / [\alpha]$.   The notation $\langle S \rangle$ indicates a symbolic segment named S, and the notation $[\alpha]$ indicates a symbolic element in the segment named α.   The symbolic segment name $\langle S \rangle$ is eventually (at run time) translated into a base-register number, and the symbolic data-element name in the segment $[\alpha]$ is going to be translated into a relative location within the segment.   In other words, a segment is a one-dimensional array, and the segment name is related to the address in logical space of this array (its base address); the symbolic element name within the segment is related to the address of the referenced element relative to start of the segment, as shown in Fig. 2.11.

Segmentation is often referred to as a *two-dimensional logical-address space* because particular elements within the logical space are ex-

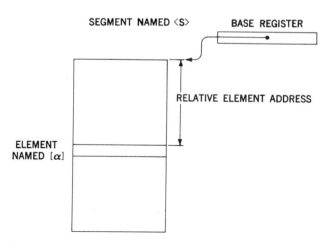

FIG. 2.11   A segment.

plicitly referenced by a pair of names.   A paging system is not considered
two-dimensional, even though the address has a page-number and a line-
number pair, because these conventions are invisible to the user.   To be
general one could consider base-register and paged systems as segmented
systems allowing one segment, and thus the segment name is implicit.   In
a general segmented system, the user programs his addresses using a pair
notation, $\langle S \rangle / [\alpha]$.   A segment is a self-contained logical entity of related
information defined and named by the programmer, such as a procedure,
data array, symbol table, or pushdown stack.   There is no logical restriction
on the length of a segment, although in any given implementation there
will be an upper bound on segment length.[7-10]   Segments can grow and
contract as needed.

A segmented system provides a logical space of nonhomogeneous
units called segments, while a base register or paged system provides a
logical space of one homogeneous unit.   Each segment is a separate logical
entity.   Some of the problems to be solved and the parameters to be determined in developing an implementation of the segmentation concept are as
follows:

1   Developing a method for mapping symbolic address pairs $\langle S \rangle / [\alpha]$ to
physical locations
2   Determining the number of segments to be allowed and their size
3   Developing a method of linking segments together
4   Developing a method for sharing segments
5   Developing a method for protecting segments

A variety of solutions to these problems have been implemented in hardware
or suggested in the literature.[7-16]   We discuss in some detail the implementation of one segmentation system, the Multics (GE-645) system,
as illustrative of the types of mechanisms presently used, and then we
briefly discuss some types of segmentation found in other proposed or implemented systems.

2.5.3   Introduction to Segmentation in the Multics System   The following
discussion and illustrations of the Multics system are based on the papers by
Glaser et al.,[8] Daley and Dennis,[12] and Organick.[15]   The logical-address
space or virtual memory of the GE-645 system can contain up to 2^{18} segments, each of which can be up to 2^{18} 36-bit words in length.   The GE-645
CPU has an accumulator register, multiplier/quotient register, eight index
registers, and a program counter, which perform the normal function of such
registers.

Additional registers used to implement the segmentation concept
are a *descriptor base register*, a *procedure base register*, and four *base-pair
registers*.   The descriptor base register points to the location in memory

of the *segment-descriptor table,* discussed below.   The procedure base register contains the segment number (name) of the procedure being executed.
Each base-pair register contains a segment-number—location-in-segment
pair and has a specific function assigned by convention, as described in
later sections.   The most general form of an address is a symbolic segment-
name—item-name pair.   Eventually this pair of symbolic names must be converted to a physical-memory location.   The discussion to follow indicates
how this mapping takes place for the common types of memory references.

Associated with each process there is a segment-descriptor table
(often called a descriptor segment), which is itself a segment.   This table
contains one word called a *segment descriptor* for each segment *known*
to the computation.   Each of the segment descriptors contains the base
address in physical space for the segment.   (We defer discussing how
paging is used with segmentation until the main concepts have been introduced.)   The segment descriptor also contains control bits used for memory
protection and other purposes not of immediate interest.

The segment-descriptor table is in effect an array of base registers,
as shown in Fig. 2.12.   The descriptor base register allows the segment-
descriptor table to be relocatable, thus giving a general mechanism by which
the segment-descriptor table can be handled like the other segments in the
system.   The segment name ⟨S⟩ or, as we shall see, a transformation of

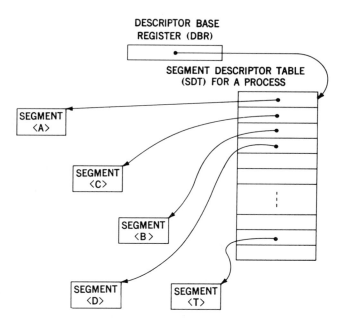

FIG. 2.12 A segmented process resident in memory.

⟨S⟩, obtained at execution time and called the *segment number,* indicates the proper segment descriptor (base register) to combine with the relative location within the segment address to yield an address in physical space, as shown in Fig. 2.13.

When a segment is loaded into the system, it is not bound in logical space because all addresses are relative to the beginning of some segment. Only when a segment is made known to a process by creating a segment descriptor does binding of the segment's location to logical space take place. This binding is caused by the transformation of the segment name into an index in the segment-descriptor table indicating the location of the newly created segment descriptor. Different processes using the same segment (and even the same process on different occasions) can have the segment descriptor in different places in a segment-descriptor table. This idea is illustrated in Fig. 2.14. The mechanism of segment-descriptor assignment is discussed below in the section on linking.

One can think of the position in the segment-descriptor table as a position in logical space. The same segment can have a descriptor, which is assigned at execution time, at different positions in the descriptor tables of different processes or in different positions in the descriptor table of the same process on different occasions. Therefore one has a system in which procedures and data can be assigned positions in the logical space of a process at the time they are initially referenced independent of the positions they may occupy in the logical space of other processes. In a paged or base-register system identical logical-space locations are assigned in all address spaces of processes using single copy shared information at the time the information is loaded into the system. The locations in the

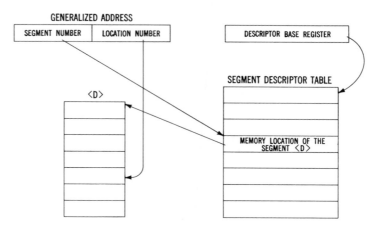

FIG. 2.13 Calculation of memory location.

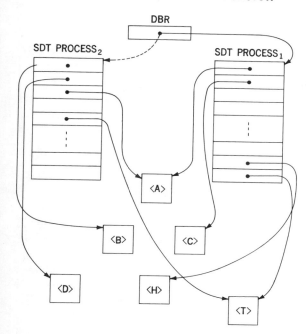

FIG. 2.14 Two processes resident in memory-sharing segments.

linkage section (Sec. 2.5.5) which hold segment numbers can be thought of as logical base registers because they point to positions in the segment descriptor table (positions in logical space). The segment descriptor contains a base address in physical space. In other words, segment descriptors are base registers which are not bound to a segment of a process until execution time, at which point a segment name is bound to a segment number or numbers usually different in each process using the segment.

If a segmentation system is to work, the segments must be properly linked together. This linkage in Multics is implemented so as to allow the realization of sharing of segments with full generality (see Sec. 2.5.5).

2.5.4 Addressing in the Multics System We now outline some of the details of addressing in the Multics system. Software and hardware are so closely interlinked that concepts on both are introduced. For the initial discussion, we assume that all segments required by a process are known and thus have entries in the segment-descriptor table. We outline later the steps required to make a segment known. The relative location within the segment table of the descriptor for a segment with symbolic name ⟨S⟩ is called the *segment number* S# of segment ⟨S⟩. The segment ⟨S⟩ may be shared by several processes and have a different segment number in each; i.e., the descriptors for segment ⟨S⟩ may appear at different relative locations within the segment-descriptor table for each computation. Figure 2.12 shows a process in memory with segments $\langle A \rangle$, $\langle B \rangle$, $\langle C \rangle$, $\langle D \rangle$, and $\langle T \rangle$. Note that the descriptor base register points to the base of the segment-descriptor table. Figure 2.14 shows two processes resident in memory sharing segments $\langle A \rangle$ and $\langle T \rangle$. Since each process has a different location in its segment-descriptor table for the segment descriptors for $\langle A \rangle$ and $\langle T \rangle$, each process refers to segments $\langle A \rangle$ and $\langle T \rangle$ by different segment numbers. The contents of the descriptor base register are changed each time a different process is given control of the machine, so that it points to the beginning of the segment-descriptor table for the currently executing process.

To make a memory reference, two numbers are necessary: (1) a segment number to make reference to the correct segment descriptor in the segment-descriptor table and (2) a location number within the segment. The segment-number–location-number within the segment pair is called a *generalized address*. The notation $S\#/\alpha$ is used, where $S\#$ is the segment number and α is the location within $\langle S \rangle$ of the symbolic element name $[\alpha]$. We now outline some of the ways in which a generalized address is formed. First consider instruction fetches. The segment number of the executing segment is contained in a register called the *procedure base register*. The location within the segment is contained in the program counter. If the procedure segment is executing a sequence of instructions that lie entirely within the segment, the contents of the procedure base register remain unchanged.

There is a bit in a GE-645 instruction called the *external flag*, which is *off* if the instruction is to make its operand address reference within the executing segment and *on* to make its reference in a segment external to the executing segment. When the external flag is *off*, the segment number is obtained from the procedure base register and the location within the segment is obtained through the normal process of address modification, possibly involving indexing and indirect addressing within the executing segment.

Instructions in which the external flag is *on* form a generalized address, as shown in Fig. 2.15. The segment tag is used to point to one of the four base-pair registers. Part of the register contains the segment number (how it got there is outlined later), and another part contains a location base within the segment, which, when combined with the address field, possibly indexed, yields the location number within the segment. Figure 2.13 indicates how the actual operand address in physical space is obtained from the generalized address. The segment number is added to the number in the descriptor base register to locate the correct segment descriptor in a segment-descriptor table, which in turn points to the base of the segment. The location number is added to the address in the segment descriptor to form the location required.

This mechanism provides the solution to the problem of allowing data structures to grow and contract at will without the programmer having to worry about physical-memory space allocation. If the data structure is a segment, it can grow to any size up to the maximum segment size imposed by the implementation or shrink at will. Only as much physical-memory space is used as presently required by the data structure. In the actual implementation, the segments are paged, and the pointer in the segment descriptor really points to the base of a *page table* containing *page descriptors* for the pages of the segment. A page descriptor contains the address in main or auxiliary storage where the given page is stored. The location number is broken into two parts, a page number and a line within the page. The actual physical address is obtained via a double table lookup, as shown in Fig. 2.16.

If the scheme were left as above, it would be unsatisfactory because

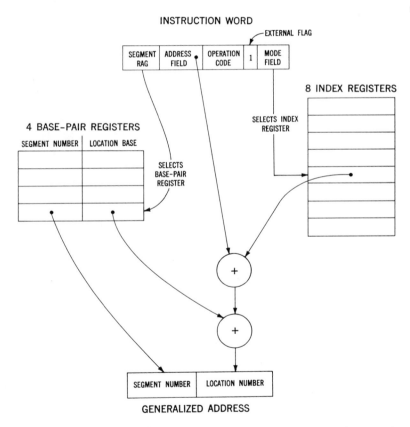

FIG. 2.15 Generalized-address calculation for an external-segment reference in the GE-645.

of the time required to compute each address. To get around this problem a small associative memory is incorporated in the processor as a memory map.[8] An associative memory was described in Sec. 2.4.4 for a paged machine in which the key was the page number. Here the concept is identical except that a longer key is required, namely, the combined page and segment number. If the double indexing described above has recently been performed, the page and segment number along with the actual page address will have been inserted in the associative memory. Then when this page-segment number is used again, the page address is retrieved directly from the associative memory and lookup in the segment- and page-descriptor tables is avoided.

Since the associative memory is restricted in size, hardware algorithms have to be implemented which determine which page-segment numbers to replace when it is full and pages not in the associative memory are addressed.[7,8]

Let us now backtrack and discuss indirect addressing. Since indirect addressing is widely used for the segment-linking scheme to be dis-

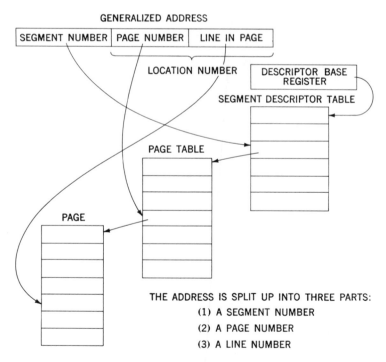

GENERALIZED ADDRESS

| SEGMENT NUMBER | PAGE NUMBER | LINE IN PAGE |

LOCATION NUMBER

DESCRIPTOR BASE REGISTER

SEGMENT DESCRIPTOR TABLE

PAGE TABLE

PAGE

THE ADDRESS IS SPLIT UP INTO THREE PARTS:
(1) A SEGMENT NUMBER
(2) A PAGE NUMBER
(3) A LINE NUMBER

FIG. 2.16 Calculation of physical location from a generalized address using paging.

cussed below, a method of indirect addressing in terms of generalized addresses is useful. Whenever an indirect address is specified, the GE-645 fetches a pair of words. The location of the indirect pair is obtained by the address-calculation method (described above and illustrated in Figs. 2.15 and 2.16). This pair, based on the setting of certain bits in the first word of the pair, can be interpreted in three ways:

1 Fetch the operand from the same segment as the indirect words; the location is given by the first word.

2 Fetch the operand from the segment which has the segment number contained in the first word of the pair and the location within the segment given by the second word.

3 Fetch the operand from the segment specified by the segment number in the base-pair register indicated in the first word and location within the segment indicated in the second word.

Indirect addressing and indexing can proceed to any level and thus pass through several segments. Indirect addressing may go several levels in one segment before reaching the operand or before passing to another segment. In effect, indirect addressing on the 645 is identical conceptually with indirect addressing on conventional machines except that one obtains a segment number as well as location number at each level.

2.5.5 Introduction to Segment Linking in the Multics System

With the above outline of addressing on the GE-645, we can now discuss the techniques used to link segments. In a system using static relocation or dynamic relocation using base registers or paging all procedures and data are linked together at the time of loading into physical or logical space. The problem resulting from these approaches was to create bindings to physical or logical space, respectively, at load time. In static relocation, this created problems with physical-space allocation at execution time, and in the base register or paged systems, it created problems with logical-space allocation. We have already mentioned that the Multics segmentation implementation allows allocation of logical space by assigning a segment descriptor (base register) at execution time. This segment descriptor and corresponding segment number is to be assigned only at the time a segment is required by a process. Prior to this point the required segment is simply a file stored somewhere within the auxiliary-memory hierarchy. The discussion to follow, based on the excellent paper by Daley and Dennis,[12] outlines the mechanisms used in Multics to assign segment descriptors and link the segments of a process together.

One of the goals of the Multics segmentation implementation is that a segment must be capable of existing in different places in the logical space of each process. This implies that each process sharing a segment must be capable of referencing it with a different segment number. Because the programmer cannot know what segment number is to be assigned at execution time, he must be able to make all intersegment references by symbolic segment name. The linkage mechanism must be able to convert symbolic segment names into segment numbers at execution time.

Another desirable feature of the linkage mechanism is that it allows reference to items within a segment to be by symbolic name rather than relative location. With this requirement, a segment may be modified and recompiled, and if its name and symbolic item names are not modified, no changes are required in the other segments which reference it.

Further restrictions are placed on the linkage mechanism by the desire to share procedure segments. To be sharable procedures must be reentrant. This means that the procedure part cannot be modified during execution and that unique data areas for temporary storage must be associated with each process calling a shared-procedure segment. Because the shared procedure may call other procedure segments unknown to the original calling procedure segment, this assignment of temporary storage should be handled in a way that avoids prior arrangement. These requirements and others are discussed further below.

Before the linkage process can proceed, a segment referenced by a symbolic name must be represented by a segment descriptor in the segment-descriptor table of the process which referenced it. In other words, the referenced segment must be assigned a segment number. The operation of setting up a segment descriptor for a segment is called making the segment *known*. Associated with each process is a symbol table called the *known-segment table*. When a segment number is assigned to a segment, an entry is also created in the known-segment table, consisting of a symbolic-segment-name—segment-number pair.

When an instruction with a symbolic segment name is first encountered, a call is generated to the supervisor, which first searches the known-segment table for a symbolic segment name like that in the instruction. If one is found, the supervisor obtains the corresponding segment number and continues with the linking process. If one is not found, a segment descriptor is created, a segment number is assigned, and an entry in the known-segment table is made. The segment descriptor is placed in the first free location in the segment-descriptor table. The segment number is just the index into this table for the corresponding descriptor. The segment number of a segment can vary from process to process and between sessions for the same process.

The segment descriptor created must indicate where the segment is located. If the search of the known segment fails to find a segment name equal to the one given in the instruction, supervisor routines called the *file system* are invoked to find the segment. The Multics file system is discussed further in Chap. 6. The file system checks a table containing the locations of all segments known to any process currently active and other tables, if necessary, called *file directories,* to find the location of the segment. The location of the segment is then entered into the appropriate segment descriptor. Movement of information within the memory system and memory allocation are topics separate from linking and are not discussed further at this time.

Let us now consider what must happen when the first reference is made to a segment. For example, consider the code

$$\underline{\langle A \rangle}$$

. . . .
     load accumulator $\langle S \rangle / [\alpha 1]$
     store accumulator $\langle S \rangle / [\alpha 2]$
. . . .

which is executing in a segment $\langle A \rangle$. The two-dimensional symbolic addresses refer to a segment different from $\langle A \rangle$.

We can recognize at this point several problems created by the requirement to use symbolic addresses. One question which probably comes to the reader's mind is: Where is the symbolic address stored? There is not enough room in the address field of an instruction for a symbolic-address pair of more than one character each. Another problem is how use is to be made of the GE-645 addressing mechanism once the first reference to an instruction is encountered. When a segment number has been assigned, one wants to use the hardware generalized-address mechanism to make further references as efficient as possible. The system must convert the symbolic address to information usable by the hardware. Because pure procedures are wanted, the linkage operation cannot modify the contents of procedure segment $\langle A \rangle$. This implies that the information associated with external references which is to be modified has to exist external to segment $\langle A \rangle$.

The linkage mechanism of Multics solves these problems by associating with every segment a set of information called the *linkage section,* which for segment $\langle A \rangle$ we call $\langle$link A$\rangle$. This linkage section is created by the assembler or compiler. The compiler creates a pair of indirect words in the linkage section associated with each out-of-segment reference. The instruction contains a reference to these words. In order to allow a transfer to the supervisor on the first symbolic reference a certain code in the indirect pair causes a transfer to take place to the supervisor if the referenced segment address is in symbolic form. In this case, the indirect pair actually contains pointers to the symbol strings.

When a symbolic segment name is encountered, the supervisor searches the known-segment table for a symbolic segment name the same as the one in the instruction. If the name is found, the associated segment number is placed in the first indirect word. If the name is not found, the system goes through the operation of making the segment known. The symbolic location within segment name, for example, $\langle \alpha 1 \rangle$ above, must now be converted to a relative location within the segment. In order to keep each segment as self-contained as possible, each segment carries with it a symbol table of all symbols which may be referenced by external segments. This symbol table is located at a standard location known to the system. Thus once the segment number is known, the segment can be located and the segment symbol table searched to find the location number of $\langle \alpha 1 \rangle$, for example. This number then replaces the contents of the second indirect word associated with the given instruction in the linkage segment. The code bits of the indirect pair are modified to indicate that a generalized address now exists there and the memory reference can be allowed to proceed as discussed in Sec. 2.5.4 for indirect addresses. All future references to this instruction automatically reference the external segment by indirect addressing through the linkage section. The supervisor is involved in only the first reference.

There is still the question: How does a segment know where its linkage segment is located? In order for procedure segments to be reentrant, the address field of instructions making external reference can contain only fixed displacements. The fixed displacement is an address relative to the beginning of the linkage section where the linkage information is stored associated with the instruction. Another generalized-address pointer must exist which points to the base location of the linkage section. The generalized address used to point to the linkage section resides in the processor registers used by the hardware in forming the generalized address. One of the base-pair registers called the *link pointer* is assigned by convention to this task. Linkage sections can be thought of as separate segments, although in certain cases several linkage sections for a process are placed in a single segment. Having seen how a procedure segment is linked to a data segment, we now examine how procedure segments are linked.

2.5.6 Linking Procedure Segments in Multics   A set of mechanisms related to those discussed in the previous section is required to link procedure segments. When one procedure calls another, conventions are required for transmission of arguments, saving and restoring the processor state again, and return of control. Because the procedures in Multics are reentrant, the called procedure must also have access to private storage associated with the calling procedure. This private storage cannot be contained within the calling procedure because it is to be reentrant itself and several processes may be using it. Therefore, the temporary storage must be external to the calling-procedure segment and associated with each process using the procedure. How is this temporary storage to be allocated automatically without the programmer's having to know the detailed execution path through the procedures of the process? Given the usual convention that a called procedure eventually returns to the calling procedure at the point of call, one can represent the execution path through a structure of called procedures in a data structure referred to as a *pushdown stack*. The convention used in Multics is to perform linkage between procedure segments with a pushdown stack. Pushdown stacks are important data structures frequently used in systems programming. Here we can only outline their use in Multics. Further background and motivation for use of pushdown stacks is given in the excellent books by Knuth[21] and Wegner.[23]

A pushdown stack is a last in, first out list. In Multics, the stack is a segment. There is one stack segment for each process. One of the base-pair registers is assigned by convention to *point* to the current entry in the stack segment and is called the *stack pointer*. An entry in the stack consists of a block of contiguous words. This stack entry is used for pass-

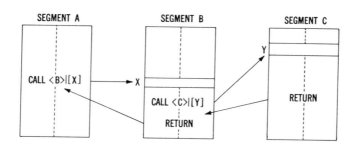

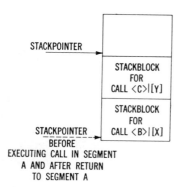

STACK SEGMENT FOR PROCESS P AFTER
CALL <B>|[X] IN SEGMENT A AND CALL <C>|[Y]
IN SEGMENT B HAVE BEEN EXECUTED

FIG. 2.17   Procedure-segment CALL linkage by pushdown stack.

ing arguments, return control, saving the processor state, and temporary storage. Information is placed in, or removed from, a stack entry relative to the stack pointer. Arguments can also be passed by placing them in the same segment as the Call, relative to the CALL, and using a base-pair register to point to the argument list. This mechanism is illustrated in simplified form in Fig. 2.17. Before the CALL ⟨B⟩/[x] in segment A is executed, the stack pointer points to the base of an entry in the stack segment, as shown by the dashed arrow. After the CALL, the stack pointer is moved to point to the base of the next entry. After the next CALL ⟨C⟩/[y] in segment B is executed, the stack pointer is as shown with the solid arrow. A procedure segment stores the processor state, fetches arguments, and uses temporary storage from words in the stack entry assigned by convention relative to the stack pointer.

When a RETURN is executed, the processor state is restored from appropriate information stored in the current stack entry and the stack pointer is automatically adjusted to point to the previous stack entry. In Fig. 2.17, the stack pointer after two RETURNS have been executed is shown with the dashed arrow. The use of a pushdown stack for a procedure CALL linkage is very general and allows reentrant procedures to be easily written. All procedures are automatically recursive; i.e., they may call themselves. Blocks of storage in the stack segment are automatically allocated and released by the CALL and RETURN mechanism.

One further point should be discussed. When transfer is made between segments, either directly or by CALL, the base-pair register pointing to the linkage section of the currently executing segment must be changed and saved in the case of a CALL. The code required to change the link pointer is most naturally associated with the segment about to be entered. To handle this situation in Multics the linkage convention discussed in Sec. 2.5.5 is modified for procedure-segment linkage as follows. Assume that a transfer from segment A to segment B is to be accomplished. The linkage to segment B could take place indirectly through the linkage section for segment A, but the link pointer would be unchanged. To get the linkage base-pair register changed automatically without introducing code for this purpose at the entry point in segment B, the linkage goes through segment A's linkage section into segment B's linkage section. Code is placed in segment B's linkage segment to change the link pointer and then transfer to the entry in segment B. The mechanism is shown in Fig. 2.18.

This mechanism is used on a CALL with the additional operations required to save the state of the processor, including base-pair registers, in the stack segment.

2.5.7 Sharing Programs and Data We are now ready to see how segmentation allows sharing to take place with full generality. The interesting ques-

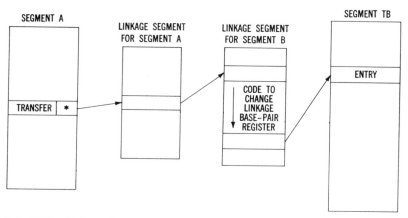

FIG. 2.18 Linkage between procedure segments.

tion is: How does the shared procedure, which must be a pure procedure, access the correct data segments for the process which is presently in control? This problem is solved by associating with the shared procedure a linkage segment for each process using it. Or, from another point of view, each process using a shared segment has a linkage segment for the shared segment. When the shared procedure is first created, a linkage segment is created. A copy of this linkage segment is obtained by the system for each process using the shared segment. These linkage sections are "filled in," as described above, to provide the proper coupling. The correct linkage section is referenced at a given time because the base-pair registers are saved and re-stored as part of the machine state.

The previous discussion showed how multiple shared procedures can be used simultaneously without conflicts of location in logical space through allocation by use of the segment-descriptor table. The solution to the problem of sharing data containing addresses now needs to be mentioned. If the addresses are internal to the data segment, they appear relative to the start of the segment. The starting point of the data segment is given by the segment descriptor, and thus no conflict of positioning in logical space can occur for this case. If the addresses refer back to a procedure segment, a linkage section is set up for each process using the shared data. The linkage section assures that no conflict can occur in positioning the data segment or procedure segments using the data. This completes our outline of the Multics segmentation implementation.

2.5.8 Other Approaches to Segmentation Implementation We now briefly examine some other implementations to become acquainted with a few possible variations of the segmentation concept. The earliest implementation

of segmentation known to us occurred on the Burroughs B-5000.   A process
in the B-5000 contains up to 1,024 segments, procedure segments may
be any length, and data segments are limited to 1,024 words.   Data structures requiring greater space use multiple segments.   The segments are
not paged and thus are the unit of physical-memory allocation.   The table
equivalent to the segment-descriptor table in the B-5000 system is called
the *program reference table*.   No attempt is made to use segmentation in
its full generality.[10]

   In a segmentation scheme, such as that of Multics, where any segment can reference in principle the entire logical-address space (all segments), many bits of address information are required in the implementation,
thus requiring base-pair registers, paired indirect words, and so forth.   In
practice any given segment need only communicate with a limited number
of segments.   A segmentation scheme of Evans and Le Clerc[13] limits any
given segment to directly addressing a small number of other segments;
each of these in turn, however, can address other segments, so that the
total address space is very large, but the addressing and protection hardware
required can be simplified.

   The Scientific Control Corporation (SCC) 6700 system, developed
at the University of California, Berkeley, by M. W. Pirtle, B. W. Lampson,
W. W. Lichtenberger, and others, along with SCC, contains a segmentation
system with several interesting ideas.[16]   The protection scheme on the SCC-
6700 is discussed in Secs. 4.1.2 and 4.1.3.   The major new idea of interest
here concerns the updating of the hardware associative map.   The SCC-6700
allows a process to access 32 segments of size 16K each.   There is an
associative map, as in the GE-645.   When a segment and page are referenced which are not in the map, instead of utilizing the time to transfer
to software routines to update the association map from the segment and
page tables, a special microprogrammed (see Sec. 4.3 for a discussion
of microprogramming) processor is invoked to perform these functions.
This special processor has access to memory and, because of its specialized
design and high performance, can update the associative map from the
segment and page tables much faster than normal system routines.   The
SCC-6700 has instruction and operand fetch overlap and thus the associative
map can often be updated without delaying the central processor.   Intersegment linking is handled through indirect addressing, as in Multics.

   The system besides Multics which has received considerable attention within the profession is the IBM 360/67[7] which is based on a scheme
developed at the University of Michigan.[11]   The segmentation system of
the RCA Spectra 70/46 is very similar.[9]   The first major difference between
the GE-645 and the IBM 360/67 is in the way a generalized address (segment number/location within segment) is formed.

   All generalized addresses in the IBM 360/67 are formed using conventional indexing and indirect addressing.   The address formed after ful

modification is broken into two parts, a segment number and a location-within-segment number (the location-within-segment number is paged, as in the GE-645, but we ignore that level of detail). In the GE-645 the segment number could not be modified by indexing. The two types of segmentation have been called *linear* and *symbolic*, respectively.[2] With symbolic segmentation (GE-645), the segments are logically independent in the sense that there are no contiguous addresses across segment boundaries. That is, there is no relationship between the last address of segment n and the first address of segment $n + 1$. There is no way using address modification through indexing to obtain an address in segment $n + 1$ from an address in segment n. With linear segmentation (IBM 360/67) addresses are contiguous across segment boundaries. The last address of segment n is contiguous with the first address of segment $n + 1$. That is, one can modify an address in segment n to produce an address in segment $n + 1$.

This difference has many implications, one of the more important being that because the segment number is the relative position of a segment descriptor in the segment-descriptor table, the position in the segment-descriptor table of a descriptor is very important in a linear-segmented system. A linear-segmented space is not two-dimensional but is a large one-dimensional logical space.

The 24-bit-address version of the IBM 360/67 can address only 16 segments, which commonly makes it necessary to pack several independent programs in the same segment. With such a usage one can reduce the number of page tables required over what a strictly paged system would demand, because the page tables of shared programs can be shared, but the full logical generality of segmentation would seem to be restricted. That is, used in this way, segmentation facilitates physical-memory utilization but ceases to be strictly a logical concept, thus losing some of its justification for existence.

As with the GE-645, the IBM 360/67 uses an associative map to try and reduce the number of times the double table lookup in segment- and page-descriptor tables is required. In the IBM 360/67, however, the instruction fetches are not made through the full map but through a separate associative register which acts like a base register for the program counter. Therefore, the situation of a loop executing across page boundaries requires references to the maps in main memory. This situation would not occur in the GE-645 because both pages of the loop have entries in the associative map. Another feature of the 360/67 is that memory protection is based on blocks of physical memory and not on logical units like segments, as in the GE-645.

2.5.9 Summary and Conclusions Segmentation is a technique for the achievement of a large logical-address space, and it can be used to achieve full generality of procedure and data sharing. The technique is based on two-dimensional addressing, symbolic segment name, and symbolic location-within-segment name. Segmentation is a technique for logical-space allocation. Segments can be paged to aid physical-space allocation. Paging is a technique for physical-space allocation.

A number of tables and mechanisms are required to implement segmentation. A central table is the segment-descriptor table. The location in logical space for a segment in a process is represented by the location of a descriptor in the segment-descriptor table. The segment number locates the appropriate segment descriptor for a segment. Different processes sharing the same segment can reference the segment with different segment numbers.

Another important concept basic to the Multics segmentation implementation is that of the linkage section and the use of indirect addressing. The linkage section provides, in effect, the connection between a symbolic segment name and a segment number for references external to a segment. The linkage section is used to achieve full generality of procedure and data sharing.

Segmentation has been developed to achieve full generality in the allocation of large logical-address spaces. To be useful, evaluation of segmentation must be performed at two levels: (1) at the level of the fundamental assumption, namely, full generality in creating and manipulating large logical spaces is truly required, and (2) at the level of a particular implementation, namely, assurance that the implementation being examined is the most effective way to achieve its goals.

In our view, segmentation is an important step in the evolution of machine organization. There is an increasing need in many areas of application to create address spaces larger than main memory and to remove from the programmer direct responsibility for keeping track of where his information is stored. Mechanisms for a generalized sharing would also seem to be important aids in decreasing the development expense of many application systems and easing maintenance. It is also our observation, however, that many classes of problems do not require full generality in manipulating large logical spaces. Systems designed specifically for these classes of problems using base registers or paging can probably meet their needs more economically than more general segmented systems.

With respect to segmentation implementation, we feel there is still room for development of additional resource-allocation aids implemented in hardware. The special microprocessor used in the SCC-6700, mentioned above, to aid updating the associative map is one such additional mechanism. Further measurement and experience with such important pioneering systems as Multics and the IBM 360/67 will undoubtedly point the way toward the type of additional hardware mechanisms which would be useful.

2.6 I/O PROCESSOR AND MONITOR-ADDRESS FORMATION

2.6.1 Mapping I/O Addresses An aspect of addressing which should be mentioned is related to I/O devices. When a process requests that certain information be written into or out of main storage in a system utilizing paging or segmentation, it uses logical addresses and thus the I/O processor should probably also access memory through some type of map.[17] This requirement is particularly important for block transfers where part of the block is in one page and the remainder is in one or more other pages. In a conventional I/O processor the starting address of a transfer and the number of words to be transferred are given to the I/O processor by the CPU, and then the specified block of information is transferred. In a paged system without mapping in the I/O processor, a new address must be sent to the I/O processor by the CPU when a page boundary is passed. This process slows down the I/O operation and on transfers to such devices as high-speed drums could result in lost information.

On the XDS-940, the direct-access communication channels (DACC) are sent two page numbers before a transfer is started so that when a page boundary is crossed, the second page number is automatically used to control the transfer. Then a signal is sent to the CPU to send the next page number, and the CPU has the time corresponding to a page transfer to respond.[18] Another approach is being taken with a cathode-ray-tube display processor to be attached directly to the 940 memory.[19] In this device a full memory map identical to that in the CPU is used.

This philosophy carried to a segmented system might require full segmentation hardware in each processor, I/O processor, and central processor or some scheme to allow all processors to share such hardware.[17] Such schemes would allow a symbolic segment-name—symbolic-location-within-segment-name to be passed to I/O processors rather than first requiring conversion to absolute addresses by the central processing unit. Developing a unified economical address-formation scheme for all types of processors in a system with dynamic relocation requires further study before additional comment can be given.

2.6.2 Mapping Monitor Addresses The remaining topic is the question of how system routines access memory. In the XDS-940 system there are, in fact, two hardware memory maps, one for user processes and the other for the system. The system would not require mapping if system routines occupied fixed core positions. Some system routines are not used frequently enough or required to give a fast enough response to need permanent residence in main memory. One would like to be able to dynamically allocate memory to these routines as they are needed. The XDS-940 system achieves this ability by using a system map. The machine uses one or the other of the two maps depending on the mode in which it is operating, system mode or user mode (discussed further in Sec. 4.1.3). Use of two maps enables the system to perform its functions without requiring changes to the user's map.

The Multics system uses a different approach. System segments are assigned to each process's segment-descriptor table and then logically become a part of each process. A potential difficulty with this approach is that system interrupts and user calls to the system which occur during the execution of a user process may cause changes to the associative map, thus necessitating frequent double table lookups to restore the map when control returns to the user process. We have seen no comment on this problem in the literature. Whether it is potentially serious depends on the frequency of interrupts and transfers to the system. There are few available published statistics on this problem, although Freibergs[20] found that for a multiprogrammed batch system there was usually a call to the system for every 100 to 1,000 instructions executed. Because of added facilities of a timesharing system, one can expect a higher rate of system calls. Collection of statistics useful in designing future systems is discussed in Chap. 7.

2.7   SUMMARY

In this chapter we have introduced a number of important concepts associated with addressing and allocation of memory, both physical-memory space and logical-memory space. The distinction between physical-memory space and virtual or logical space has become very important in the design of timeshared systems. User and system processes can usefully be viewed as running on virtual processors, each having its own logical-memory space.

Base-register and paging concepts create the same one-dimensional form of logical space and are techniques to aid allocation of physical space. These techniques run into logical-space-allocation problems, if procedures and data are to be shared with full generality. Segmentation, a technique developed to overcome logical-space-allocation problems, creates a two-dimensional logical space. The motivations for these concepts were examined in some detail.

The other major idea introduced is that of a map from logical space to physical space. The map can be implemented in hardware or software or (usually) a combination of both.

REFERENCES

1   **McGee, W. C.:** On Dynamic Program Relocation, *IBM Systems J.*, vol. 4, no. 3, p. 184, 1965.

2   **Randell, B., and C. J. Kuehner:** Dynamic Storage Allocation Systems, *Commun. ACM*, vol. 11, no. 5, p. 297, May, 1968.

3 Corbato, F. J., et al., An Experimental Time-sharing System, *AFIPS Conf. Proc., Spring Joint Computer Conf.*, vol. 21, pp. 335–344, 1962.

4 Amdahl, G.: Unpublished simulation study, IBM Corporation, 1965.

5 Kilburn, T., et al.: One-level Storage System, *IEEE Trans.*, vol. EC-11, no. 2, p. 223, 1962.

6 Dennis, J. R.: Segmentation and the Design of Multiprogrammed Computer Systems, *J. ACM*, vol. 12, no. 4, pp. 589–602, October, 1965.

7 Gibson, C. T.: Time-sharing in the IBM System/360: Model 67, *AFIPS Conf. Proc., Spring Joint Computer Conf.*, vol. 28, p. 61, 1966.

8 Glaser, E. L., et al.: System Design of a Computer for Time-sharing Applications, *AFIPS Conf. Proc., Fall Joint Computer Conf.*, vol. 27, pp. 197–202, 1965.

9 Oppenheimer, G., and N. Weizer: Resource Management for a Medium Scale Time Sharing Operating System, *Commun. ACM*, vol. 11, no. 5, p. 313, May, 1968.

10 Wald, B.: "The Descriptor: A Definition of the B5000 Information Processing System," Burroughs Corp., Detroit, Mich., 1961.

11 Arden, B. W., et al.: Program and Addressing Structure in a Time-sharing Environment, *J. ACM*, pp. 1–16, January, 1966.

12 Daley, R. C., and J. B. Dennis: Virtual Memory Processes, and Sharing in MULTICS, *Commun. ACM*, vol. 11, no. 5, p. 306, May, 1968.

13 Evans, D. C., and J. Y. LeClerc: Address Mapping and the Control of Access in an Interactive Computer, *AFIPS Conf. Proc., Spring Joint Computer Conf.*, vol. 30, pp. 23–30, 1967.

14 Graham, R. M.: Protection in an Information Processing Utility, *Commun. ACM*, vol. 11, no. 5, p. 365, May, 1968.

15 Organick, E. I.: A Guide to Multics for Subsystem Writers, *Project MAC Doc.*, March, 1967.

16 "6700 Time-sharing Computer Reference Manual," Scientific Control Corporation, Carrollten, Texas, February, 1969 (additional information also obtained at a public presentation of the 6700).

17 Smith, Arthur A.: Input/Output in Time-shared, Segmented, Multiprocessor Systems, (thesis) MAC-TR-28 *MIT Project MAC Doc.*, June, 1966.

18 Pirtle, M. W.: Modifications of the SDS-930 for the Implementation of Time-sharing, *Univ. Calif. Berkeley Project Genie Doc.*, M-1, April 4, 1967.

19 Watson, R. W., et al.: A Display Processor Design, *AFIPS Conf. Proc., Fall Joint Computer Conf.*, vol. 35, 1969.

20 Freibergs, I. F.: The Dynamic Behavior of Programs, *AFIPS Conf. Proc., Fall Joint Computer Conf.*, vol. 33, pt. 2, pp. 1163–1168, 1968.

21 Knuth, D. E.: "Fundamental Algorithms: The Art of Computer Programming," Addison-Wesley Publishing Company, Inc., Reading, Mass., 1968.

22 Conti, C. J.: Structural Aspects of the System 1360 Model 85, *IBM Systems J.*, vol. 7, no. 1, pp. 2–29, 1968.

23 Wegner, P.: "Programming Languages, Information Structures and Machine Organization," McGraw-Hill Book Company, New York, 1968.

24 Corbato, F. J.: System Requirements for Multiple Access Timeshared Computers, Project MAC Document MAC-TR-3.

chapter THREE

Communications

3.1 COMMUNICATION PROBLEM AREAS

3.1.1 Introduction The purpose of a timeshared computer system is rapid time multiplexing of computer-system resources on behalf of user requirements. The system attempts to perform this multiplexing so as to satisfy user completion and response-time needs and to utilize system resources efficiently. A useful point of view toward these systems is that they are large communication-switching centers which control the transmission and transformation of information as it moves between the large number and variety of devices attached.

3.1.2 Communication with Main Memory The central point through which the information passes in present organizations is main memory (with a possible side journey to the CPU for transformation) as it moves from one device to another. Main memory is a prime system resource and consequently a potential source of communications problems. In timesharing systems, multiple CPUs, high-transfer-rate secondary storage devices, and numerous I/O devices share access to main memory. The processors which control the secondary storage and I/O devices and communication with memory are usually referred to as channels, I/O controllers, or I/O processors. A design problem is to provide the various processors with an adequate data-transfer capability to and from main memory. Ideally each processor should be able to transfer a datum to or from main memory at its convenience without regard for the memory's ability to accept or supply the datum at that particular moment or the ability of the processor-to-memory transfer-addressing path (memory bus) to effect the transfer. Unfortunately, economic and technical considerations relegate the above ideal to a standard against which practical systems can be compared. Concepts related to communication with main memory are discussed in Sec. 3.2.

3.1.3 Communication with Auxiliary Storage and I/O Devices

A basic communication problem with auxiliary storage and I/O devices is gaining access to a direct-transfer path to main memory. A timesharing system contains a variety of devices attached to it. Associated with these devices is a range of data-transfer rates. Direct-transfer paths to main memory require logic to resolve conflicts for access to a memory module and require sending and receiving circuits at each end of the path; therefore, it is usually uneconomical to provide a separate path for each device. It is possible, however, using the fact that the attached devices have a range of transfer-rate requirements, to design I/O processors which enable many devices to share one direct-transfer path to main memory concurrently. This problem is discussed in Sec. 3.3. Besides the data-transfer needs, there are also control communication needs associated with auxiliary storage and I/O devices (see Secs. 3.3 and 4.2).

3.1.4 Communication with Remote Devices

Three major communication problems are associated with remote devices:

1 The transmission of information between the central facility and the remote devices
2 The interface between transmission lines and the central facility
3 The interface between transmission lines and the remote devices

We are concerned in this book only with the logical problems and the concepts they present the designer of timesharing systems; we are not concerned with the many other signal-transmission and interface problems of interest to an electrical engineer generally. Along with the transmission of information we must consider techniques for utilizing standard telephone lines for digital information, sharing lines among several devices, and synchronizing communication between remote points. Associated with the interface between transmission lines and the central facility are the problems of identifying, controlling, and addressing communicating devices and converting the transmitted information to a form usable by the central machine and vice versa. Associated with the interface between transmission lines and the remote devices are problems of encoding and decoding information and providing identification. These problems are discussed in Sec. 3.4.

3.2 MAIN-MEMORY COMMUNICATION

3.2.1 Multiple Memory Box and Bus Organization

The technological problem to be solved in the design of a memory communication system is to provide adequate transfer capability between main memory and all processors

requiring access. In practical systems, the rate at which data can be transferred between processors and main memory is limited by the transfer
capabilities of the memory itself and the memory busses. The rate at which
the memory can transfer information is often referred to as the *memory
bandwidth,* usually measured in words per second. Bandwidth limitations
also exist for the memory busses. Because the memory system is shared
by several processors, care must be taken in the design to keep performance
from being seriously degraded due to *interference* caused by simultaneous
attempts on the part of the several processors to utilize a facility such
as a memory bus or portion of memory itself. Figure 3.1 shows a common
method for organizing the memory structure in a resource-sharing system.

The memory, instead of being considered one monolithic unit with
one set of addressing circuitry and one set of read/write circuits, is broken
into some number m of smaller boxes each with its own set of addressing
and read/write circuits. In the XDS-940, for example, a 64K memory
is broken into four 16K boxes. Accessing each box are up to n data-address
busses. Each data-address bus has cables for data to and from memory
and for the required address. The quantity n in present systems usually
varies from 2 to 5 because many devices can share a bus, because there
are a limited number of processors, and because of memory-bandwidth limitations. The number of busses required and bus organization are discussed
further in Sec. 3.3. A schematic of one representative memory box is
shown in Fig. 3.2. Any combination of busses 1, 2, 3, or 4 may request
access to the memory box simultaneously. The priority access control must
decide which bus is to be given access on this particular memory cycle,
and the requests on the other busses must remain pending until the next
cycle or be canceled and renewed on the next cycle. The term *bus structure*
is frequently used to refer to the bus-priority control complex. The memory-system bandwidth has two bounding numbers associated with it.

The maximum memory-system bandwidth for the system shown in
Fig. 3.1 is $p \times R$, where p is the smaller of the number of memory modules
m and the number of access paths n, and R is the maximum transfer

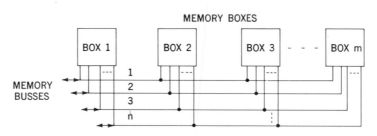

FIG. 3.1 Memory organization in a resource-sharing system.

rate of each box. In other words, the maximum transfer rate is acheived when each path requests access to a separate module.

The minimum transfer rate is just R and occurs when all paths request access to the same module. There is *interference* in this case.

The scheme shown in Fig. 3.1 cuts interference by allowing simultaneous access to more than one box. That is, if bus 1 requests access to box 2 at the same time bus 2 requests access to box 3, both accesses are granted because each box has its own addressing and read/write circuitry. Even given the scheme shown in Fig. 3.1, serious interference can result when memory addresses are contiguous in the boxes, e.g., box 1 having addresses 1 to 16K and box 2 addresses 16K $+$ 1 to 32K. Consider the case of a high-speed drum processor which transfers at the memory rate. If this device has a higher priority for memory access than the arithmetic unit, then during a block transfer the arithmetic unit could be denied memory access for a prolonged period if it tried to access the memory box being used by the drum processor. To get around this problem designers have developed the technique called *interleaving*.

In an interleaved memory, consecutive addresses are in different memory boxes. For example, in a two-memory-box system all the even addresses might be in one box and all the odd addresses in the other. With an interleaved memory, the probability of one processor's tying up the memory for a significant time is greatly decreased. The design problem is to determine the size of each box and whether or not interleaving is to occur over all boxes or over groupings of boxes. These questions can be studied with simulation techniques.[1]

To make a memory reference in one of these multibus configurations, a processor first makes a request for use of its memory bus; and when this request is granted, it uses this bus to transmit its memory reference request to the appropriate memory module. If either of these requests is rejected, the processor repeats the procedure or leaves its request pending.

To resolve conflicting requests for either a memory bus or memory

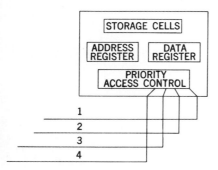

FIG. 3.2   Detail of a memory box.

box some type of priority mechanism must be employed.   Priorities typically are assigned to processors and to memory busses; the latter are used to resolve conflicting requests for a memory module.   The design of the total memory structure including the priority scheme is critical if bottlenecks in this important area are to be avoided and the possibility of expansion is to be provided for the addition of new I/O devices and processors.

3.2.2 A Restrictive Memory-bus Organization   In contrast to the memory organization discussed above, let us consider a memory organization which seems inadequate to meet the demands placed on it in a timesharing system. A schematic of the memory-access path is shown in Fig. 3.3.   This organization is commonly found on many small- to medium-scale machines.   The memory is not interleaved, and there is only one access and addressing path to memory, which the CPU and I/O processors share.   In such systems the I/O processors usually have priority over the CPU for access to memory because they may lose data if they cannot access memory when needed. When an I/O processor requires access to memory, the CPU is halted during memory addressing and access.   With such a memory organization there is the possibility of serious interference with the CPU.

Another type of processor available on many such machines is called a *multiplexor processor*.   It allows multiple slower-speed I/O devices to be connected to a data path concurrently.   The hardware for assembly of characters from the slower-speed devices into words uses CPU registers. Further, temporary storage for memory addresses associated with the transfers of the slower-speed devices and for the partially assembled words is part of main storage.   Thus, during character transfers from the slower-speed devices, additional CPU interference results.

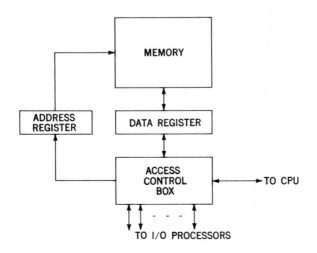

FIG. 3.3 Single memory-access path.

3.2.3 Synchronous and Asynchronous Communication

One can classify memory systems into two types, *synchronous* and *asynchronous*. In synchronous systems, requests for memory can occur only at discrete time points, and thus the concept of *simultaneous requests* can be used. The point of request is usually just prior to the start of a memory cycle, and at this time all processors requesting a memory reference place their requests on the lines and the priority mechanism arbitrates between them. In asynchronous systems, a processor can request a memory reference at any point in time, and the concept of simultaneous requests loses meaning. In systems such as the GE-645, asynchronous memory access is used, while the XDS-940 is an example of a synchronous system.

The argument for using asynchronous memory references and asynchronous communication among major system modules is that it allows replacement of modules with others having different performance characteristics without requiring modification of unreplaced modules. Further, asynchronous communication can take place at maximum rates not restricted by the times fixed for synchronous systems. In asynchronous systems, the concept of priority has little meaning because the requests for access generally are handled on a first in, first served basis. Therefore, physical and statistical properties of the various processes cannot be easily taken advantage of to improve the performance at a given cost point by sharing memory busses or by allowing variable-priority requests. Synchronous systems can make use of variable-priority information.

3.2.4 Multics System Memory-bus Organization

A typical asynchronous system is shown in Fig. 3.4, where each CPU has its own bus to each memory box. Note that the fast secondary storage device used for swapping (the drum) has its own bus to each memory module. Finally a processor called the GIOC (general I/O controller) has a separate bus to each module (the GIOC is discussed further in Sec. 3.3.2). One of its major functions is to schedule access to its bus to each memory module. Because the system is asynchronous, access to a memory module is on a first in, first served basis. The memory modules are interleaved. This asynchronous approach provides ease of replacement of CPUs or memories with faster units with little or no hardware and software modification. One problem with gaining full bandwidth from an asynchronous system is that memories operating continuously are inherently synchronous, and therefore an access decision must be made at a point in time and cannot easily be revoked even if a higher-priority request comes along slightly later.

3.2.5 XDS-940 Memory-bus Organization

An example of a synchronous system which can inexpensively use simple priority schemes to increase memory and bus bandwidth is the XDS-940, a schematic of which is shown in Fig. 3.5.   This system also illustrates a number of other concepts usable with asynchronous systems.

There are two busses to 940 memory.   The memory is interleaved four ways.   In the XDS-930, which served as the basis for the 940, the bus called B_2 (second path) in the figure always has priority over bus B_1 (first path).   This arrangement of priority is common in second-generation and many third-generation machines and is based on the idea that high-speed devices such as drums and disks must have access to memory when required or data can be lost.   Data can be lost because these devices are constantly sending data due to their rotation.   In the direct-access communications channel (DACC) of the 930 there is a one register buffer, as shown in Fig. 3.6.   On input from a device the assembly register packs

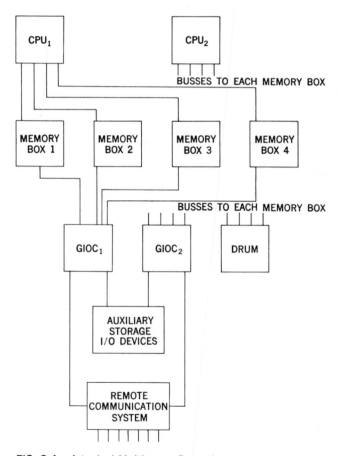

FIG. 3.4   A typical Multics configuration.

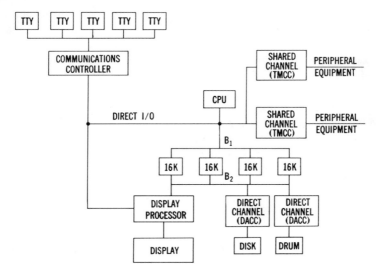

FIG. 3.5   XDS-940 configuration.

four 6-bit characters in a 24-bit word and then transfers the word to the buffer register.   At this point the 930 DACC requests a memory cycle to store the contents of the buffer register into memory.   Because the second path has priority over the first path, this request is granted and the potential value of the buffer register is not obtained.   On output to a device an analogous operation results in the opposite direction.

When the assembly register transfers a word to the buffer register,

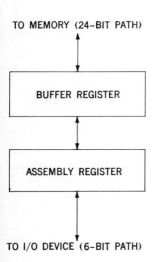

FIG. 3.6   A typical Multics configuration.

the buffer register has at least three memory cycles in which to transfer its contents to memory before the assembly register transfers its next word to it.   Therefore, during any one of these three cycles, the buffer register can accomplish its transfer.   The purpose of buffering is to gain time. Therefore, what the developers of the 940 did was to take advantage of this potential buffering action by allowing the second path to request memory access with either a higher or lower priority than the first path.   For example, after the assembly register transfers its contents to the buffer register, the DACC makes its first request for memory with low priority.   If this request is granted, one knows that no interference resulted.   If this request is not granted, a second low-priority request is made.   If this second request is not granted, the third request is a high-priority one.   Simulations have shown that with this system memory interference with the CPU is very low.[1]

Before leaving the XDS-940 we should point out one further mechanism found on other computers also, namely, *direct I/O*, shown in Fig. 3.5.   By direct I/O we mean that the CPU directly inputs or outputs a single word or unit of information from or to a device by executing a single instruction.   The destination or source of this word within the central system is either a register of the CPU or a memory address given in the instruction. Each word transmitted is under direct control of the CPU.   This mechanism is in contrast to that of an I/O processor or channel, which, once started by the CPU, can transmit information to and from memory independently of the CPU operation.

3.2.6   Increasing Memory Bandwidth with Buffer Stores   One of the factors creating memory-communication bottlenecks is the speed differential between main-memory access time and processor logic.   Processor logic is faster than memory access time.   A method used frequently to overcome this problem is to fetch from memory several instructions at once and to overlap the fetch of operands with the instruction fetch.   This approach is a form of buffering and has been quite successful in increasing the memory bandwidth to the central processors, but it does not come to grips with the problem of increasing the memory bandwidth to I/O processors as well.   A different form of buffering coming more into consideration can be used to increase the total memory bandwidth as seen by all processors.   This approach is to associate with each memory box or with each processor a high-speed buffer store.   The first approach is represented by a system developed by M. W. Pirtle and others, at the University of California, which we call the Berkeley system.   Many ideas of this system appear in the SCC-6700 and other machines under development.[2]   The second approach is represented by the IBM 360/85.[3]   At present the IBM 360/85 associates the buffer memory only with the CPU, but the basic idea is capable of generalization. The goal is to use this high-speed buffer storage in such a way that the processor "thinks" that all the storage is constructed of this high-speed solid-state memory. Before making a comparison between the systems a brief description of each is given. The discussion of the Berkeley system is based on the form appearing in the SCC-6700.[2]

3.2.7 The IBM 360/85 Memory Organization

A schematic of the model 85 memory system is given in Fig. 3.7. Main storage in this system has a cycle time of about 1 microsecond. For storage configurations of 500K and 1,000K words (32-bit), storage is interleaved four ways. For smaller storage configurations, storage is interleaved two ways. Note that the buffer storage is available only to the CPU and not to the I/O or other processors. The buffer storage has a cycle time of 80 nanoseconds. The buffer storage is either 4K, 6K, or 8K words. The design of this system was oriented toward increasing the effective speed of memory as seen from the CPU. The importance of high data-transfer rate between all processors and memory has not been highly developed in this machine because, in our view, it is still seen as primarily a batch-processing machine for CPU-bound scientific applications. The memory bus is four words wide in order to achieve the bandwidth required for the main applications envisioned. For I/O oriented systems, this organization offers little advantage, but the basic ideas can be extended.

Main memory and the buffer storage are organized into sectors of 256 words. During operation, a correspondence is set up between buffer-storage sectors and main-storage sectors, in which each buffer-storage sector is assigned to a single different main-storage sector. Because of the limited number of buffer-storage sectors, most main-storage sectors do not have any buffer-storage sectors assigned to them. Each of the buffer-storage sectors has a 14-bit sector address register, which holds the address of the main-storage sector to which it is assigned.

The assignment of buffer-storage sectors is dynamically adjusted

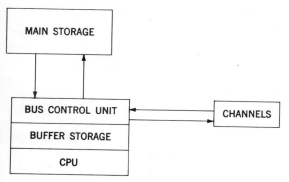

FIG. 3.7 IBM 360/85 memory system.

during operation so that they are assigned to the main-storage sectors that are currently being used by programs.   If the program causes a fetch from a main-storage sector that does not have a buffer-storage sector assigned to it, one of the buffer-storage sectors is then reassigned to that main-storage sector.   To make a good selection of a buffer-storage sector to reassign, enough information is maintained to order the buffer-storage sectors into an activity list.

When a buffer-storage sector is assigned to a different main-storage sector, the entire 256 words located in that main-storage sector are not loaded into the buffer at once but each sector is divided into 16 blocks of 16 words each, which are located on demand.

Storage operations always cause main storage to be updated.   If the main-storage sector being changed has a buffer-storage sector assigned to it, the buffer is also updated; otherwise no activity related to the buffer takes place.   Since all the data in the buffer are also in main storage, it is not necessary on a buffer-storage-sector reassignment to move any data from the buffer to main storage.

Two 80-nanosecond cycles are required to fetch data that are in the buffer.   The first cycle is used to examine the sector address and the validity bits to determine if the data are in the buffer.   The second cycle is then used to read the data out of the buffer.   If the data are not in the buffer, additional cycles are required while the block is loaded into the buffer from main storage.

Simulation was used extensively during the design of this memory system as well as that for the Berkeley system.   There are many important parameters, such as choice of a replacement algorithm, buffer size, sector and block sizes, which must be determined.[3]

With the simulation running a representative scientific-oriented job mix, it was found that mean performance of this system as compared to an ideal system consisting of only 80-nanosecond memory was 81 percent.[3] That is, on average, the CPU obtained information from the buffer storage on 81 percent of its references.

3.2.8   The Berkeley System Memory Organization   The group at the University of California which developed the Berkeley system is the same one which developed the XDS-940.   The designers of this system recognized that a memory organization which treated both main and secondary memory as an integral unit and which minimized interference between all processors was a central problem.   A schematic of the Berkeley system memory organization is shown in Fig. 3.8.

The basic system has eight memory boxes containing 16K of 1-microsecond core memory and six fast 200-nanosecond register sets, to be described.   Additional memory boxes can be added.   The memory is interleaved eight ways, and a 48-bit double word (instructions and fixed-point data are 24 bits) is always fetched. It is beyond the scope of this book to go into all the details of the addressing and priority scheme, but some highlights can be mentioned. The six fast register sets in each box consist of storage for a double word, an address, and various status and priority bits.

It was mentioned earlier that sophisticated priority schemes cannot be used with an asynchronous system because the concept of simultaneity cannot be made precise. Yet synchronous systems which have a memory cycle as a basic unit of time cannot run as fast as asynchronous systems. The designers of this system have chosen to make it synchronous, but in order to give the processors greater freedom to proceed at their own pace and to use the 200-nanosecond memory effectively, the machine uses 100-nanosecond intervals as the basic timing unit and as the points at which requests can be made to a memory box.

Two main priorities are involved in this system, priority for access to a memory box and priority for access to the core part of each box. The first priority problem is handled in two ways: (1) each request for memory is made either with high or low priority; (2) if two or more processors request access to the same box at the same time with the same priority, a hardwired priority among the busses resolves the conflict. However, if a bus with a low hardwired priority requests a cycle indicating it wants it with high priority, it gets access even if a bus with a higher hardwired priority is requesting a cycle with low priority. Once access to a box is granted, the address is compared to the addresses in the fast memory during the first 100-nanosecond period, and if it is found on a fetch and the status bit indicates that the data portion is valid, the data are delivered to the processor during the second 100-nanosecond interval. Otherwise a hardwired algorithm releases a register set to this request. Additional core-access priority information comes with the requests to indicate whether a low, warning, medium, or high priority is required for access to core. This priority information is stored with the request in the fast registers and

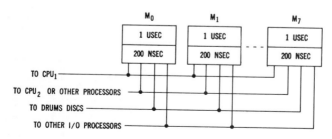

FIG. 3.8 Berkeley system memory organization.

is used to determine which request in the fast registers to service on the next core cycle. The warning level is used to reserve a fast register set by processors which know ahead of time in which box their next request will occur. When a second warning request comes to a box, all previous warning requests in the box are reset to high priority.

Because the CPUs are designed around instruction and operand fetch lookahead, they can make requests far enough in advance for the required information to be in fast memory by the time it is actually required. Similarly the drum and disks on block transfers know ahead of time which boxes are going to be required. On stores, the information is left in fast memory by a processor, and this information is later used to update core. If a fetch to the same location is then made at a slightly later time, the information can be obtained from fast storage. For tight loops all information may reside in the fast storage. The result of this memory organization is that simulations have shown that more then 15 million words per second can flow to and from memory to keep all processors running at close to full capacity. The decision to use six fast register sets was arrived at through simulation.

Besides the memory organization given above, the Berkeley system has another unique design approach. The various I/O processors are microprogrammed to allow them considerable independence of the CPU to perform tasks previously requiring software. An example is the drum processor, which can handle swapping functions previously involving the CPU. A useful way of thinking about the multiple processors is to view them as forming a hierarchy much like that of the various storage media. An example of such a processor is discussed in Sec. 6.1.

In our view, the main advantage of the memory buffer organization of the Berkeley system over the 360/85 is that the fast memory is available to all processors and not just the CPU. Further, stores in the Berkeley system are made to fast memory and not to the slower core memory. In a timesharing system, transfers between main storage and secondary storage are frequent, and thus this system approach of the Berkeley system is particularly important. The scheme of the Berkeley system should probably require less hardware and therefore be less expensive. The synchronous approach of the Berkeley system also allows development of a priority scheme which uses all available information to decrease interference for core requests. As mentioned earlier, the scheme of the 360/85 can be generalized to remove a number of the possible disadvantages mentioned above.

3.2.9 Summary We have introduced a number of concepts associated with achieving increased memory bandwidth—multiple memory boxes, interleaving, and high-speed buffers. The advantages and disadvantages of synchronous and asynchronous communication as approaches to achieving increased memory bandwidth were also discussed.   Many design tradeoffs are available to the designer involving size of memory boxes, number of memory busses, and choice of mode of communication.   Use of high-speed buffers further increases the number of design parameters which must be determined.   These design decisions may be difficult to make without adequate statistics on past system performance and probably require the aid of simulation experiments.

3.3   AUXILIARY STORAGE AND I/O COMMUNICATIONS

3.3.1   Methods of Connecting n Devices to m Memory Modules

DIRECT CONNECTION   A basic problem with auxiliary storage and I/O devices is gaining access to a direct-transfer path to main memory.   Further, logic is required to determine where in memory to transfer to or from and to determine how much information to transfer.   Theoretically, one could solve these problems by providing a direct-transfer path, addressing, and count logic for each device to each memory module.   Such an approach is represented by Fig. 3.9.   This approach may be unsatisfactory because of its cost in terms of line-selection logic and line-driving circuits.   To reduce the cost we need to use the information available to us about device

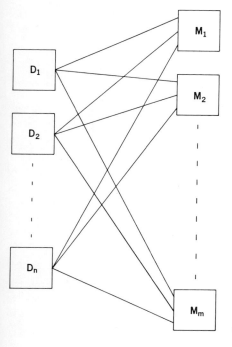

FIG. 3.9   Direct communication of n devices with m memory modules.

and memory information-transfer rates.   Starting with Fig. 3.9, we observe
that a memory module can transfer information to only one device at a
time and devices can transfer to only one memory module at a time.   Transfer can take place over a maximum of n or m lines, depending on which
is larger, but there are $n \times m$ lines.   Therefore, most of the access lines
are idle, and the logic and driver circuitry associated with these lines is
not being effectively used.

CROSSBAR CONNECTION   Using the observation above, one could take
the logic associated with each device to determine which access line to
use and the logic associated with each memory module to arbitrate between
competing requests for access and centralize it in the interconnection scheme
of Fig. 3.10.   The logic required, in this scheme, for determining the path
between devices and modules is called a *crossbar switch*.   The circled points,
called *switchpoints*, determine the connection path from devices to modules.
Conflicts for access to a module line would be resolved by a priority scheme.
The use of a crossbar switch has reduced the number of line drivers required,
but the switching logic required to set up a transfer path is probably as
great as in Fig. 3.9.   The crossbar switch has the disadvantage over the
direct-connection scheme in that localizing the switching logic in one central
unit makes the system highly dependent on the reliability of the crossbar
switch.

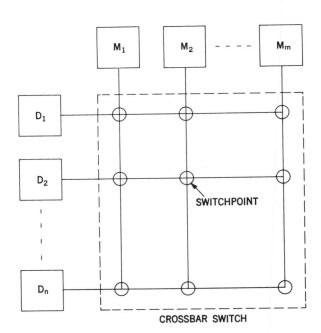

SWITCHPOINT

CROSSBAR SWITCH

FIG.   3.10   A crossbar
switch for n devices to
communicate   with m
memory modules.

DISTRIBUTED CONNECTION   The logic of the crossbar switch can be distributed into the memory modules to increase reliability.   The resulting organization is shown in Fig. 3.11, which, as the reader has probably noticed, has the same organization as Fig. 3.1.   In a practical system n is probably going to be larger than m.   This implies that not all devices can have access to memory simultaneously.   This observation, coupled with the observation that the devices transfer at varying rates, allows one to share access paths between devices.

SHARED CONNECTION   Some devices transfer at very low rates of a few information units per second, and others transfer at very high rates of hundreds of thousands to millions of information units per second. Therefore, slower devices can share access paths.   The scheme of Fig. 3.12 results.   This scheme uses timeshared (multiplexed) busses.

The limitation on the number of devices which can multiplex a transfer path is determined by the bandwidth of the path and the transfer rates of the devices.   The maximum transfer rate of a device must be less than the bandwidth of a path.   The maximum transfer rate of all devices on the system which can transfer concurrently is a function of the memory-bus and memory-box bandwidths.   This function is a statistical function based on traffic-flow observations.   If at peak transfer points the transfer rate exceeds that of a bus or a memory box, *saturation* is said to occur.   For example, all memory busses may be operating below saturation, but the system can be saturated because all busses are trying to access the same memory module.   The design goal is to have the system operate near satura-

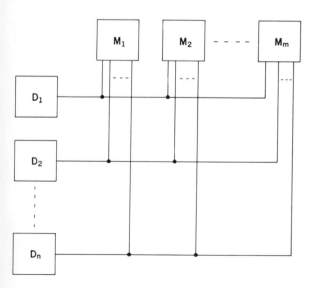

FIG. 3.11 Communication switching distributed into the memory modules for connecting n devices with m memory modules.

tion at all times. Without buffering (temporary storage) of information,
a saturation condition may cause information to be lost. The amount of
buffering required for a device depends on the statistical properties of the
system (the distributions of transfer-rate requirements to the memory modules and busses), the transfer rate of the device, and the cost or possibility
of losing information from the device.

There are many tradeoffs available to the designer of any communication system between numbers of access paths, bandwidth of access paths,
buffering, and the costs of each of these, in order to meet a given information-transfer rate. The concepts in this section apply to memory-bus structures and to other I/O busses connected to I/O processors, as discussed
in the next section.

3.3.2   Multiplexing an Access Path

INTRODUCTION   Access to a shared transfer path is commonly governed
by a control line which runs serially through all devices on the path
(Fig. 3.12). The simplest scheme is probably to assign priority by position in

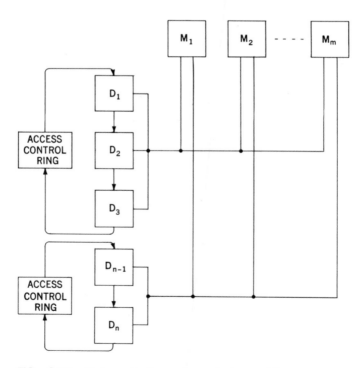

FIG. 3.12 Communication of n devices with m memory
modules sharing access paths.

the control ring. When a transfer is completed, control goes to the device requesting access in the highest priority position. With this approach, devices are assigned positions based on worst-case transfer conditions. However, using such a scheme may prevent the path from utilizing its maximum bandwidth. This rigidity is unnecessary if devices can request access to the path with variable priority. For example, consider the case of the XDS-940.

THE XDS-940 SHARED PATH The reader will recall from the discussion of Sec. 3.2.5 that the DACCs could request access to memory with a variable priority based on the fullness of the assembly register. The DACCs and other devices directly accessing memory are attached to the second memory bus, as shown in Fig. 3.13. In the 940, devices are strung on the second bus in a series connection. If position were the sole determinant of priority, $DACC_1$ could tie up the bus even if it required access with low priority and $DACC_2$ required access with a high priority. Therefore, simple changes to the logic were made so that devices on the second path request access to the bus with an A, B, or C priority, with A being higher priority than B and B being higher priority than C. The device requesting with the highest priority gains control of the bus. If two or more devices request access with the same priority, physical position is used to distinguish among them. Priority between the second and first paths for access to a memory box is determined as follows. A second-path A request has higher priority than the first path, and a second-path B or C request has lower priority than

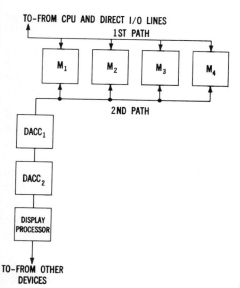

TO-FROM CPU AND DIRECT I/O LINES

1ST PATH

M_1 M_2 M_3 M_4

2ND PATH

$DACC_1$

$DACC_2$

DISPLAY PROCESSOR

TO-FROM OTHER DEVICES

FIG. 3.13 XDS-940 second-bus structure.

the first path.   Such a variable priority scheme works for both synchronous and asynchronous systems.

MULTIPLEXOR PROCESSORS   Up to this point we have assumed that each device has its own memory-addressing, assembly, and transfer-count logic.   Additional cost savings can be made by observing that it may not be necessary to operate all devices concurrently.   Therefore, we can provide one set of addressing, assembly, and count logic and attach several devices to this box, which we call an I/O processor.   Means are also provided to select which device is actually to perform a given set of transfers.   Requests for access to devices attached to this I/O processor are queued by the software system.   Devices making requests for service do so through the interrupt signal system discussed in Sec. 4.2.

If we had to tie up an I/O processor while a very slow device transferred many units of information, it would be an ineffective way of utilizing the I/O processor.   To utilize the I/O processor more effectively, we can transfer one unit of information to one device and keep track of this transfer and the memory-transfer address with software and then switch to another device for a transfer.   When the first device is ready for another transfer, it can send a signal to stop present processing and branch to the program controlling transfer to the device.   Such a scheme is used frequently but does require interference with the CPUs computing work.

To make it possible to share one set of addressing, assembly, and transfer-count logic without requiring service by the CPU, a special I/O processor called a *multiplexor processor* is used.   This piece of hardware is logically many I/O processors.   Each logical I/O processor has a fixed set of memory locations, where the memory address of the next transfer, partially assembled word, and count are stored.   One set of such locations is associated with each line attached to the multiplexor processor.   The multiplexor processor services the current highest-priority device.   On input it services the device by fetching a transfer address, partially assembled word, and count.   The information unit from the device is assembled.   If a word is completely assembled, a transfer between multiplexor processor and memory is made.   The memory address is then incremented, the word count is decremented, and they, along with the contents of the assembly register, are stored away in their fixed locations.   On output the multiplexor processor services the device by fetching a transfer address, partially disassembled word, and count.   An information unit is taken from the disassembly register and sent to the device.   If the disassembly register is empty, a word is fetched from memory at the transfer address and stored in the disassembly register.   The transfer address is incremented, the word count is decremented, and these words along with the contents of the disassembly register are stored away in memory in their fixed locations.   The device with the highest priority is then serviced next in the same way.

THE MULTICS GENERALIZED I/O CONTROLLER Multiplexor processors and I/O processors servicing higher-rate devices for a block transfer in one time span can share a single memory bus. These devices may be individual units on a bus, as shown in Fig. 3.13, or may be integrated onto one generalized I/O processor (GIOC) as in the Multics system (Fig. 3.4). The GIOC is shown in more detail in Fig. 3.14. The GIOC is constructed of modular functional building blocks: common control, adapter control, and adapter channels, as described by Ossana et al.[4] Adapter channels provide the proper termination with I/O devices and may perform assembly or provide other data buffering. The adapter control comes in two varieties, direct and indirect. The direct adapter control contains address and word-count registers for directly controlling memory transfers. The indirect adapter controls contain minimum control and are for slow- and medium-speed devices. The address and word-count information is stored in memory and must be accessed on each transfer. Indirect adapters correspond to multiplexor processors, and direct adapters correspond to I/O processors, allowing single devices to be attached for a block transfer.

The common control unit, using fixed-priority information assigned to each adapter control, determines which adapter control may be attached to a memory-data bus either for a data transfer or for a transfer of command information to an adapter channel from the program. The common control provides assembly and word-count updating for indirect adapter controls. The common control, at the completion of a transfer to memory, examines all adapter controls currently requesting a transfer and determines which

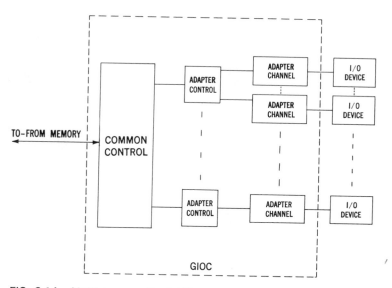

FIG. 3.14 Multics generalized I/O controller.

has the highest priority.   The allocation of priority and design of buffering
in the adapter channels must ensure that no information can get lost in
worst-case situations where several high-priority high-speed devices are operating simultaneously.   The common control can preempt the operations of
an indirect adapter control to perform a transfer for a direct adapter control,
then return to complete the indirect-adapter-control transfer.   Indirect adapters require several memory cycles for each transfer.   Data may be lost
from high-speed devices attached to direct adapters if preemption is not
possible.

USE OF MULTIPLE PROCESSORS FOR I/O   In Sec. 3.4.4 the use of a
separate small computer to control communications with remote terminals
is discussed.   The concept can be extended to handling other I/O as well.

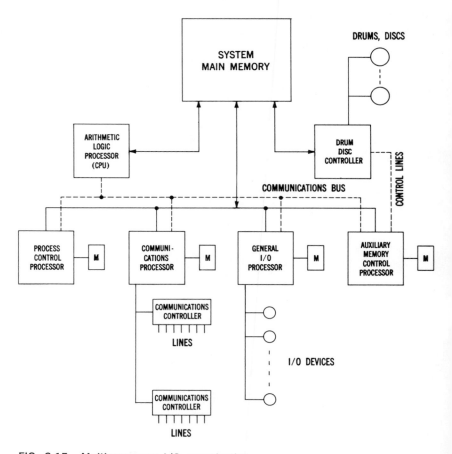

FIG. 3.15   Multiprocessor I/O organization.

Such an approach is taken on the SCC-6700.[2]   The idea is represented in simplified form in Fig. 3.15.   All I/O processors are identical, but they are given different names to indicate function.   These processors have a subset of the instruction set of the CPU, and they also can execute normal I/O instructions.   Each I/O processor has its own memory, and there is an instruction in all processors to transfer a block of data from system main memory to an I/O processor memory.   Each I/O processor can contain the allocation and control programs to handle the set of devices attached to it.   The auxiliary-memory control processor controls a special high-speed channel to system main memory for handling memory extension through drums and disks.   The process control processor handles process scheduling functions.   Each of the I/O processors is microprogrammed (see Sec. 4.3) for inexpensive implementation of the extensive instruction set. Because all processors in the system obey a common subset of instructions, the system can probably be developed with the same ease as if one were working with a single processor and then appropriate sections of code can be moved to the I/O processors.

The University of California researchers who developed the XDS-940 and participated in development of the SCC-6700 have founded the Berkeley Computer Corporation (BCC) to produce a timesharing system.   In description to follow is based on conversations with M. W. Pirtle.   In the BCC system there are a number of independent processors as in the SCC-6700, except that each in the BCC system is attached to the common central memory.   Each processor has a prescribed task.   Two of these processors are identical and execute user processes; they are not capable of directly performing I/O.   The other processors are thought of as resource managers. The number of resource managers depends on the application mix of the system.

Normally there are three resource-management processors, one for managing main and auxiliary memory, one for managing the two processors executing user processes, and one for managing communication facilities and remote devices.   Another processor may be required for managing local I/O devices such as tape drives, card equipment, and printers.   These resource-management processors are individually programmed to perform their assigned tasks.   They also make use of special hardware features, such as microprogramming (see Sec. 4.3) to aid them in performing their functions.   There is little direct communication capability between processors.   Most intercommunication and control between processors takes place through tables in the common main memory.   Intercommunication in the BCC system is discussed further in Sec. 4.2.4.

3.3.3 Summary We have seen several methods of connecting auxiliary storage and I/O devices to memory.   The discussion has illustrated how a designer can take advantage of his information on device transfer-rate requirements to minimize cost by sharing transfer paths and addressing, assembly, and count logic. The problem of determining device priority in a shared approach was discussed. The suggestion was made that the use of a variable-priority scheme might increase flexibility and utilization of a transfer path. The use of multiple processors to control I/O was introduced. This approach seems to offer a number of advantages in improving system performance.

The detailed design of I/O processors and system conventions to send commands to devices and receive status information from devices was not discussed. This is an important subject which must be considered in a complete design. In the XDS-940 and other systems, command and status information are transmitted by a separate bus wired in parallel to all devices. Each device has an associated device number used for an address. In the Multics system and others, command and status information pass directly from memory through the I/O processor to the device over the same lines used for data transmission. Indication whether a transfer is data or a command is given in the instruction setting up transmission. If a device wants to send status information, a particular signal is given. The details of I/O processor design, like those of central-processor design, are beyond the scope of this text.

3.4 REMOTE-TERMINAL COMMUNICATIONS

3.4.1 Introduction In this section we consider some of the concepts of communication with remote terminals and the equipment required at the interface between user and system and between computer and communication lines. Communications is a complex subject with many specialized areas. In this section we consider only those basic concepts with which we feel system programmers and computer hardware designers should be familiar.

Communications costs, both for equipment and for line rentals, are a considerable portion of the expense of a timeshared computer system. Therefore, this subject should be given careful attention by the system designer.

3.4.2 Transmission Concepts

CLASSES OF LINES Transmission *lines*, also called *channels* or *circuits*, are classified as simplex, half duplex, and full duplex. A *simplex* line can transmit information in only one direction. A *half-duplex* line can transmit in either direction but can transmit in only one direction at a time. A *full-duplex* line can transmit in both directions simultaneously.

The speed of transmission is described in *bauds,* 1 baud normally being 1 bit per second.   Common carrier corporations such as the telegraph and telephone companies supply a variety of transmission services either serial by bit or serial by character, with transmission rates ranging from around 110 bauds to several hundred thousand bauds.   The grade of a communications line refers to the rate at which information can be transmitted over it.   For example, a normal dial-telephone line, called a *voice-grade* line, can transmit up to about 2,000 bauds.   Rates (tariffs) and interface equipment vary of course, depending on the rate of transmission required.   For higher than 2,000 bauds one may not be able to use the dial-telephone lines, also referred to as the *switched network,* and one may have to lease private lines instead.

MODULATION   Computer equipment normally generates and utilizes direct-current (dc) binary signals, as shown in Fig. 3.16.   If the terminals are local to the computer, within a $\frac{1}{2}$ mile for example, these dc signals can probably be directly transmitted just by stringing wires.   If the terminals are at greater distance, it is usually impractical, if not illegal, just to string wires.   The only economic, and often legal, approach is to utilize the lines provided by the common carriers.   The common carriers usually do not transmit dc signals but utilize a technique called *modulation,* which converts the dc information into other electrical forms more efficiently transmitted and less prone to errors introduced by noise signals.   A common type of modulation is *frequency modulation.*   In this type of modulation, the amplitude of the source signal is converted into frequency variations within a constant-amplitude signal.   The mechanism commonly used for computer communication is very simple.   At each end of the communication line, the computer or terminal equipment is connected to circuits called *modems* (modulator demodulators) or *data sets,* which convert the two dc levels to two frequencies at one end and then convert the two frequencies back to dc levels at the other end.   This process is shown in Fig. 3.17.   A 1 bit (true) might be represented by a frequency of 2,000 hertz and a 0 bit (false) might be represented by a frequency of 1,000 hertz, for example.   At these frequencies, one can think of the conversion as having two tones.   As shown above, transmission is serial by bit.   By using a range of frequency pairs, one line can be used to transmit several bits in parallel, usually a character.   Thus, one line has been divided into several transmission channels.

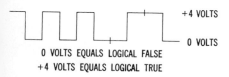

0 VOLTS EQUALS LOGICAL FALSE
+4 VOLTS EQUALS LOGICAL TRUE

FIG. 3.16   Logical signals in digital equipment.

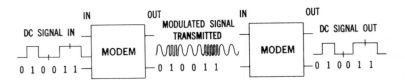

FIG. 3.17   Use of frequency modulation for digital transmission.

CODES   Character information must be coded into a string of bits, both for handling by the computer and for transmission.   Many codes are in use, but one code format, the ASCII (American Standard Code for Information Interchange) is being used more and more.   It encodes 128 characters into 7 *binary information units* (bits), and then some equipment uses 1 additional bit to give an error-detection ability, thus encoding characters in 7 or 8 bits.   In our examples we consider the 8-bit case.

SYNCHRONOUS AND ASYNCHRONOUS TRANSMISSION   Data transmission can be either *synchronous* or *asynchronous*.   In asynchronous transmission, characters can be sent with varying time intervals between them.   The character code is preceded by a bit called the *start bit,* which signals the receiving device to decode the following 8 bits of character code.   The character code is followed by a *stop* bit or bits to signal the receiving device to stop receiving and reset to await the next start bit.   Normally for teletypes, the line is in the 1 state while awaiting a new character. The start bit is a 0 bit.   The stop signal is at least two 1 bits in length to allow time to reset.   Thus an 11-bit code is sent for each character.   The above concept is shown in Fig. 3.18.   When the receiving device receives the start signal, it starts a timing mechanism to decode the incoming character.   The receiving device must be able to decode strings of 1's or 0's represented by constant voltage levels over a given time length equal to some multiple of a bit time, as shown in Fig. 3.18.   The bit time of a teletype is 10 milliseconds, for example.

Asynchronous transmission is used by teletypes and other terminal

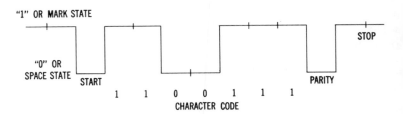

FIG. 3.18   Bit string for an asynchronous transmission.

devices on which the operator sends characters at more or less random intervals and is used for continuous transmission on low- or medium-speed devices where one wants to avoid the problem of synchronizing the timing generators on the sending and receiving equipment.

Synchronous transmission is used where two machines transmit to each other continuously or where high data rates are desired. The asynchronous method requires 3 bits of synchronizing information which do not contain useful code information and thus 3 extra bit times for each character. In synchronous transmission, sending and receiving devices have timing generators in exact synchronism, so that there is no need for start and stop bits. The receiver decodes a new character every 8 bit times. Synchronous equipment is more expensive because of extra complexity and care required to maintain synchronism. If the receiver slips 1 bit time, it still extracts what it thinks is a character every 8 bit times. The use of an error-detection bit can often detect this situation, however. The two timing generators are synchronized by special character codes sent at the start of each message.

3.4.3 Line-sharing Techniques

THE CONCENTRATOR Rental of communication lines, particularly high-speed lines over long distance, is expensive and therefore a number of techniques have been developed to share this resource among several terminals. For example, a commercial timesharing service might have a machine in Chicago and want to obtain customers in Minneapolis, New York, and other cities. These customers will probably not be willing to pay long-distance rates and therefore, the timesharing firm will lease one line between each market area and the central computer and place a *concentrator* in each market area. A customer dials the computer with a local number and is connected with the concentrator. As far as the customer is concerned, he has made direct contact with the computer. The concept is illustrated in Fig. 3.19.

The concentrator is usually a small computer which collects messages from the users in its area over low-speed asynchronous lines then transmits the messages over the high-speed leased line to the computer, either asynchronously or synchronously. A message is delimited by a special character or characters, such as a carriage return, recognized by the concentrator. When the concentrator recognizes an end-of-message character from a user, it enters the user's message, preceded by information to identify the user, in a buffer used as the source by the high-speed line.

Similarly, messages from the central computer are sent to the concentrator preceded by appropriate identification. The concentrator then sorts the messages into buffers for each user and transmits to the user at slow speed. With this technique, an expensive resource is shared by several users, in keeping with the philosophy of the total timesharing system design.

THE MULTIDROP AND POLLING TECHNIQUES One may wish to have several concentrators on one line or attach several terminals to one line. One can accomplish this with a technique called *multidrop* for sending information to terminals and called *polling* for receiving information from terminals. With multidrop, the message is preceded by a device address and followed by an end-of-message character or characters. The message is sent down the line, and all devices decode the address; only the device addressed connects itself to the line. When the end-of-message character is received, the device disconnects itself. The network may be able to precede the message with several addresses or have a *broadcast* code indicating that several or all devices should receive the message. The concept is illustrated in Fig. 3.20.

In transmissions to the computer, only one device can transmit at a time, and the line is organized by polling the devices under computer control. A *polling message* is sent down the line, which asks "terminal X do you have anything to transmit?" Terminal X replies with a code for

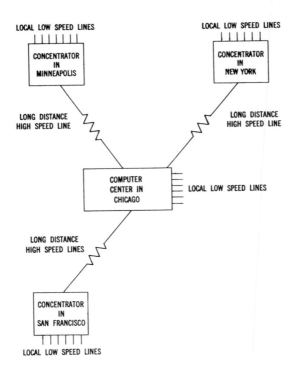

FIG. 3.19 Communications using concentrators to multiplex high-speed lines.

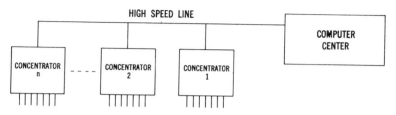

FIG. 3.20   Communications where several concentrators share one line.

yes or no.   If the answer is "no," the next polling message is sent.   When the distance from the computer to the terminals is long, the time taken to send a polling message to a terminal and receive a message back may become great.   In this case a modified technique causes "no" replies to be sent ahead to the next terminal and so on until either a message is sent to the computer or the last terminal sends a "no" back to the computer. In this case, the terminal must preface its message with its address for proper identification.

The central computer usually organizes the polling from a *polling list* which contains the polling sequence.   By placing a terminal's address in several places in the list one can vary the frequency with which various terminals are polled.   This is a commonly used technique for handling vary- ing-data-rate devices in a uniform manner.   Polling is becoming more widely used in timesharing systems collecting data from specialized terminals, as well as for handling cathode-ray-tube terminal systems in which the individual consoles can be more economically organized around multiple control units than treated as stand-alone units.   The concepts introduced in this section are also used in the design of the computer I/O system.   For example, the direct I/O lines of the XDS-940 use the multidrop technique.

3.4.4   The Computer Interface

THE LINE BUFFER   At the computer interface, the incoming serial string of bits must be converted into 8 parallel bits representing a character and must be stored in a buffer register.   To accomplish this function requires stripping off the start and stop bits on asynchronous transmission.   The error-detection bit may also be utilized to check the transmission at this time.   Similarly on output, the parallel bits representing a character must be converted to serial form and have the start/stop bits added.   An error- detection bit may also have to be added if the character is represented in the computer without the error-detection bit.   These functions are per- formed by a device commonly called a *line buffer*.   The concept is illustrated in Fig. 3.21.   The line buffer has additional tasks of sending and receiving

control signals to data sets to connect, disconnect, and for proper synchronization.   The line buffers also receive status information from the modems
indicating, for example, whether or not they are still connected to the line.
This status information can be tested by the computer, or it can be used
to generate a signal if the state of the line changes.   These functions are
important for automatic answering of the line and to avoid system difficulties
on accidental or erroneous disconnect.   When such a disconnect occurs
it is important that the user on that line be automatically logged out, in
order to free the line and protect the user.   There is one line buffer for
each line.

THE COMMUNICATIONS CONTROLLER   The line buffers must in turn
communicate with main memory.   This communication is handled by attaching the line buffers to a device commonly called a *communications controller*

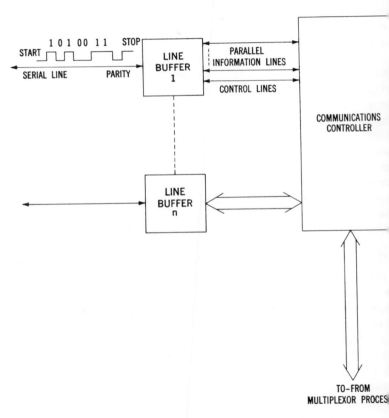

FIG. 3.21   The communications-line interface at the computer.

The communications controller in turn can be attached to a multiplexor channel (indirect adapter control), as is on the GE-645, it can be attached to the direct I/O lines, as on the XDS-940, or it can be attached to a separate small computer which in turn is connected to the central machine, as on the GE-265. The small computer can also be designed and programmed to handle the functions of line buffer and communication controller directly.[5]

The communications controller of the XDS-940 works as follows. First consider input. When a line buffer has received a character, it raises an input flag. The communications controller sequences continuously through the line buffers, and when it finds one which has raised its input flag, it stops and assembles a word containing the character code and the address of the line. The word also contains a data-overrun bit, which is set if two characters had arrived before the line buffer was serviced. After assembly, the controller generates an interrupt signal, and the XDS-940 issues a direct input command to fetch the assembled word to memory. If the controller were on a multiplexor channel, it would indicate a request for service and the multiplexor channel would store the word in memory.

On output, a slightly more complicated procedure is required. When the line buffer has completed outputting a character, it raises an output-completed flag. The communications controller stops its scan at this line when the output-completion flag is sensed and sends an interrupt to the XDS-940. The XDS-940 fetches the address of the line and checks to see if additional characters are to be output. If so, the 940 assembles a word containing the next character and this line number and sends it to the controller. The controller deposits the character in the appropriate line buffer and continues its scan. In a system with a multiplexor channel, the request for service would directly cause a memory reference to obtain the next character. The communications controller, as can be seen, is a device automatically polling and performing a multidrop function.

The use of the direct I/O lines, as on the XDS-940, requires about 300 microseconds of CPU computation for each character handled. This time is not a serious interference if a limited number (under 32) of low-speed lines is used, but it would be a serious problem if several high-speed or many low-speed lines were in use. Therefore, attachment of the communications controller to a multiplexor channel or small computer is probably a better approach.

Timesharing systems are increasingly called upon to handle terminals with a variety of transmission speeds from 110 to several thousand bauds. It is important that new devices be easily interfaced without major hardware or software modifications. These goals cannot be easily achieved with the simple communications controller described above, which scans each line in sequence, and a communications controller with a variable priority system is usually required. Such a device, after completing a service request, would simultaneously scan all line buffers requesting service and service the one with the highest priority next.

Connecting the communications controller to a separate small computer allows a number of processing tasks to be performed, such as editing, message assembly, file creation, and so forth, without interfering with the work of the central machine. This useful function is discussed further in Sec. 6.2.5.

3.4.5 The Terminal Interface The terminal is the point of interface between the user and the system. It is here that the capabilities of the man and the machine must be matched. There are many terminals available from manufacturers which can usefully be classified into typewriter, cathode ray tube, and special-purpose terminals. We indicate some characteristics of terminals to give the reader an idea of the complexity facing the software designers in handling the wide variety available.

Typewriter terminals transmit and receive from 110 to around 400 bauds, depending on the terminal. Some of these terminals can operate in half-duplex mode, in which case the keyboard is directly connected to the printing mechanism; and when each key is struck, it immediately produces a record on the paper. Others can operate in full-duplex mode, in which case the printing mechanism is logically disconnected from the keyboard. When a key is struck, the character is sent to the computer which in turn echoes the character back, causing it to be printed. In full-duplex mode, one can input and receive output simultaneously. Full-duplex mode is also useful to check that the character was received correctly. If the correct character returns, one knows it was received correctly. Some typewriter terminals send individual characters to the computer, and others transmit only lines or messages. Some can perform carriage return or line feed in one character time; others require different lengths of time to move the carriage. A variety of control and character codes are in use.

Cathode-ray-tube (CRT) terminals vary from character-oriented terminals, which can receive transmissions up to 2,400 bauds, to general purpose graphic terminals, which can draw lines and characters in microseconds. These general purpose graphic terminals can be directly interfaced to the memory bus, I/O processor, or to a small terminal computer, which in turn can be interfaced to the central computer in many ways, including voice or higher-grade lines. The design of general purpose graphic terminals and their interface is a special topic in itself.[6] The character-oriented CRT terminals have local buffer memories and usually function in half-duplex mode and transmit blocks of information. Some newer terminals operate in full duplex, with the keyboard handling performed as with a full-duplex typewriter terminal and the output to the local memory for display handled like other CRT terminals.   CRT terminals can be stand-alone units, or multiple terminals can be connected to one or more control units, which are in turn attached to a single line.   A variety of character and control codes are used.

Special terminals are similar in variety to those mentioned above and have keyboards or other code-generating mechanisms for input and printers or CRTs for output.

The special requirement placed on the terminal interface is that there be some way of identifying the type of terminal requesting service so that the software can handle its requirements.   The basic hardware concepts mentioned earlier on transmission and computer interface apply equally well to a wide variety of terminals, but each terminal type creates special problems for the software.   Therefore, terminal-type identification on initial contact with the system is essential.   At present there is no standard way of providing this information to the system.   On answering a call from a teletype, the system can wait for the terminal to transmit, but other terminals, such as many CRT terminals, must be polled to receive information. Without standard code sequences for polling, serious problems are created. How should the system know whether to poll or wait for information?   One approach is to wait 30 seconds, for example, and then poll.   A common solution to identification problems is to require each type of terminal to dial a separate number.

3.4.6 Summary   In this section we have introduced the common concepts involved with transmission of information to remote terminals interfacing the transmission lines to the central facility, and we have considered terminal characteristics and identification problems.   Many of the ideas such as concentrator, multidrop, and polling apply to other areas of the I/O system design as well.   The outline of terminal characteristics and identification problems should alert the reader to the need for careful consideration in the design of line interface equipment if the system is to accommodate with ease the variety of devices users are beginning to demand.

REFERENCES

1 **Pirtle, M. W.:** Intercommunication of Processors and Memory, *AFIPS Conf. Proc., Fall Joint Computer Conf.,* vol. 31, pp. 621–633, 1967.

2 "6700 Time-sharing Computer Reference Manual," Scientific Control Corporation, Carrollten, Texas, February, 1969 (additional information was also obtained at a public presentation of the 6700).

3 **Conti, C. J., et al.:** Structural Aspects of the System/360, Model 85, *IBM Systems J.,* vol. 7, no. 1, pp. 2–29, 1968.

4   Ossana, J. F., et al.: Communication and Input/Output Switching in a Multiplex Computing System, *AFIPS Conf. Proc., Fall Joint Computer Conf.*, vol. 27, 1965.

5   Newport, C. B.: Small Computers in Data Networks, *AFIPS Conf. Proc., Spring Joint Computer Conf.*, vol. 34, pp. 773–775, 1969.

6   Watson, R. W., et al.: A Display Processor Design, *AFIPS Conf. Proc., Fall Joint Computer Conf.*, vol. 35, 1969.

chapter FOUR

Protection and control

4.1 SYSTEM PROTECTION

4.1.1 Introduction Many levels of protection are required in a resource-sharing system, both hardware and software.[1,2] Even though resource-sharing systems have been in operation for a decade, they are still in developmental stages and the full range of protection mechanisms and the costs of the various protection mechanisms which are implemented or could be implemented is not fully known. Computer-system design practice is usually to put in hardware only the most general purpose mechanisms or to solve clearly seen system bottlenecks with hardware. Thus, many of the protection mechanisms exist in software routines rather than in hardware. As experience is gained with present systems, and as designers gather statistics on the cost of the various protection mechanisms and see how they can be generalized and related to one another, more hardware protection will evolve. In this section we examine protection methods which presently exist in hardware and leave for Sec. 5.4 discussions of protection mechanisms existing in software. The following varieties of protection have been distinguished by Lampson:[12]

> **1** Protection of the system from user processes. It is imperative that users not be able to take actions which would stop the system from running or destroy information essential to the system.
>
> **2** Protection of the users from each other. A user must not be allowed to take any action which would harm the operation of another user's process.

3   Protection of users from themselves.   A user may have several processes in execution or one process with several subprocesses, all of which are in intercommunication.   A user may want to protect these processes from each other in terms of memory access, execution times, or interaction paths.

4   Protection of the system from itself.   A timesharing system is a complex entity which is constantly evolving.   It is essential to have protection mechanisms which limit the damage which a malfunctioning module can perform.

For hardware design purposes, the above protection requirements have been reduced to two main areas:

1   Protection against accessing, changing, or transferring control to certain words in the physical memory of the machine (memory protection)

2   Protection against executing certain instructions (control protection)

Given a set of hardware features, the software designer can use these features in many ways to develop a total protection scheme for the system.   In this section we present various hardware protection features found on current or proposed machines, and later (Sec. 5.4) the subject is treated again from the software point of view.

4.1.2   Memory Protection

INTRODUCTION   In memory-protection schemes, areas of memory can be given different classifications such as:

1   Inaccessible
2   Read write
3   Read only
4   Execute only

Some examples of uses for the various categories of protection follow.   Many programs, as well as the monitor system, may be residing in main memory at a given time, and therefore some areas of store must be made inaccessible to other areas.   Full read/write privilege is required by most system programs.   Some subsystems, such as compilers, text editors, and debugging aids, as well as library routines, may be shared by many users and thus, by making them read-only, they can be properly protected.   In a computer utility, renting time for use of special programs will probably be a significant business.   In order to protect proprietary programming or other techniques, one wants to prevent users from reading the code, but one does want the user to be able to execute the code, thus illustrating a situation requiring execute-only protection.

PROTECTION OF PHYSICAL-ADDRESS SPACE   Memory protection can be applied to the physical-address space or to the logical-address space.   To protect the physical-address space, the physical memory can be broken up into blocks of a fixed size, and a protection key can be assigned to each block as a hardware register. This key indicates the type of access allowed to its corresponding block. The difficulty with this approach is that it does not distinguish among processes. Any process can write in a block with a write attribute key or execute a block with an execute attribute key. In a system using shared information, some people need write privileges to certain codes and other persons are to be allowed only read access to the same codes. To use such a system, the software monitor would probably have to examine memory, changing the protection keys each time the system switched control to a different process. Such an approach might increase system overhead and result in an awkward design.

In an attempt to improve the situation somewhat, some systems use a key-and-lock method. A set of locks is assigned to memory blocks, as described above, and a key is kept as a status word with each process. Access of a particular degree is granted to a block, if the status word bears a specified logical relation to the lock of the block. This scheme is still probably not as desirable as the methods to be described below because any process which has a key which might inadvertently bear a write relation to a block can write in that block. To guard against this would require very large keys. Several existing systems use a 4-bit key, which gives only 16 combinations. Adequate protection using such a system probably requires extensive software intervention.

PROTECTION ON LOGICAL-ADDRESS SPACE A much better place to apply protection, which gets around the type of problem discussed above, is to protect the logical-address space rather than the physical-address space. In systems which use relocation or base registers to map the logical space to the physical space, protection is often provided with *bounds registers*. A bounds register splits the memory into two parts, a contiguous region between the area pointed to by the base register and bound by the bounds register, and the remainder of memory. This scheme is illustrated in Fig. 4.1. Access is granted a process in the former area and denied the process in the latter area. There is usually a bounds register associated with each base register. This approach is an improvement over the previous memory-protection scheme because protection is more easily changed as processes controlling the machine change, but it still suffers from a limitation. The type of protection offered by the bounds-register approach is all or nothing. In a timesharing system finer distinctions of protection are usually desirable. Because protection is limited to contiguous areas, the sharing of procedures will require frequent changes of base-register—bounds-register pairs unless at least two such pairs are used.

The best approach to protection, we believe, is found on those systems having paging and/or segmentation hardware. The IBM 360/67 has, in our opinion, an awkward design feature in that protection is maintained on physical blocks of memory, even though the system has elaborate segmentation hardware.[4] In a protection scheme based on the paging or segmentation hardware, a procedure can more easily be given access only to those procedures and data segments necessary to accomplish its task and then only the type of access required for its task.

The XDS-940, for example, has a simple protection scheme utilizing the map registers described in Sec. 2.4.2.[3] It will be recalled that each map register contained 6 bits but only 5 were used for the block address, the remaining bit being used to define a protection classification. If the protect bit is a 1, the page is read-only; i.e., information can be retrieved from the page, but no information can be written into it. If an attempt is made to write into a read-only page, a fault interrupt is generated, which transfers control to the proper system routine. If the protect bit is a 0, the user can read from the page or write on it if it has been assigned to the user. Map registers corresponding to pages not assigned to the user have the protect bit set to a 1 and the other bits set to 0. This means that the user could never be assigned real block 0, which is always used by the system. The map registers are set to the type of access to be granted from information maintained in other tables.

A more general system of protection is employed on the GE-645, where protection is at the segment level.[1] Part of the information stored in the segment-descriptor word is the type of access to be granted the segment—write-only, read-only, read/write, execute only, no access, access only by system-level processes. This protection information is set into the

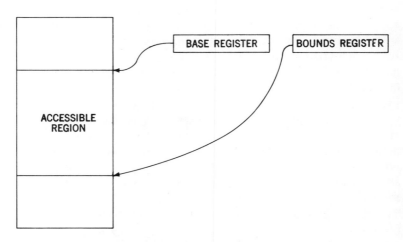

FIG. 4.1   Protection of logical space using a bounds register.

segment descriptor at the time a process requests access to the segment. The segment is located in the file system through a directory, which indicates not only where on auxiliary storage the segment is stored but also which users can access the segment and with what type of access. Based on this information, a segment-descriptor word is set up.

Another level of protection exists on the GE-645, and a similar mechanism exists on the IBM 360/67.[4,5] The descriptor base register and segment descriptors have associated with them a bounds field indicating the maximum defined segment number and segment length, respectively. These bounds are compared against the two components of a generalized address, and a failure to be within these bounds generates memory-access violation. Entries in the associative map also contain appropriate protection information.

There is a potential difficulty with the above approach; protection is defined on the segment rather than on the access path to the segment. That is, any segment in a process has the same access rights to a given segment as defined in the given segment's descriptor. The difficulty can be seen using the example of a debugging program. The debugging segment requires read/write access to itself and to the program being debugged. The user-program segment should have no access to the debugging segment and full access to itself. Both debugging segment and user-program segment form a process having one segment-descriptor table. The question then is: What access rights should be placed in the segment descriptor of the debugging segment? In the GE-645 system, the issue is sidestepped through the design chosen for the total software protection system rather than through hardware protection of the access path to the segment.

The directed segmentation scheme of Evans and LeClerc[6] places protection on the access path by use of a protection connection matrix. A similar result could be achieved in a system such as the GE-645. A process can have n possible segments. Each segment can have n possible access paths to the other segments (including reference to itself). Thus each segment can be assigned an access vector consisting of n sets of capabilities. A segment will be given access to the jth segment in the segment-descriptor table in a manner defined by the jth entry in its access vector. The access vector can be stored in memory with the descriptor segment and implemented in the hardware map.

The connection-matrix approach to segmentation is implemented in the SCC-6700. Access protection is placed on the connection path between segments and is either no access, read-only, read or indirect (not write), or any type of access. Associated with the hardware map are four intersegment access registers (ISAR) which define for each of four segments their access privilege to eight other segments. If a segment which is assigned an ISAR accesses a segment not listed in its ISAR, a special microprocessor (Sec. 2.5.8) updates the ISAR from access information stored in software tables. The concept of protection applied to the access path is shown in Fig. 4.2. Figure 4.2a shows an access-protection matrix for a process with 10 segments. The access vector for a segment n is given by row n of the matrix. The access rights of segment n to segment m are given by the entry at row n, column m. For example, segment 3 has

SEGMENT \ SEGMENT	1	2	3	4	5	6	7	8	9	10
1	3	0	3	2	0	0	1	0	0	0
2	1	2	1	1	0	0	1	0	1	2
3	0	1	3	1	0	1	0	2	0	3
4	1	2	2	3	0	1	0	0	1	2
5	0	1	3	1	3	0	1	2	0	1
6	3	3	3	0	1	2	3	0	3	2
7	0	0	1	0	1	3	3	1	3	0
8	1	1	3	1	2	1	0	3	2	1
9	1	0	3	0	1	0	2	3	3	1
10	0	1	2	3	3	3	1	1	0	3

0 NO ACCESS
1 READ ONLY
2 EXECUTE ONLY
3 READ WRITE EXECUTE

(a) ACCESS PROTECTION MATRIX

3	0	0	1	3	1	0
8	1	1	0	3	2	1

A B C

FIELD A INDICATES SEGMENT ROW OF ACCESS PROTECTION MATRIX
FIELD B INDICATES WHETHER C FIELDS CONTAIN ACCESS RIGHTS TO FIRST FIVE
  SEGMENTS OR SECOND FIVE SEGMENTS: 0 = FIRST FIVE OF THE ROW
                                     1 = SECOND FIVE OF THE ROW
FIELD C INDICATES ACCESS RIGHTS OF SEGMENT IN THE A FIELD TO
  FIVE SEGMENTS (EITHER SEGMENTS 1,2,3,4,5 OR SEGMENTS 6,7,8,9,10)

(b) TWO INTERSEGMENT ACCESS REGISTERS

3	1	1	0	2	0	3
8	1	1	0	3	2	1

A B C

(c) TWO INTERSEGMENT ACCESS REGISTERS

FIG. 4.2 Protection mechanism on access path between segments.

execute-only access to segment 8.   The full access-protection matrix would be implemented in software.   It is probably uneconomic and unnecessary to implement the entire access-protection matrix in hardware.

Figure 4.2b shows how two hardware intersegment access registers could be implemented.   The mechanism is essentially that of the SCC-6700. The access rights to five segments are contained in hardware.   If access is made to a segment in the other five segments, from segment 3, then the ISAR presently associated with segment 3 would be reset to hold the access rights to the other five, as shown in Fig. 4.2c.

One could also implement the concept by explicitly associating segment numbers and access rights in the ISAR.   This approach would allow individual entries in the ISAR to be changed rather than replacing all entries if a segment not in the ISAR was referenced.   Extra hardware complexity would probably be required to determine which entry in the ISAR to replace and to hold the extra information.

Systems such as the GE-645, which do not apply hardware protection to the access path between segments, create such protection with software, as shown in Sec. 5.4., where an additional hardware aid is described for a protection system such as that used in Multics.

4.1.3   Control Protection

INTRODUCTION   Certain instructions in the machine are usually not generally available for any process to execute.[3-5]   For example, processes are usually prevented from directly performing I/O instructions because other processes may be using a particular device.   All attempts to perform I/O operations generally go through the system so that these requests for service can be scheduled.   Further, user processes must be prevented from halting the machine or executing any other instructions which might interfere with the system or other users.

USER AND SYSTEM MODE   To handle the above problem, many machines are designed to operate in two modes, usually called *system mode* and *user mode*.   In system mode, all instructions in the machine are executable.   In user mode, certain classes of instructions, called *privileged instructions,* are prohibited.   If an attempt is made to execute a privileged instruction, a fault interrupt is generated which transfers control to the system.   For example, in the XDS-940, the following instructions are privileged: all I/O instructions, all instructions to control interrupts, all instructions to sense conditions of I/O devices or console switches, all unused operation codes, and the halt instruction.

To perform any operation requiring execution of a privileged instruction, a user process executes a call to the system.   This ability to interact with the system gives great flexibility to the user in developing his own systems to run under the timesharing system. Further, depending on the addressing scheme used, addressing may be different in the two modes. For example, in the XDS-940 there are two memory maps, one for the system routines and one for the user routines. A simple scheme exists in the 940 to allow the system to use the user map also, which facilitates communication between modes and simplifies writing reentrant routines. Many systems require system routines to make absolute physical-address references. Thus, all system routines have full read and write access. This approach leaves the system vulnerable to software and hardware errors. If the system references memory through a map, system routines requiring read/write access can be placed in one set of pages and system routines requiring read-only access can be placed in another set of pages. This approach permits hardware and software errors to be localized more easily.

SWITCHING BETWEEN USER AND SYSTEM MODE The problem of communication between modes is one requiring careful consideration, because if the design of the mode-switching scheme has not been carefully considered, programming can be awkward and time can be wasted in extra checking on the validity of the calls between modes.

A straightforward mode-switching scheme, implemented on the XDS-940,[3] utilizes *programmed operators*. The programmed-operator concept is in effect a method for making subroutine calls logically appear to the user as machine instructions. When a bit in the instruction word signifying a programmed operator is detected, the bits which are normally interpreted as the operation code are then interpreted as an address to which control is transferred. Two types of programmed operator exist on the XDS-940: (1) a system programmed operator in which the transfer is made to locations in the system code and the mode is switched to system mode (the previous mode is saved) and (2) a user programmed operator in which transfer is made to locations in the user's process. All calls to the system for assistance are thus made with system programmed operators. To return from system mode to user mode, the system executes a jump instruction addressed through the user map rather than the system map. While in system mode, the system can access locations in user processes by use of the user map. Besides giving a simple interface between modes, the programmed-operator concept allows the user to think he is programming a machine different and more powerful than that provided by the bare hardware.

A different mode-switching mechanism is used in the Multics system. In Multics, shared system segments are assigned to each process and have entries in each user's segment-descriptor table. Transfers to the system are handled in the same way as normal intersegment references.

The control bits of the system-segment descriptors indicate that system segments operate in system mode. The Multics mode-switching mechanism is general and integral in the sense that system calls are treated uniformly with all intersegment references.

CONTROL PROTECTION ASSOCIATED WITH AREAS OF MEMORY

In the user-monitor-mode approach above, the mode classification is associated with a process. Other schemes have been suggested such as associating mode classification with areas of memory, thus tying the problem of control protection to the memory-protection system. Such a suggestion has the advantage of increasing flexibility in the software design. In a user-monitor-mode approach only two protection classifications exist: either a process has full access to the system, with all the potential for damage implied, or a process has limited access. Further, processes having user-mode classification must call on system routines to perform any function requiring execution of a privileged instruction. Responsibility for determining the right to make such a request falls upon the system routine. This form of checking can be time-consuming because checking must be performed for each call.

Providing control protection as part of memory protection eliminates this checking on each call and increases flexibility of protection application. The checking problem is very similar to that which resulted when protection was assigned to a segment rather than to the access path to the segment. Checking access rights to system routines is a software implementation of protection placed on the access path to the system routines. The method to be described provides hardware assistance for placing protection on the access path.

A method of control protection suggested by Lampson[2] works as follows. The system places privileged instructions required by a process in an area of memory marked execute-only, with the additional status that privileged instructions can be executed. The process accesses these privileged instructions with execute instructions. (An execute instruction causes the instruction in the location specified in the address field to be fetched and executed, but the program counter is not modified unless the instruction is a branch.) The question remains how these privileged instructions get set up initially. One answer is that a mechanism like that used for linking in Multics can be used. The location to contain the privileged instruction can contain a code such that when the location is first executed, a transfer is made to the system. The system can check the validity of the attempt and set up the privileged instruction if allowed.

Therefore, the system has complete control over which instructions a process can execute; different processes can have the use of separate sets of privileged instructions depending on what operations they need to perform, and much of the extra checking associated with each system call is avoided. The system can even allow a process direct access to areas of auxiliary storage by placing the appropriate I/O instructions in the execute-only section of memory. This scheme is used on the SCC-6700, where it exists at the page level. A page in the SCC-6700 can be read/write, execute-only, or execute as privileged instruction.

4.1.4 Summary The concepts of memory and control protection have been introduced as forms of hardware aids to the solution of the protection problems listed in Sec. 4.1.1. Memory protection can be applied to physical or logical space. Protection of logical space is easily accomplished as part of schemes for dynamic relocation. Memory areas could be assigned various modes of access such as read/write, read-only, and execute-only.

In review, control protection is associated with the class of instructions a process can execute. User and system modes are common on many machines. In user mode, a restricted set of instructions can be executed. In system mode, all instructions on the machine are executable. Methods of switching between modes were discussed. Applying control protection to areas of memory rather than processes has the advantage of increased flexibility in allocating control protection.

In other words, there are two places where protection of a resource can be placed: (1) on the resource itself or (2) on the access path to the resource. Greater flexibility and system efficiencies seems to be obtained if hardware protection is placed on the access paths to various resources.

4.2 INTERRUPT SYSTEM

4.2.1 Introduction An important feature of any resource-sharing system is some means for the various processors and devices of the system to communicate with each other. One of the mechanisms which has evolved to handle this requirement is the priority interrupt system. The basic concept of the interrupt is very simple, but it did not exist in developed form on most machines until third-generation equipment. The CPU starts and stops various I/O processors and, for some devices, effects detailed control over the device. Without an interrupt system, the CPU may spend much time testing sense bits associated with the devices to determine when they require service. With an interrupt system the CPU ignores a device until an explicit signal is received from it.

This motivation for the development of a priority interrupt system is probably valid as long as the same processors which handle user processes also handle resource management. When one develops system organizations such as that of the BCC system (Sec. 3.3.2), where certain processors are dedicated to handling user processes but no I/O and other processors are dedicated to various resource-management tasks, the hardware intercommunication system can be simplified. We discuss the BCC approach in Sec. 4.2.4 after first exploring the types of intercommunication signals usually required in a resource-sharing system and focusing on the priority interrupt system.

The simplest thing that happens when a device signals on an interrupt line is that the CPU branches to a fixed location and executes the instruction there, which in turn is usually a subroutine branch to a routine to handle the interrupt. This routine stores in temporary locations the contents of any CPU registers which it may need to use and then re-stores these registers when it is finished. A transfer is then made back to the program which was interrupted.

Most present systems have several interrupt lines with priority levels associated with individual lines or groups of lines, such that if an interrupt on level four occurs and before the routine associated with this level is finished an interrupt occurs on a higher level two, then control is transferred to the routine associated with this higher-priority level. When the level-two routine finishes, control passes back to the level-four routine, which, when finished, returns control to the program originally interrupted.

The process of handling interrupts can be considered as a major driving point of resource-sharing systems. Algorithms for scheduling I/O and resource allocation are started, stopped, and conditioned by the various interrupts. All interrupts are explicit calls to the system for action or assistance.

A user program can be considered to be in one of three states: (1) ready to execute, (2) blocked while waiting for some I/O or other process to finish, or (3) running. When the system receives an interrupt, the effect is to change the state of one or more user programs and the system. There are two major classes of interrupts: (1) interrupts generated external to the CPU, for example, I/O interrupts, and (2) interrupts generated within the CPU, for example, arithmetic overflow or illegal instruction executions.

4.2.2 Types of Signals Let us examine briefly four types of signals and see the effect they have on the system and programs.

I/O SIGNALS These interrupts are generated by the successful or unsuccessful completion of an I/O operation. Such an interrupt is generated when a channel has completed transmission of a block of data or a device has completed some operation such as a tape rewind or disk-arm positioning. In most systems, the interrupt level identifies the device requesting attention, but the exact meaning of the signal can be determined only by obtaining additional status information contained within the device itself.

Upon receipt of the signal and determination of the meaning of the signal several things can happen; some typical examples follow:

1   A device may be ready to transmit information to or from an I/O buffer in system memory.

2   A device may be finished with a transmission, which causes the device to be freed for other users and changes the status of a user from blocked to ready.

3   An error condition may occur requiring system attention.

TIMER SIGNALS   Timesharing systems have attached to them one or more hardware clocks which generate an interrupt at fixed intervals.   The clock on the 940 generates an interrupt every 16 milliseconds.   (A clock with a finer time interval is desirable because events often require smaller time intervals for adequate control.)   These timing marks are used for accounting purposes, as system protection, and as major input into the scheduling routines.   The system-protection uses are varied but usually involve periodic checks of I/O operations to be sure that they are completed within expected times and that no hardware or software malfunction has occurred which could tie up an important piece of equipment.

USER PROGRAM SIGNALS   Two subclasses of interrupts can be generated, one from arithmetic operations resulting in signals such as divide check or arithmetic overflow or underflow and the other from attempts to execute illegal instructions or reference illegal memory locations, for example.

HARDWARE-FAILURE SIGNALS   These interrupts result from hardware failures such as errors detected on data transmission or power failure.

TRAPS   Let us examine the two major classes of signals mentioned above, those generated external to a CPU and those generated internal to a CPU.   A distinction is often drawn between *interrupts* and *traps*.   Though it is not always clear, rigorous, or formal the distinction is useful in gaining insight into different design problems.   Both types of signals have the same hardware effect; a processor is forced to execute an instruction at a fixed location, which may be a branch to a subroutine.   We can see the distinction more clearly in a multiprocessor system.   Interrupts are signals generated external to the processors.   Traps are signals generated within a processor.   Signals from I/O devices can be called interrupts.   Signals such as timers, user program signals, and hardware failures can be called traps.   Interrupts can be handled by any processor in the system, but traps are usually handled by the processor in which they originate.   Interrupts indicate that certain conditions on which processes have been waiting are satisfied, but traps force a process to transfer to a location within itself.   The difference in design problems between these two classes of signal is that, in a multiprocessor system, interrupts are usually routed to the first processor executing

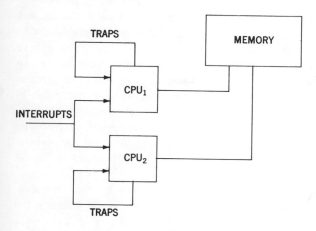

FIG. 4.3 The distinction between interrupts and traps.

a lower-priority function than the incoming signal. This processor then transfers control to the appropriate interrupt-handling routine. Trap signals affect only the processor in which they originate. The idea is shown in Fig. 4.3.

4.2.3 Accounting during Interrupt Processing Accounting during interrupt processing is handled in two ways. In the XDS-940 system, the user whose program is running during an interrupt is charged for the interrupt processing time even if the interrupt is serving another user's program. The justification is that over a given period of time the interrupt time required for each program will average out and thus the hardware-software expense required to sort out interrupt processing charges is not worth attempting.

In the Multics system, on the other hand, interrupt processing time is charged to the user whose program is being serviced.

4.2.4 Priority Assignment Most systems preassign the priority level associated with the various interrupt signals. This creates a dichotomy between the priorities of the other processes in the system and the priorities of the interrupt routines. The hardware interrupt routines automatically get priority over other processes executing in the system, which means that interrupt routines must be treated differently from other processes in the system and that the interrupt routines cannot easily utilize facilities provided other processes. Many hardware interrupt signals do not need a fixed priority and instead can have a priority based on the particular function being performed or the state of the system. Further, the number of mechanisms required in the system is increased by treating hardware signals differently from other signals generated in the system. Theoretically, there is no reason why signals from hardware devices cannot be treated like signals from software processes.

One approach to unifying the hardware and software signals has been suggested by Lampson.[2]   His proposal is to move scheduling functions to a special microprogrammed processor (see Sec. 4.3) which can access main memory, create processes, manipulate the queues of processes waiting to use a central processor, and switch a central processor from one process to another.   This special processor would perform all the functions of present interrupt systems: monitor a large number of signals, recognize priorities among signals, and see that a processor is executing instructions of the highest-priority process ready to execute, as indicated by the signals. Related to the last function is the requirement for high-speed switching of a processor from one process to another.

All hardware signals would initially be handled by the microprogrammed scheduling processor.   This special processor would examine the present priority of the signal and either create a queue entry for a process to handle the service request or, if priority was high enough, switch a central processor to a process to handle the signal.   Using such a special scheduling processor, the concept of an interrupt routine is no longer needed, and all scheduling functions are unified.

An objection to this approach is likely to be that building an algorithm into hardware creates a design difficult to change.   Use of a microprogrammable processor with an easily modifiable memory does allow flexibility. One can achieve the same level of flexibility in this approach as in present systems.   The cost of making modifications in terms of design and programming effort may be greater, however.

Another objection is that switching a processor from one process to another, in a unified system, requires switching more of the state vector than is done with present interrupt systems.   The state vector consists of processor central registers, address map, and other status information, as discussed in Chap. 1.   Storing and reloading all the various registers could be time-consuming and create difficulties in handling signals which require response within a few microseconds.   There are several possible answers to the problem.

One approach is to use only a few central registers and to keep a hardware pointer to the remaining table of state information.   Special instructions for switching the state information in one operation are possible. This type instruction requires several memory cycles or subcycles for the stores and loads but requires only one for instruction fetch.   Another approach is to use multiple sets of central registers, as is done on the XDS Sigma 7 system.   Normal processes would share one set of registers, and the few processes requiring high priority would have their own sets.   A hardware pointer to the remaining table of state information would also be necessary.

Lampson's suggestion in a slightly modified form has been implemented in the BCC system, in which a number of independent processors are attached to the common central memory, some processors are dedicated to handling user processes, and other processors are dedicated to specific resource-management tasks (see Sec. 3.3.2). In the BCC approach there are no interrupts to processors. There is only a single attention line over which other processors can acquire the attention of a given processor; for those processors which handle I/O or auxiliary storage devices, there is a second line over which an attached device, such as a communications controller, can acquire the controlling processor's attention. These lines do not cause an interrupt but instead set an attention flag (flip-flop) in the receiving processor. These flags can be interrogated at the receiving processor's convenience.

When the processor finds an attention flag set, it either goes to tables in the common main memory or inputs a status word from a device, where the processor or device identification and other information to be communicated is stored. In other words, the BCC system has gone back to using the type of communication mechanism found in early computers. The BCC designers feel that a priority interrupt mechanism is unnecessary in a system organized like theirs. Let us examine the BCC system more closely to see why a priority interrupt mechanism is superfluous.

First consider the processors which handle user processes. These processors do not control I/O or auxiliary-storage functions and perform only limited resource-management functions. The main signal these processors require is a signal to change processes. However, these processors do have to communicate with the other resource-management processors. The signal to change processes is like an interrupt in that it forces the processor to go to a specific memory location to find the information required to change processes.

When one of the user processes requires assistance from one of the resource-management processors, a message is placed in main memory and a signal is placed on the attention line to the appropriate resource-management processor. Depending on the nature of the service request, the calling processor may either wait for the request to be completed or may switch processes. The processor would wait only for those types of request which could be satisfied within a few microseconds.

When a resource-management processor completes its current task, it checks its attention flag to see if there is further work to be accomplished. If the flag is raised, the processor takes the highest-priority tasks as indicated in the interprocessor communication tables in memory.

In a similar manner, a resource-management processor can check and interrogate the attention flag associated with attached devices. All I/O to devices other than auxiliary memory devices, such as drums and disks, is by direct I/O instructions. The auxiliary-memory resource manager controls special high-speed direct memory-access channels for drum and disk transfers.   Because each task of a resource-management processor is quite simple, there are well-defined points for checking the attention flags, and because the resource-management processors are fast, the simple inter-communication mechanism outlined above leads to no serious delays.   The reader may want to review the discussion above after reading Chap. 5, where scheduling is discussed in more detail and the problem of unifying the treatment of hardware and software signals is amplified.

Present systems offer mechanisms to make some adjustment in priorities, by allowing the interrupt levels to be selectively turned off or saved and temporarily ignored.   To increase the priority of one level, one can issue an instruction to the interrupt system which sets the interrupt system to temporarily store incoming higher-priority interrupts but not allow them to enter the system and cause a transfer of control.   This approach to priority adjustment is rather inflexible and potentially dangerous because the system remains ignorant of the existence of pending requests for service during the time the interrupts are disabled.   Further flexibility is gained if interrupt levels can be triggered by software as well as hardware.   For example, on the XDS-940 the interrupt from the communications equipment is given a high priority so as not to lose characters coming in from the terminals.   There is a certain amount of processing required on each incoming character to convert it to an internal-system code, echo it to the teletype, check to see if it is a control character having special significance to the system, and to place it in a buffer associated with the proper job.   If all the above functions were carried out in one routine, other equal- and lower-priority interrupt signals would be ignored during the entire time.   The only time-critical operation is bringing the character into memory initially; the remaining functions are of low priority.   The way this problem is handled in the system is to bring the character, along with terminal identification, into memory as part of the high-priority interrupt routine and then with software to trigger a lower-priority interrupt level and exit from the higher-priority routine.   The lower-priority routine then performs the remaining functions but is interruptable by higher-priority signals.

Another approach exists on the Digital Equipment Corporation PDP-10 system, which has several interrupt priority levels, each represented by a wire on the I/O bus running through each device.   Each device can be assigned a priority number by software which indicates on which line(s) it is to send its interrupt signal(s).   This approach gives flexibility to the system designer in assigning priorities based on function and system condition.

4.2.5 Summary A timesharing system needs a flexible-priority interrupt system or some other appropriate method of interprocessor and device communication.   Attention signals are major inputs to the resource allocating (scheduling) processes. The hardware signals are not the only inputs to the scheduling routines, and treating the hardware signals in a different manner from the software signals requires extra mechanism in the system design. A reexamination of the design of the hardware interrupt system in the light of the total resource-management function seems to be indicated.

4.3 THE MICROPROGRAMMING CONCEPT

4.3.1 Review of the Control Problem

The dividing line between hardware and software concepts is an ill-defined constantly shifting area. A technique being used more frequently and with increasing generality in the design of processor control units, called *microprogramming*, has the potential of blurring this area even further. The term microprogramming has no universally accepted definition. We supply one for use in this text within the context of the following discussion. The term seems to have originated in 1951 with M. V. Wilkes in discussing a machine whose operation codes would be programmer-definable.[7] Wilkes observed at that time that there probably was no need for such a machine and reconfirmed his view in 1958.[8] Since that time, however, changes in hardware technology and increased complexity in operating systems and other systems software have opened this question up again.

This section introduces the concept of microprogramming and briefly indicates some of its implications for systems designers. The reader can then evaluate the merits of the technique in light of a specific system with which he may be involved. The material of this section parallels the excellent presentation of Flynn and MacLaren.[11]

First, it is necessary to review the nature of the control problem. Figure 4.4 shows a processor from the control point of view. The basic resources of the processor are a set of registers and their contents, execution logic, and access to main memory. The basic control problem is to allocate these resources to perform the function specified in the operation code of each instruction. The execution unit performs ordinary combinatorial logic (time-independent, without storage of its own) on the contents of the registers presented to it. The functions required to perform an instruction execution are:

1 To open and close gates to control data flow between the processor registers and the execution unit

2 To control which logic function is being performed by the execution unit on the operands presented to it

3 Possibly to sequence through several iterations of functions 1 and 2

In other words, an operation specified in an instruction is made up of one or more elementary operations which are defined in terms of the basic

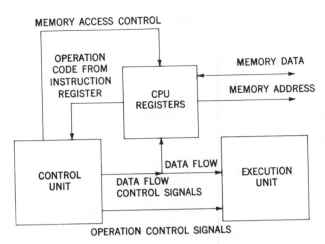

MEMORY ACCESS CONTROL

OPERATION
CODE FROM
INSTRUCTION
REGISTER   CPU
                 REGISTERS

MEMORY DATA

MEMORY ADDRESS

CONTROL   DATA FLOW   EXECUTION
UNIT   DATA FLOW   UNIT
               CONTROL SIGNALS

OPERATION CONTROL SIGNALS

FIG. 4.4   CPU organization from the control point of
view.

hardware logic of the processor.   These elementary operations are referred
to as *microsteps* or *microoperations*. The set of microsteps required to
specify an instruction execution is called a *microprogram*.   A microstep
is completely defined by the states of some number of gates N.   This
number may vary from tens of gates to thousands, depending on the processor.   However, since many operations work on entire register contents, fewer
actual gating descriptions are actually required to specify each microstep.

The operation code of an instruction contains an encoding of combinatorial and sequential logic required to perform the specified operation.   At
each microstep in the execution the control unit must send the signals
to the gates which specify that microstep.   Some mechanism must sequence
the control unit through the required steps.   In a standard control-unit
implementation, a counter is used.   The states of the counter and the operation code of the instruction specify the microsteps.

To review, the basic logic level operations of the processor are to
gate information from registers to the execution unit, to perform a simple
combinatorial-logic transformation on the operands presented to the execution unit, and to place the result back in a register or registers.   Similar
types of steps are required to perform an address calculation and to access
memory.   We ignore these steps and for purposes of illustrating the microprogramming concept consider only operation of the execution unit during
instruction execution.

4.3.2   Uses of Random-access Memory in Control Design   These control
functions are naturally handled using a fast random-access memory as part

of the control unit.   Questions of cost and performance are discussed later. The combinatorial information required to specify each microstep can be given in a stored word.   The sequential information can be given by the sequence of words fetched.   Each word is called a *microinstruction*.   A sequence of microinstructions to perform a normal instruction operation as specified in the operation code is called a *microprogram*.   It is this use of random-access memory which we wish to associate with the concept of microprogramming.   A standard microinstruction may be organized as shown in Fig. 4.5.   The *gating specification* specifies the current microstep to be performed.   The *test code* specifies a condition which, if true, indicates that the next microinstruction is to be fetched from the control-memory location given in the *next address* field.   If the condition is false, the next microinstruction would be fetched from the next higher address.   The conditions tested, for example, could be overflow on a simple addition, sign of a result, or more elaborate combinations of signals.

The address of the initial microinstruction in a sequence required for an instruction is given by the operation code or some function of the operation code.   This description is highly simplified but illustrates the basic concept.   More elaborate schemes have been devised using addressable bits or words for temporary storage, microindex registers within the control unit itself, several alternate addresses in a microinstruction, or other methods for forming the next address based on current or past execution unit states. A particularly useful feature, in our experience, is a microprogram subroutine facility.   The exact design parameters for making the many possible choices are generally based on considerations of control-memory cost, performance required, types of instructions being implemented, and data-path layout of the processor.[9]   Conceptually the operations performed by the microprocessor are similar to those performed by higher-level processors, the main difference being that the microprocessor uses more internal-logic conditions as data and can effect address-logic signals and exercise detailed control over processor data paths and registers.

The memory access time of the control memory must be about half that required to gate registers into the execution unit, execute the combinatorial function, and gate the result back to a register to achieve proper performance.   To meet this performance requirement economically, choice of memory technology for implementing the control memory has favored read-only stores in the past.   The advent of relatively inexpensive high-performance integrated-circuit memories now makes it economical to

GATING SPECIFICATION	TEST CODE	NEXT ADDRESS

FIG. 4.5   A typical micro-instruction word.

use read/write memories for control functions. The memory size required depends on the processor design but is probably around 1,000 to 2,000 words with around 100 bits per word for medium to large machines. Efficient use of microprogramming requires a speed differential of from 4 to 10 between main-memory and control-memory access time. This differential is to enable several microinstructions to be executed per main-memory cycle.

4.3.3 Implications of Microprogramming The implications of the above discussion are clear. The software designer working with a machine based on microprogramming can have more freedom in specifying the structure of the machine with which he is to work.[11] If we call the instructions in the instruction set seen by the assembly language programmer *macroinstructions*, we see that the software designer can have more freedom to choose his macroinstruction set, because once the basic microprogramming logic and facilities have been implemented, new or modified instructions can be easily created by writing new microprograms. Many frequently used operations required within the operating system involving manipulation of tables and basic list processing for handling of resource and allocation queues and character manipulation can have appropriately designed macroinstructions implemented by microprogramming. In other words, macroinstructions can be implemented oriented toward the data structure desired by the designer. A microprogram sequence used in place of a normal subroutine can save several memory cycles.

An example of the power of implementing frequently used critical functions in a microprogrammed sequence is the evaluate (EVAL) instruction added to an IBM 360/50 used in the Rush Time-sharing System.[10] This instruction evaluates a PL/I expression directly in hardware in its standard form. One can conceive of frequently used sections of the operating system being moved entirely into microinstruction sequences, e.g., the handling of the associative map on the SCC-6700, as described in Sec. 2.5.8. Other examples are interrupt-handling routines and parts of the processor, and main-and auxiliary-memory management functions.

Another area for microprogramming techniques in system design is that of special processors oriented toward such functions as allocation and access of auxiliary storage, particularly that required for extending main memory. Examples are discussed in Sec. 3.3.2, and another example is outlined in Sec. 6.13. Lampson has proposed that the entire processor interrupt-handling and scheduling function be integrated into a special microprogrammed processor,[2] as discussed in Secs. 4.2.4 and 5.2.8. If microprograms are easily changed, flexibility still exists to experiment with different allocation algorithms and parameters.

Writing microprograms is more difficult than conventional programming because of the greater detail of hardware knowledge required and large number of conditions controlled and tested by a single microinstruction. Because one of the motivations for use of microprogramming is efficiency, the use of higher-level microprogramming languages at the level of ALGOL or FORTRAN may not be possible. The basic concepts of programming extend to microprogramming, however.

REFERENCES

1 **Graham, R. M.:** Protection in an Information Processing Utility, *Commun. ACM*, vol. 11, no. 5, p. 365, May, 1968.

2 **Lampson, B. W.:** A Scheduling Philosophy for Multi-processing Systems, *Commun. ACM*, vol. 11, no. 5, May, 1968.

3 **Lichtenberger, W. W., and M. W. Pirtle:** A Facility for Experimentation in Man-Machine Interaction, *AFIPS Conf. Proc., Fall Joint Computer Conf.*, vol. 27, 1965.

4 **Gibson, C. T.:** Time-sharing in the IBM System/360: Model 67, *AFIPS Conf. Proc., Spring Joint Computer Conf.*, vol. 28, p. 61, 1966.

5 **Glaser, E. L., et al.:** System Design of a Computer for Time-sharing Applications, *AFIPS Conf. Proc., Fall Joint Computer Conf.*, vol. 27, pp. 197–202, 1965.

6 **Evans, D. C., and J. Y. LeClerc:** Address Mapping and the Control of Access in an Interactive Computer, *AFIPS Conf. Proc., Spring Joint Computer Conf.*, vol. 30, pp. 23–30, 1967.

7 **Wilkes, M. W.:** The Best Way to Design an Automatic Calculating Machine, *Manchester Univ. Computer Inaugural Conf., Manchester*, July, 1951, pp. 16–18.

8 **Wilkes, M. V.:** Microprogramming, *AFIPS Conf. Proc., Fall Joint Computer Conf.*, vol. 12, pp. 18–19, 1958.

9 **Tucker, S. G.:** Microprogram Control for System/360, *IBM Systems J.*, vol. 6, no. 4, pp. 222–241, 1967.

10 **Babcock, J. D.:** A Brief Description of Privacy Measures in the RUSH Time-sharing System, *AFIPS Conf. Proc., Spring Joint Computer Conf.*, vol. 30, pp. 301–302, 1967.

11 **Flynn, Michael J., and Donald M. MacLaren:** Microprogramming Revisited, *Proc. ACM Natl. Conf. 1967*, pp. 457–463.

12 **Lampson, B. W.:** Scheduling and Protection on Interactive Multi-processor Systems. *Univ. Calif. Berkeley Project Genie Doc.*, 40.10.150, Jan. 20, 1967.

part THREE

Software concepts

chapter FIVE

Processor and memory allocation

5.1 INTRODUCTION TO SOFTWARE CONCEPTS

The software system not only has the job of allocating the system hardware resources to meet user requirements but comprises an important set of resources in itself. The user views the system through a software window which gives him the view of a system with many more capabilities then could be easily attained if he had direct access to the hardware.

The user has access to a file system which enables him to store his work from terminal session to terminal session, serves as a communication link between programs he is developing or using, acts as a link between other devices, and permits him to share his work with others and in turn to build on their efforts. The file system is probably the most important system element from the user's point of view.

The user has access to language translators, text editors, debugging aids, library routines, and system functions. These software subsystems and aids ease his job of instructing the hardware to perform the information-processing tasks of interest to him.

A command system is available to the user to help him instruct the system in how to meet his needs. This software system constitutes one of the user's main points of contact with the system.

That part of the software system of concern to the designer involved in solving the technological problems of economically sharing the total system resources among many users is usually of little direct interest to the user as long as it works and enables him to meet his information-processing requirements. To the user, the system is a black box, which through subsystems, command language, file system, and other software routines provides him with capabilities he could not easily achieve with direct access to the hardware. The user appreciates the internal workings of the resource-sharing aspects of the black box only because he knows that by sharing resources with many others he can attain capabilities which he could not otherwise afford.

These points are useful for the system designer to keep in mind. The designer's function is to provide a service; his skill and knowledge are useful only to that end and not in and of themselves. The user probably cares little for the clever N-dimensional, web-threaded scheduling algorithm of which the designer is so proud and which he is planning to publish, particularly if the one-dimensional one would work and provide the same function and cost as seen by the user. It would seem good practice for the designer to keep conceptual simplicity, integrity, and uniformity as goals while being aware of the tradeoffs which a given state of technology makes available to him at each design step. The user, his information-processing requirements, and his need for privacy, reliability, and easy interface with the system should be constantly borne in mind. These points are stressed here because the designer of the software system operates under fewer constraints than the hardware designer. The result has often been poor software and human engineering. With these words of concern we turn now to a discussion of the software system.

The software system is most naturally discussed under functional headings, such as processor and memory allocation, the file system, handling of I/O, the command system, subsystems such as compilers, text editors, debugging aids, and so forth. This approach is the one taken in this part of the book. Subsystems are not discussed except to indicate briefly how they are connected to the rest of the system. Within the above functional areas one can recognize two subclasses of functions: (1) those functions which must permanently reside in main memory because they are used frequently or must react quickly to the changing demands for system resources and (2) those functions which are swapped in and out of memory as part of the system or as part of user processes.

The resident functions handle requests to service I/O devices, schedule processes, allocate memory and I/O devices, handle communications with user terminals, and all other tasks which occur at a great enough frequency or require sufficiently fast response. Associated with these resident routines are many tables containing status information about user processes and system resources.

The swappable functions are associated with less frequently required services, such as allocation of subsystems, logging users in and out of the system, accounting, file-system manipulation, and other resource-allocation functions which do not require immediate system attention. One of the technological design problems is to determine the boundary between these two classes of functions and to organize the design so as to minimize the amount of main memory required for the resident functions while meeting the intrinsic needs of the users.

Looking at the implementation details of an operating system, we see that they consist of a set of routines, usually reentrant, which manipulate a system data base. The system data base consists of various kinds of tables, queues, buffers, and list structures, some of which reside in main memory permanently and some of which can be moved between main memory and auxiliary storage. Just as understanding how to interconnect logic modules, flip-flops, registers, and control signals is required by the hardware designers to convert a system design into functioning hardware units, it is the system programmer's job to understand how to create and manipulate the various basic types of data structures mentioned above. A few basic types of data structures are introduced at appropriate points in the discussion.

Part three covers reliability, maintenance, recoverability, measurement, and evaluation as well as the obvious functions of processor and memory allocation, protection, the file system, I/O, and the command system; the former topics are as vital to the success of a design as the latter and must be taken into account from the earliest design stages. All these topics are considered in some detail in this chapter and those to follow.

5.2 PROCESSOR ALLOCATION

5.2.1 Introduction The central problem is this. Only as many processes can be executing at a time as there are hardware processors in the system. Hardware processors must be assigned to processes in such a way that they meet user response requirements and achieve balanced utilization of other resources. When a new process is to begin execution, main-memory allocation must take place. In multiprogramming systems, where several processes reside in main memory concurrently, processor and memory allocation are interrelated and cannot be treated independently in the design. The framework for the solution to the above problems centers around the concept of a process and virtual processor introduced in Chap. 1. At this point it might be useful to review Sec. 1.5.

In brief, the basic idea is that a given configuration of hardware is converted by software into many virtual processors, each of which has its own memory space, an instruction repertoire, and access to the I/O and file system and can intercommunicate and share memory with other virtual processors. Processes can be created or destroyed by the system or by other processes by calls to the system. A process and virtual processor are defined by a set of information called the *context block* or *state vector,* to be described in detail below.

We first discuss the allocation of physical processors to processes under the assumption of unlimited physical-memory space in order to bring out certain basic concepts; then we discuss the problems involved in allocating memory and processors when physical-memory space is limited.   Closely related to physical-resource allocation is the intrinsic problem of interprocess communication.   The discussion of processor allocation which follows has been strongly influenced by the excellent work of Saltzer[1] and Lampson.[2]

5.2.2   Basic Process Intercommunication Functions   To see the intrinsic intercommunication problems, let us first consider a simplified case, two processes executing in two separate processors but sharing memory.   Assume further that process A places work for process B to do on a *work queue.*   An example might be a computation process which from time to time places characters to be output in a buffer, which are then output by another process.   When process B finishes all the work on its queue, what should it do?   It could loop looking at the queue, finding nothing look again.   When process A places work on the queue, process B would find it immediately and perform the appropriate function.   Looking requires, at a minimum, memory cycles to be utilized.   Utilizing memory cycles causes a potential system drain and, more seriously for the cases we are to consider later, ties up a processor.   Therefore, a better answer to the question is to have a process *block* itself until some new work arrives

Blocking is the ability to cease executing until further work arrives In the two-process two-processor situation, process B could block itself by executing a *halt* instruction or by an explicit call to the system to perform this function.   When a process blocks, there is the opportunity, as we shall see later, to switch the processor to another process.

When a new task is added to the queue, process B must be un blocked or *awakened* by some mechanism.   Process A must send a signal to the system indicating that process B should be awakened.   This awakening function is thus an interprocess communication function which must be provided by the system.   For the simple case of two processes running on two processors this signal could be a simple interruption of the halt state.   Thus, we have seen that a process is in one of two states, *running* or *blocked.*   The process is *running* if it is executing instructions and is *blocked* if it is waiting for a *wake-up* signal to resume execution.   Furthermore, two processes, in order to work together, must be able to intercommunicate data and control information.

In order to prevent loss of information, wake-up signals which occur while a process is executing must be saved, and a process must not b allowed to block until all wake-up signals have been handled. Such a function is provided in the hardware interrupt or intercommunication system by storing each signal as it comes in until it has been acknowledged. A similar function must be provided in handling software intercommunication signals. If these signals are not stored, *race* conditions can occur, in which the first signal to arrive is processed and later signals arriving during the processing of the first are lost. Saltzer refers to such a mechanism for saving wake-up signals as a *wake-up waiting switch.*[1]

In a two-process system, an awakening signal sent by one process always goes to the other, and no explicit address of the signal destination is required. To generalize this concept to a situation involving many processes requires a *process identification tag* to identify the process to receive the awakening signal.

In summary to this point, a process can be in one of two states, *running* or *blocked*. A blocked process is one which cannot run until some signal arrives to unblock it. These unblocking signals are referred to as *wake-up* signals and change the status of a process from blocked to *ready to run*. A signal which causes one process to be unblocked may also cause another to be blocked. These signals can come from many sources: system processes, user processes, hardware interrupts, such as the terminal communications equipment, a timer, completion of a disk seek, or execution of an instruction with an illegal memory address.

The wake-up signals are sent along with related status information to a part of the system often called the *scheduler.*[2] In the Multics system, the term *traffic controller* is used.[1] One of the defining differences between classes of multiprogramming systems, besides the range of available facilities, is the design of the scheduler. In an online file-management system or other I/O-oriented system, the prime wake-up signals are associated with the I/O devices, while in a general purpose timesharing system the signals from clock sources are given increased importance, as we see below. From the point of view of the system, the life history of a process is an alternation of running and blocked periods. Each running period is terminated by a signal to block this process. This blocking signal may be made by the process itself, a system process, or some other user process.

A simple example is a request by a process for a character from an I/O device. If the character is not available, the process may be blocked until the character arrives. The request for the character may wake up a system routine to refill a buffer from the required I/O device.

During the discussion of the handling of various specific resources, additional examples of signals for blocking and wake-up are given. One of the basic design problems is proper handling of the communications of blocking and wake-up signals.

5.2.3 Scheduling

INTRODUCTION   If there are more processes than there are physical processors on which to run them, some processes will be unblocked but not running. This state is called the *ready-to-run* or *ready state*. Therefore there are three states, running, ready, and blocked. It is necessary to have some algorithm for deciding which of the several processes that are ready to run should be run next. This algorithm is often called the *dispatching* or *scheduling* algorithm. The dispatching algorithm is an important part of the scheduler but, as we have seen above, is by no means the whole of the scheduler.

Useful criteria for the design of a dispatching algorithm are[2] (1) to minimize the effort expended by the system in switching processes and (2) to be able to react rapidly to the changing collection of processes ready to run, so that the most important process is being run at every instant.

There is much discussion in the literature about what features a dispatching algorithm should have to meet the above criteria.[3] The goals of designing a dispatching algorithm which is both responsive and inexpensive of system resources are often contradictory, and therefore tradeoffs in both areas are required for practical algorithms. We discuss dispatching algorithms further in Sec. 5.2.6 Our approach in this chapter is to repeatedly discuss certain concepts at greater levels of detail.

THE READY LIST AND PROCESS PRIORITIES   Basic to any dispatching algorithm is some scheme for keeping track of the processes which are ready to run. A list of such processes is called a *ready list*. We can now see the general framework of processor allocation. A wake-up signal sent to a process causes that process to be placed on the ready list. When a process blocks, it allows the hardware processor to be temporarily switched to a process on the ready list. The dispatching algorithm must choose which process on the ready list is to be run. One can recognize two times when the actual decision can be made of the order processes are to be run in: (1) when the processes are placed on the ready list and (2) when a process is to be removed from the ready list.

The mechanism chosen must allow flexibility to explore different dispatching strategies and at the same time require little effort on the part of the system to make the decision. Any scheduling mechanism which requires a large fraction, say 20 percent, of total computing time in deciding what to do next can probably be rejected.

The general approach to dispatching usually taken is to order the processes on the ready list according to a *priority number*. The dispatcher is thus a simple routine which always chooses the highest priority process to run next. We now describe three common alternatives available in handling process priority.

The simplest mechanism is a *first in, first serve* priority ordering. When a process is awakened, it is placed on the end of the ready list. The dispatcher always takes its next process to be run from the top of the list. Thus, priority increases with time spent on the ready list.

The second technique is called the *fixed-priority technique*. Here a process is assigned a fixed-priority number when it is created. When the process is placed on the ready list, it is placed ahead of lower-priority processes and behind processes of equal or greater priority. Again the dispatcher picks the next process to be run from the head of the list. Both these approaches are simple and require little system scheduling effort, but they are inflexible and insensitive to other system information which may allow better response to users or more balanced utilization of system resources.

A third approach, called the *variable-priority technique*, assigns a computed priority to a process at the time the process is assigned to the ready list. The priority computation can take into account whatever information is determined by the designer to be relevant, such as amount of processor resources used in the past, size of memory required, reason for having been blocked, and so forth. The concept can be generalized so that each process can have a different priority-assigning procedure, in other words a private scheduler. This private scheduler is provided by the system, as chaos would result if each user could try to write a scheduler to maximize his benefit. The idea would be to allow processes controlling real-time operations to compute their priority in one way, which might frequently place them at the head of the ready list, while other classes of service would have priorities computed in different ways. Even with a computed priority scheme, if processes are ordered on the ready list according to priority, the dispatcher can be a simple procedure taking the top item from the list when a new process is to be run.

THE TIMER AND PREEMPTION With the above ideas established, we can examine two additional complicating questions: (1) What if a process which is placed in a running state does not block itself? (2) What if a new process added to the ready list has an importance, as determined by the scheduler, greater than one which is running?

The first question is answered by noting that once a process is started running, it cannot be allowed to run as long as it might require if responsiveness to all users is to be maintained. Therefore, one of the important sources of scheduling signals is a *clock source* or *interval timer*. A *clock source* is a device for producing an interrupt at some fixed frequency which can be used to increment registers for recording elapsed time. Similarly, an *interval timer* is a device which when set will send a signal after a given elapsed time, possibly variable under program control.

The length of time which a process is allowed to run before it is blocked is called a *quantum* or a *time slice*. The quantum size is one of the important parameters of a scheduling algorithm.[4,21] It may be fixed or variable, depending on some other parameters such as process size, process priority, or the length of time the process ran last time. In general, the average response time can be decreased if one can adjust the quantum size so that the majority of processes can satisfy their processing needs in one quantum period. One can get an intuitive feeling for why this may be true by considering a simple example suggested by Saltzer. Assume there are five processes to be run each of which requires 10 seconds of computing. Assume further that there is no overhead or lost time in switching the processor from one process to another and that the scheduling algorithm runs one process for a fixed quantum, switches the processor to the next process for the same quantum period, and so on until all the processes are completed.

Consider what happens if a 1-second quantum is used. Each process will compute for 1 second before the processor is switched to another process; after 10 seconds each process has computed 2 seconds; after 45 seconds each process has computed 9 seconds; and after 46 seconds the first process completes, followed at 1-second intervals by the other processes. The average response time is 48 seconds.

Now consider what happens if a 10-second quantum is used. After 10 seconds the first process completes, after 20 seconds the second process completes, and so on until after 50 seconds, as before, all processes are completed. The average response time is 30 seconds. Increasing the quantum size to one in which the processes could complete decreased the average response time. In a real situation, where overhead or idle time is associated with switching the processor, the improvement would be greater.

In an actual situation, the problem of picking a quantum size and scheduling strategy is complicated by the wish to balance total system resources and to give good response to highly interactive processes without seriously increasing the response time to more computer-oriented processes. Minimizing the average response time is not in itself a sufficient criterion. Therefore, more complicated scheduling strategies and variable quantum sizes are often used, for example, those discussed in Sec. 5.2.6.

When a running process is blocked by a signal from an interval timer, it is immediately ready to run and must be assigned some priority and returned to the ready list. The processor is then reassigned to the next highest priority process in the ready list.

One additional piece of information is now needed on the ready list besides a process identification tag and priority number, namely, the quantum interval which this process is to be allowed to run when it gains control of a processor. The additional design problem of determining this quantum interval for each process has been introduced.

When the scheduler places a process on the ready list which it determines is more important than one which is running, the lowest-priority running process can be blocked and returned to the ready list as discussed above and the processor switched to the more important process.[1,2] This *preemption* concept should be handled carefully to avoid unbalanced utilization of system resources. For example, when swapping is involved and considerable system resources are expended in bringing a process into main memory, the scheduler must maintain some deferral power over incoming blocking signals to avoid situations where a process is brought into main memory only to be immediately blocked.

SUMMARY We have now introduced the major concepts involved with processor scheduling:

1 The concept of process state: running, ready, blocked
2 The concept of an awakening signal
3 The concepts of ready list, priority number, and dispatcher
4 The concepts of an interval timer and quantum length
5 The concept of preemption scheduling

The next step is to discuss interprocess communication, priority number, and quantum length in further detail.

5.2.4 Interprocess Communication There are two basic sources of awakening and blocking signals. A prime source is external hardware interrupt signals, which are initially handled by system routines called *interrupt handlers*. The interrupt handlers determine what action to take and must send appropriate awakening and blocking signals to the correct processes.

A second source of blocking and awakening signals is generated internally by software. For example, the XDS-940 and Multics systems allow processes to create parallel or subsidiary processes which in working together may need to *interlock* with each other by sending blocking and awakening signals. These latter signals are implemented by a mechanism in the XDS-940 which can be considered as a *software interrupt* system.[22] The processes must contain their own interrupt handlers, but the system must provide the mechanism for transmitting the signals. Adequate interprocess communication also requires that status information be available to the process to which the software interrupt is directed.

There seem to be two main approaches to the communication of blocking and wake-up signals in present systems. In one approach, the process generating the signal must be explicitly aware of all the processes affected. In the other approach, the process generating the signal need not be explicitly aware of which processes are affected but need only perform simple actions such as incrementing a certain memory cell. Both approaches can be used for communicating software and external hardware-originated signals.

Consider a variation of the software interrupt system of the XDS-940.[22] One can associate a number of bits of information, an *interrupt field,* with the information about a process already kept by the scheduler. These bits correspond to software interrupts. A process communicates an interrupt by sending to the scheduler a process identification tag and an interrupt number for the process to be interrupted. The scheduler sets the appropriate bit in the interrupt field of the designated process and returns. The process sending the signal may then continue or block itself until it receives an interrupt. The process which received the interrupt is placed on the ready list if it was blocked.

When the dispatcher gets around to assigning a processor to a process with a software interrupt pending, it does not restart it at the location indicated by the stored-program counter but at some location, established by convention, associated with the highest-priority pending interrupt number. The process returns from this routine to the scheduler to get back to where it was previously. Additional elaboration, such as software interrupt masking, can be added. In other words, the mechanism is very similar to that found in hardware except that now it is handled by the scheduler.

Status information can be stored either as part of the information kept about each process by the scheduler or in shared memory. Processes can also signal each other through shared memory. A type of interprocess communication facility which can be used either to explicitly signal particular processes or to implicitly signal other processes is the *event channel* approach used in different forms on the Multics system[36] and the CAL system.[35] The basic idea is quite simple, but very general and powerful. Processes with appropriate status are allowed to request that the system create named objects called *event channels.* There can be many event channels in the system. Event channels can be protected such that only authorized processes can communicate with a given channel. The event channel in its simplest form is just a first in—first out queue of information. The amount of information which can be placed on the queue can be variable, but is usually restricted to being a status word or words. Shared memory can be used for transmission of bulk information.

During the programming of processes, conventions are established as to which event channels are to be used by cooperating processes. Several processes may utilize a common event channel. When a process wishes to communicate with other processes, it sends a message addressed to a given event channel or channels through a call to the system. The system places the message on the end of the queues of the addressed channels. When a process reaches a point where it is expecting communication, it requests the next item on an addressed event channel queue. If one is available, it is removed from the queue and passed to the requesting process. If the queue is empty, the requesting process is blocked, and the name of the requesting process is stored in the event channel so that when a message is received, the process can be awakened. This discussion has presented the concept of an event channel in one of its simplest forms. Elaboration and other variations of the idea are possible.

The routines handling external interrupts can also explicitly send the scheduler a process identification tag and possibly a priority number. This communication method requires that requests for service to routines handling external devices also be accompanied by the process identification tag.

An implicit communication approach is taken with the XDS-940 system.[2] When a process is blocked, a word in its state vector is set indicating the reason for its being blocked. This word also has an address to be checked by the dispatcher and bits indicating what condition the dispatcher should find in order to awaken the process. The I/O or other routine which is to awaken the process at the completion of some action does not know explicitly which process it is servicing but does know that it is to store some value in a particular location when it is finished. The indications are usually simple—greater than, equal to, or less than zero. Using the implicit communication approach, the list of blocked processes and processes ready to run is the same. The dispatcher must search the list checking each process to see if its awakening condition has been met.

The explicit communication approach seems to us more natural and is the one primarily used in hardware communication between modules, but it may require more code when implemented in software. The implicit communication approach results in code which may be easier to modify because of the decoupling possible between system modules but requires extra time to determine which process to run next, because the appropriate scheduling routine must check one or more cells designated by each process in some order until it finds a process to run. A detailed example of the communications involved in an I/O request is given in Sec. 6.2.3.

5.2.5 The Context Block Let us now consider in more detail the nature of the information which must be saved when processors are switched. The information to be saved when a processor is switched is the context block introduced in Sec. 1.5.2. The context block consists of the program counter, contents of the processor central registers and indicators, possible additional registers if address mapping is used, some indication of the process's current address space, and possible indications about certain I/O device status. How much of this information must actually remain in main memory while the process is blocked or on the ready list? This is an important question because one would like to have blocked and ready processes create as small a drain as possible on processor and memory resources. There is the additional requirement that the time required to switch a processor be as small as possible in order to minimize processor idle time.

Besides the above information there is usually associated with each job or process some amount of memory not accessible to the process but accessible to the system for storage of temporary values, buffer space, constants, and tables unique to this process. This memory area is called the *temporary storage area;* it is a page in the XDS-940 system and must be resident in main memory before computation can begin. The sum total of all information required to run a process is the context block.

The context block contains tables, or pointers to tables, like those described in Sec. 5.3.2 defining the process's virtual memory space. If this information is on auxiliary storage, one access must be made before the system knows where the rest of the process-memory space is stored. On many systems, such as the XDS-940, which have relatively few active processes (running, ready, or blocked) and relatively small memory spaces for each process, some of the context-block information is kept in main memory at all times. This approach places restrictions on the number of allowable active processes because of preallocated table space but does allow switching to take place with fewer references to auxiliary memory. If several processes or parts of processes are kept in main memory concurrently, in order to try and overlap computation and swapping, as described in Sec. 5.3, then the context block should probably be in main memory also; otherwise idle time might result while bringing back enough information to enable the process to continue.

The important point is that very little of the context-block information is required to be in main memory for ready and blocked processes and that tradeoffs in speed of processor switching and use of main memory exist.

5.2.6 Structure of the Ready List—Dispatching

THE READY-LIST ENTRY We now turn our attention to the structure of the ready list. The information in the ready list about each process must include explicitly or implicitly process identification tag, priority number, quantum number, possibly wake-up waiting switches or software interrupt fields, and any other information required by the scheduling framework decided upon.

The approach taken in the XDS-940 system is to group this scheduling information together with some of the context-block information into contiguous cells. This information constitutes an entry in a table of like entries called the process-activation table. The process identification tag is implicit in the position in the table of the entry for the process. This identification can be called the *process number*. This is a common approach throughout operating system design to use table position as the identification for various types of entities.

USE OF LIST PROCESSING Priority is conveniently handled by position within the ready list. To avoid physically moving these entries about in

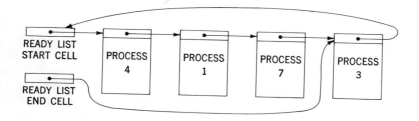

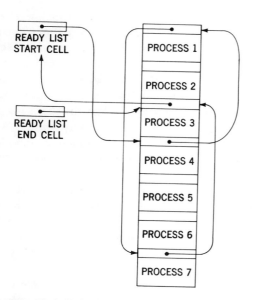

FIG. 5.1 Simple list-structured ready list (*a*) as it appears logically and (*b*) as it appears in the table.

main memory, the ready list in the XDS-940, as is common in other systems, is a linked list. Thus, each entry in the ready list contains a pointer to the next successor entry. Other pointers are kept in the table entries to link related processes. Structuring tables and queues as lists is a common technique used in operating system design. The simplest form of a ready list is shown in Fig. 5.1a as it appears logically and in Fig. 5.1b as it appears in the table. Each entry consists of several contiguous computer words to hold the state information for a process. Common ways of implementing tables are discussed in appropriate places in the remainder of the book.

One can keep track of blocked processes by placing them on another list. Again no movement within core is required if list processing is used. Changing the priority of a process or adding a new process to the ready list at any priority point is done simply by inserting a new element in the list. Insertion requires modification only of the values stored in the pointer word associated with each entry affected.

ASSIGNMENT OF PRIORITIES   The assignment of priorities and quantum numbers by the simple *first in, first served* scheme was mentioned earlier. This scheme places a process on the bottom of the ready list when it is removed from the running state or when it is awakened. Each process is run for a fixed quantum unless it blocks. This scheduling method is often referred to as *round robin* scheduling.

Another common approach is to use some sort of multilevel priority scheme and variable-length quantum. We discuss two variations in common use, but many other variations are possible. More sophisticated schemes are also possible within the framework of the discussion given earlier.

The motivation behind the use of multilevel schemes is to make the system very responsive to interactive users. The common feature of multilevel schemes is that computer-oriented processes drift to lower-priority levels. Interactive-oriented processes drift to high-priority levels. A multilevel strategy splits the ready list into sections with different priorities. A process added to a priority level is usually added at the end. Within a level, service is first in, first served. Thus, at the point where a process must be chosen to run, the dispatching algorithm always starts looking at the highest-priority section first. The processes on the lower-priority levels get run only if there are no processes ready to run on the higher-priority levels. For example, no level-two process gets run until all processes at level one have been run, even if processes continue to be added to level one, and so forth. There is always the possibility, unless additional features are added to the scheme as discussed below, that some processes on the lower-priority levels may not get run or may run so infrequently that the response is not acceptable.

THE XDS-940 MULTILEVEL SCHEME   One multilevel scheme represented by the XDS-940 system is discussed in a somewhat simplified form here.[2]   There are four levels, in order of priority, called teletype, I/O, short quantum, and long quantum.   A list processing implementation of such a multilevel list is shown in Fig. 5.2.   Processes which blocked because of a request for a teletype character which was not available or because their output teletype buffer was full are added to the teletype level when they are awakened.   Similarly, processes which block for various reasons for other I/O service are added to the I/O level when they are awakened.

The system has two quantum lengths, a *short quantum* and a *long quantum*.   A process is always allowed to run for a short quantum, and

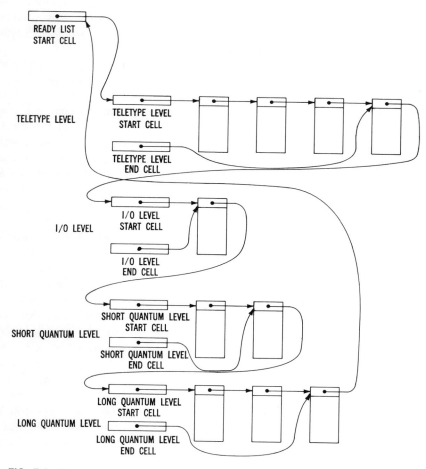

FIG. 5.2   List-processing implementation of a multilevel ready list.

if at the end of this time no other process is ready to run, it can continue. The purpose of the short quantum is to assure that some useful computation takes place, in order to justify the expense of swapping the process in.   This scheme also allows higher-priority processes to preempt the processor if they appear during or after a short quantum.   When a process is dismissed after a short quantum, because a higher-priority process has become ready, it is placed on the short-quantum level.   During the time a process is running, the number stored in the machine associated with the long quantum of this process is decremented on each clock pulse.   When the process is blocked, the present value of the long quantum is stored and the decrementing is continued next time the process is run.   Thus, eventually the long-quantum number is reduced to zero and the process is moved to the lowest-priority level, the long-quantum level.   This method ensures that all processes will run with reasonable response to each.   This scheme is just one of the many which could be devised to limit the number of times a process can appear on the high-priority levels of the ready list.

One refinement in the XDS-940 scheduling algorithm should be mentioned.   The same technique is used on other systems as well.   When a process makes an I/O request, it is not immediately blocked.   Instead, a table is consulted which contains the expected time to complete the requested I/O service.   If this time is less than the amount of the quantum remaining, the system allows the I/O request to proceed and waits without blocking the process.   The motivation is that if the I/O operation can be completed, there will be a greater return on the investment of swapping the process in.   If the process were blocked, it would probably be swapped out only to be awakened immediately and require swapping back in.

MULTILEVEL PRIORITY ORGANIZED BY RUN LENGTH   Another variation of the multilevel strategy assigns several levels, each with a different quantum length.[4,25]   When a job is run, it can run for the length of time specified by the quantum length of the queue it was on unless it blocks earlier.   One might, for example, adjust the quantum length of a level according to some criterion, e.g., that the majority of processes which reach the level can complete in the chosen quantum period, as suggested by the discussion of Sec. 5.2.3.   When a process is created, it is placed at the end of the top level.   When a process reaches the end of time specified for its level, it is placed at the end of the next lower level.   Computer-oriented jobs thus drift down the levels.   When a job blocks for teletype or other I/O and then is awakened, it is again placed on the end of the top level. Setting quantum lengths is a function of the system characteristics and can be determined only by experiment with the actual system or by simulation.   Quantum length is an important parameter and should be carefully considered because system response and utilization seem to be sensitive to it.[4,21]

Additional complexity can be added to a scheduling algorithm to take into account maximum utilization of memory or any other resource.[24] In the discussion of memory allocation given in Sec. 5.3, we indicate that effective scheduling algorithms probably cannot be designed independently of the algorithms chosen for swapping and memory allocation. All the algorithms probably should be chosen to reflect the performance characteristics of the hardware and to some extent the characteristics of the user community at a particular installation.

SUMMARY   Scheduling can be performed at two points, when processes are placed on the ready list and when processes are to be dispatched to processors. Practical scheduling probably should not require much computing. The usual approach is to perform scheduling when processes are added to the ready list. The ready list can be structured to handle priority levels, and there are many ways of assigning priorities to processes. There is no general agreement on a best approach, although most methods try to give high priority to interactive processes. Dispatching then becomes a matter of simply choosing the highest-priority process on the ready list.

5.2.7   Scheduling of System Functions—Interrupt Routines   This discussion of scheduling has applied primarily to user processes. The scheduler must also control system processes. Many system routines do not run on virtual processors as user processes do. As a result, many system routines have a different character from user processes. The discussion of the interrupt-handling routines given below points out these differences. The system routines can be thought of as being blocked and unblocked by interrupts, by requests for service by user processes, and by status information from I/O devices. Much of the system activity is performed by resident routines which do not require swapping. When an interrupt or user request arrives, control is transferred to the appropriate routine, the required action is performed, and control is returned to the user process. The system may have ready lists of its own to handle requests for I/O and other services on devices which can be used by only one process at a time. Scheduling of I/O is discussed in Chap. 6 and a detailed example of these ideas is given in Sec. 6.2.3.

There is a problem associated with scheduling system routines when a quantum runout occurs in the middle of the system routine. If the system routine is an interrupt-handling routine, it is necessary to complete it before entering the scheduler. Some mechanism must exist, however, to return from the interrupt routine to the scheduler rather than to the interrupted user process.   If the system routine is handling a direct request for service from a user process and the quantum runs out, two common courses of action are open, depending on system design.   If the system routines are not reentrant or can leave the system in a dangerous state if not executed to completion, the quantum runout signal must be ignored until the routine is finished.   Return, however, must be to the scheduler rather than the user process.   Again some mechanism must be provided to return to the scheduler.   Such a mechanism is described below.   If the system routine is reentrant and is not required to complete, the scheduler can be directly entered on quantum runout.

A hardware mechanism used on the XDS-940 to transfer from the system routine to the scheduler rather than back to the user process when a quantum runout occurs during processing of the system routine is called the user-mode trap.   It works as follows.   When the clock interrupt routine finds that quantum runout has occurred and a system routine is being executed, the user-mode trap is set and a return is made to the system routine rather than to the scheduler.   Then when the system routine completes and tries to return from system mode to user mode, a trap signal is generated transferring control back to the system.

During the discussion of interrupts in Sec. 4.2 it was pointed out that present interrupt systems seem to require treating interrupt routines outside the system's normal process-scheduling and priority-assigning functions.   Unlike other processes in the system, interrupt routines usually do not run on virtual processors.   They run on the hardware processors as part of the basic system.   As a result, the system facilities and mechanisms available to virtual processors—protection, access to the file system, communication between virtual processors, access to the user's terminal, and access to utility processes—are not easily available to the interrupt routines.   On the other side, processes running on virtual processors cannot easily be allowed to handle signals entering the system through the normal interrupt mechanism.   In effect, the scheduling function is split into two parts, one part to handle signals entering through the hardware interrupt system and the other part to handle signals generated by virtual processors. The priorities assigned to the hardware signals are usually fixed among themselves, and unless the interrupts are disabled, the hardware interrupt-handling routines always take priority over processes running on virtual processors.   Mechanisms can be developed to interface these two parts of the scheduling function.   The scheduling system which results from the dichotomy between the interrupt routines and other processes is workable but runs counter to the desired goal of minimizing mechanisms and treating functionally related tasks in a uniform manner.

The reason interrupt routines do not usually run on virtual processors is that switching a hardware processor from one virtual processor to another is a time-consuming task. Conceptually what is involved is switching state vectors. The state vector consists of the central registers of the machine, the virtual processor's memory map, quantum length, possibly temporary storage for system routines, I/O device and other status information, and so forth.

The virtue of present interrupt systems is that they allow the hardware processor to be switched to the interrupt-handling routine with a minimum of state information being saved. The interrupt-handling routine can be given the responsibility of saving any other state information with which it may interfere, such as various central registers.

Therefore, if hardware and software awakening and blocking signals are to be treated in a uniform manner, one requirement is to develop mechanisms to switch virtual-processor state vectors very rapidly when necessary. Lampson's suggestion[2] of implementing a special microprogrammed processor to perform scheduling and aid in processor switching was discussed in Sec. 4.2.4. This special processor would have access to memory and could manipulate the ready list and perform dispatching and other scheduling functions. The previous discussion covered system routines normally resident in main memory.

When a system routine is required which does not normally reside in main memory, it can be swapped into main memory. If time is not a pressing factor, a state vector for this system process can be set up and this process placed on the ready list. Both Multics and the XDS-940 make use of processes which are created by the system to perform some low-priority checking or other operation. A state vector is created for each of these processes, and it is placed on the ready list. An example of such a process is one which is awakened every few seconds to check the consistency of system tables or to see that an I/O device or channel is not hung up in some way. In the XDS-940 system, the major part of the nonresident system is considered a process which is assigned to all users. It is written as reentrant code so that only one copy is required in main memory.

In the Multics system, system segments are assigned as part of the user's process. The system segments are reentrant. Some are permanently resident, and others are nonresident.

5.2.8 Interlocking Another subject requiring brief mention is that of interlocking,[2,15,32] which has a number of aspects. First, consider a common situation. When several processors (hardware or software) are sharing a common data base, certain precautions are required. When the data base is being modified by one process, it is dangerous to allow other processes to read or write it. Several processes may read a common data base concurrently, without risk. It is therefore necessary for the process which intends to modify the data base to *lock* out other processes which may want to access it.   To have such a lock implies that there is one routine used by all accesses to the data base.

When a routine is going to access the common data base, it first checks the lock.   If the lock is set, the routine must wait.   If the lock is not set, the routine sets the lock, accesses, and modifies the data base. After modification, the lock is cleared.   It is important that the locking mechanism be so implemented that between the time of checking the lock and setting it no other processor can also check the lock.   If this situation could arise, two processes could simultaneously gain access to the data base, which is the very situation the lock is to prevent.

A variety of hardware and software mechanisms can be used to implement a lock.[2,15,32]   Lampson[2] has suggested providing a machine instruction which:

1   Tests the contents of the addressed memory word.
2   If it is negative, skips.
3   If it is positive, sets the addressed word negative and does not skip.

If the instruction is called TSL, for test and set lock, then the following sequence of instructions implements an interlock:

TEST   TSL   LOCK
              BRANCH   DATA BASE
              BRANCH   TEST

The data base is locked to other processors if the contents of LOCK are negative.   When the contents of LOCK become positive, the data base is unlocked and a processor can gain access and set the lock in the same instruction thus ensuring that no other processor can also reach the data base simultaneously.   The above scheme, as pointed out by Lampson, has one disadvantage, and that is that processors locked out are utilizing main-memory cycles constantly testing the lock.   To get around the problem of expending memory cycles continuously checking the lock, the process locked out of the data base can block itself by placing itself on a list to be awakened when the lock is cleared.   The routine presently accessing the data base can exit through a standard routine which clears the lock and awakens the next process waiting for access to the data base.

Lampson has suggested another interlock mechanism, sufficient to lock another processor out of a block of code for a given length of time, which does not require either that memory cycles be expended checking the lock or that the software mechanism block a process until the lock is cleared.[2]   The idea is to implement a special instruction he calls PRO-TECT, which, when executed by one processor, cannot be executed again for a given length of time.   If another processor tries to execute this instruction, it is temporarily idled until the waiting period is up.

One possible implementation would be to set a counter by the execution of the PROTECT instruction.   The counter would then count down at a given rate to zero in a free running mode.   If any other processor tried to execute the PROTECT instruction while the counter value was greater than zero, it would be halted until the counter reached zero.   At that point the waiting processor would execute the PROTECT instruction and proceed.   In a multiprocessor system, priorities for access to the PROTECT instruction must be assigned to take care of the case of several processors halted waiting for the PROTECT counter to reach zero.   The mechanism described above would be quite useful for locking out processors while a few instructions were executed to change a system table or change a queue entry position.   One additional feature is required, however, to provide adequate protection.   The interrupt system signals must be automatically ignored during the time the PROTECT counter is nonzero.

This mechanism has a problem if the code executing while a PROTECT operation is in force accesses a page not in memory and generates a page-fault interrupt.   This interrupt cannot be ignored.   Lampson has suggested that the problem can be handled by ensuring that all addresses generated during a PROTECT operation fall in the same page, or in pages guaranteed to be in main memory, or in one other page which is first referenced before critical operations are performed.   In the latter case if the return from a page fault executes the PROTECT operation, no danger will result.

There are other interlocking problems.   If two processes A and B are sharing one processor, the following situation could result.   Process A sets the lock and gains access to the data base and is blocked.   Process B enters the lock-test loop.   The machine could get hung up at this point in a *deadlock* unless process A gets control of the machine again.   In a timesharing system process, B would eventually run out its quantum, and process A could get control of the machine again.

Two processes can deadlock each other in other ways.   Assume process A is using resource X and process B is using resource Y.   Process A could request access to resource Y, without giving up X, and block waiting for Y.   At a later point process B could request access to resource X, without giving up Y, and block waiting for X.   At this point both processes are deadlocked unless the system can gain release of resource X or Y.   The situation could have been avoided if the processes could access only one resource at a time.   If processes can gain control of more than one resource at a time, the design must provide means of recognizing potential deadlock situations.   The interlocking problem in its many forms is a troublesome area which the designer must be aware of.

5.2.9 Summary Many important concepts were introduced in this section. We saw that processes are in one of three states: running on a hardware processor, blocked waiting for some condition to be satisfied, or ready to run. Processes ready to run are commonly kept on a ready list positioned by priority. Processes are dispatched to processors from the ready list according to priority. The ready list can be structured into several priority levels in an attempt to satisfy response or other requirements. Many other possible scheduling mechanisms can be used within the framework presented.

Processes are prevented from running for long periods by use of a timer and quantum number. Means are also usually provided for higher-priority processes on the ready list to preempt a processor from a running process.

Means must be provided for processes and system routines to inter-communicate. Explicit and implicit communication mechanisms were discussed. The concept of software interrupts is one mechanism allowing processes to intercommunicate, the concept of an event channel is another. The lack of uniformity, in present systems, in handling hardware and software blocking and awakening signals was brought out.

The idea of resident and nonresident system routines was introduced. Resident routines permanently reside in main memory to meet frequent or high-priority requests for service. Nonresident routines are used less frequently or with low priority and can reside in auxiliary storage.

The potentially troublesome area of process and processor interlocking was presented. Interlocks must be carefully designed to ensure proper isolation of one process from another in handling a common data base. It was shown that without forethought processes can get into deadlocked situations where neither can proceed because of the condition of the other.

Finally, it was pointed out that processor scheduling design probably cannot be considered in isolation from other resource-allocation problems in the system.

5.3 MEMORY ALLOCATION

5.3.1 Introduction The memory-allocation problem can be viewed as being divided into two main parts: (1) a record-keeping function of keeping track of the virtual-memory space of each process in the system, whether it is in main memory, on auxiliary storage, or both, and where, and of keeping track of which areas of main memory and auxiliary storage are free and (2) a main-memory allocation (swapping), decision-making, and strategy function, required if more than one process is residing in main memory at a given time, of deciding which process(es) or parts of processes are to be moved to auxiliary storage to make room for the new process about to be run. The problem of keeping track of free space on auxiliary storage is discussed in Sec. 6.1.3. The problems of keeping track of the virtual-memory space of systems like Multics were discussed in some detail in Chap. 2. The XDS-940 record-keeping functions are discussed in more detail here because they further illustrate some of the basic problems. After this discussion we examine the problem of memory allocation and swapping in greater detail.

5.3.2 Memory-space Tables

INTRODUCTION Two sets of tables are required. One set of tables keeps track of the virtual-memory space of processes, and the second keeps track of utilization of real memory. There must be a link between these sets of tables. To understand the following example, the reader should be familiar with the XDS-940 paging mechanism and relabeling (map) registers described in Sec. 2.4.2.

KEEPING TRACK OF REAL MEMORY When a process is running, the actual physical blocks in main memory, in which the logical pages of the process are stored, are indicated by the real relabeling registers or map. To determine the physical blocks in main memory to be assigned to an incoming process, the memory-allocation routines work with two tables. One table is called the *real-memory table* (RMT), which contains information about which logical pages of which processes are using the various physical blocks of main memory and which blocks are *free*, not occupied by a page of some process. The RMT is ordered by physical block number. The other table is called the *real-memory counter* (RMC), which contains information about the number of processes using the code stored in the various physical blocks. For example, the text-editing system, which is reentrant, may be being used by several users, and thus efficiencies are gained if it is not swapped unless absolutely necessary. Additional counters are used to indicate frequency of physical-block use to assist in determining which blocks should be selected for assignment to an incoming process. A discussion of this type of counter is given in Sec. 5.3.3. Each of the above tables contains one entry for each physical block of main memory.

KEEPING TRACK OF VIRTUAL MEMORY In Chap. 2 we saw that virtual memory is kept track of in segment- and page-descriptor tables. In the XDS-940, the actual pages or memory space associated with a job, possibly containing several processes, are kept track of in a table called the *program-memory table* (PMT).[22] That is, there is one PMT for each job. There is a word of storage in the PMT (page descriptor) for each of the user's logical pages. Separate page tables are not kept for each process in a job because processes may share pages, thus creating duplicate entries. The logical effect of separate page tables is created, however, by the mechanism to be described. The motivation for this approach is discussed further in the next section. The word (descriptor) in the PMT indicates where that page is located in physical storage (main memory or auxiliary storage). When the page is in main memory, this PMT word indicates the starting physical address (physical block) in which it is stored; when it is in auxiliary storage, the physical address is given there.

The PMT entries have no particular ordering; i.e., the position of the entries in the PMT does not necessarily correspond to the logical ordering of pages in a process, although all pages belonging to one job are in con-

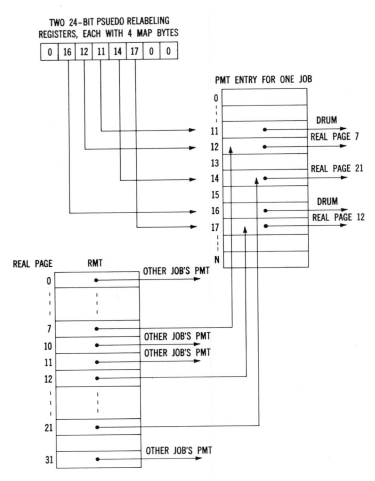

FIG. 5.3   Relation of memory-allocation tables in the XDS-940.

tiguous PMT cells. The logical ordering is stored in two words of the state vector of the process. These words have the same format as the two real relabeling registers and are referred to as *pseudo relabeling registers*. There is one pair of pseudo relabeling registers for each process. The difference between the real relabeling registers and the pseudo relabeling registers is that the map bytes of the pseudo registers point not to real memory but to PMT entries. The order of the map bytes in the pseudo relabeling registers is the logical order of the program's pages. That is, byte 1 points to an entry in the PMT where information about logical page 1 is stored, and so on. The pseudo-relabeling-register bytes and the appropriate entries in the PMT to which they point give the effect of a separate page table for each process.

The RMT does not actually contain explicit information but pointers back into the PMT. The pointers in the RMT and the page address in physical memory contained in a PMT entry are the connection between real and virtual memory (this topic is discussed further in this section). When the memory-allocation routines determine that certain physical blocks are to be assigned to an incoming process, any information of value in the blocks must be removed to auxiliary storage. By use of the RMT, the system can reset the address in the proper PMT entry to indicate the auxiliary-storage location to which the page has been removed. The mechanism is illustrated in Fig. 5.3. By calls to the system, processes can change the contents of the pseudo relabeling registers or PMT entries and in this way perform overlays.

In capsule form the following events take place in the XDS-940 when a process is blocked and another process is to be run. Similar events are required in other systems.

1 A check is made using the pseudo relabeling registers and the PMT to determine whether the process to be run is already in main memory and, if not, how many physical blocks are required. If the new process already resides in memory, transfer of control takes place immediately.

2 Using the RMT, RMC, and usage counters, the memory-allocation routines determine which blocks are to be freed (this point is discussed further in Sec. 5.3.3).

3 Using the pseudo relabeling registers and the PMT, the location and logical order of the pages to be brought into main memory are determined.

4 I/O commands for transferring pages into and out of memory are prepared, and the swap takes place.

5 The real relabeling registers are set up.

6 The machine registers are re-stored from the values stored in the state vector, and the process is started. The methods for allocating space on the auxiliary storage device are important concepts and are discussed in Sec. 6.1.3.

MORE ON THE CONNECTION BETWEEN REAL AND VIRTUAL MEMORY In a system with paging, conceptually the simplest way to keep track of the pages for a process is with a page table for each process. If processes share pages, there will be a separate entry in each page table for the shared page. The extra space required may not be a serious problem if the page tables are not kept permanently in main memory.

The XDS-940 designers decided to keep the virtual-memory information in main memory in order to speed up switching the processor from one process to another. This is one motivation for the pseudo relabeling registers and PMT mechanism. Use of this mechanism has one further motivation. Assume page tables are used. There is a separate entry in each page table of processes sharing a page. When a shared page is moved, each page table containing a descriptor for the page must be updated. Where should the entry in the real-memory table point? It could point to a connection block of words or to a connection list of words each word pointing to the appropriate place in a page table of a process using this page. When the page is removed from main memory, the information in the connection block is used to indicate which page-table entries to update. This bookkeeping is eliminated by using the approach taken in the XDS-940. Only the one PMT entry need be modified when the page is moved.

This mechanism covers the case of several processes in a job sharing a page. The case of processes in several jobs sharing a page still needs discussion. With the PMT approach above, each job sharing a page needs an entry in its PMT for the shared page. This requires extra space and still leaves the problem of updating several entries when the shared page is moved.

This problem is solved in the XDS-940 system by a table called the shared-memory table (SMT), used for keeping track of pages sharable between jobs. Examples of such sharable pages, in the XDS-940, are those of compilers, text editors, and other subsystems. The entries in the pseudo relabeling registers, which represent shared pages, are coded to point to the appropriate SMT entry rather than a PMT entry.

In a system with segmentation, shared segments have only one page table, which contains the only information needing change when a page is moved. However, if the page table itself is moved, the appropriate segment descriptors for all processes using the shared segment must be modified.

Another mechanism for keeping one copy of changing information used by several processes useful for both the segmentation case and the strictly paged case is that of the *hash table* or *association table*,[26] which we discuss in the context of a paged system. There is a page table for each process. The page table could contain an entry for each page in the address space of the process if it is addressed using the page number as an index.   The page table could also be organized and addressed as a simulated associative or content-addressed memory (in the manner described below) addressed by the page number.   Such an organization would allow the page table to contain one entry for each logical page in use rather than one entry for each page of the address space.   To simplify the discussion to follow, assume that the former organization is used.   A page-table entry in the scheme to be described contains only an auxiliary-storage address where the page normally resides and protection information but no main-memory location.

No core address for the page is kept in the page table.   Main-memory contents are kept track of by another table called the hash table, or association table.   Each entry of the hash table contains an auxiliary-storage address and real-memory address for a page residing in main memory.   The entries of the hash table are not ordered by real-memory block number, as for the real-memory table discussed in Sec. 5.3.2.   Instead the entry position is determined by a *hash-coding* algorithm.

Hash coding is a method of table lookup used to simulate a content-addressable memory.   The concept of a content-addressable memory was discussed in Chap. 2, where such a memory was used as a hardware map.   A word or record in a content-addressable memory consists of several fields. The contents of one or more of these fields can be used as a key to retrieve all words or records containing that key.

In hash coding, a transformation (hashing) is applied to a key used to access a table.   The result is a table address in which to put the record containing the key.   Hashing the key on retrieval yields the same address where the record containing the key is stored.   Several keys can hash to the same address, in which case a *collision* is said to result.   There are many ways to handle collisions.   One simple method is the following.   If a location already has an entry, the next free slot below this location is used to store the new entry.   Then on retrieval, the contents of the field used for the key in the location corresponding to the hashed key are compared against the access key.   If they are equal, the entry contains the desired information.   Otherwise a linear search is made of the entries below the address produced by the hash until an entry containing the desired key is found.   The hash table is usually considered to be circular; i.e., the first entry logically follows the last entry.   The size of the hash table and hashing algorithm are factors determining the probability of two auxiliary-storage addresses hashing to the same hash-table address.   If the hashing algorithm produces random addresses, placement of collision entries can be out of line, on average, a distance of less than two even when the table if 75 percent filled.   Retrieval is clearly quicker if no collisions result.   Choice of table size and hashing algorithms are discussed further in the literature.[28,29]   With this brief introduction to one approach used for a hash table, let us see how the idea is used to keep track of pages in main memory.

The auxiliary-storage address of a page to be placed in main memory is hashed to determine its entry in the hash table. If there is an entry at the address produced, the first free entry below this point is used. At the location determined by the hashing, or the first free location beyond this point, an entry is created which contains the main-memory address of the page, the auxiliary-storage address of the page, and possibly the access rights granted this page.

When a page is to be removed from main memory, a search can be made of the hash table until an entry is found having the same main-memory address as the page under consideration. This entry contains the auxiliary-storage address at which to store the page. A real-memory table could be used with a pointer into the hash table, in order to speed up the location of the auxiliary-storage address of the page. The entry for the page swapped out is then removed from the hash table.

When a process is to be brought into main memory, the system must check to see if any pages of the process are already in main memory. This check is accomplished as follows. The auxiliary-storage address of each page is hashed. The hash table is then searched starting at the address produced by the hashing. The auxiliary-storage address of the hash-table entry is compared against that of the page to be brought into main memory. If they are equal, the page is already in main memory and the main-memory address contained in the hash table entry indicates its location. If the auxiliary-storage addresses do not match, the hash table is searched further. A linear search of the entire hash table results if the entry is not there. If no entry in the hash table has an auxiliary-storage address equal to that of the page under consideration, the page is brought into main memory from auxiliary storage and a hash table entry is created.

This mechanism has the following desirable features:

1   Each page in the system has a unique identifier (its auxiliary-storage address) by which it can be referenced, whether it is in main memory or not.

2   Only one structure, the hash table, needs to be modified when a page changes main-memory location or is removed from main memory.

3   Shared pages are properly handled without special consideration.

This scheme could be inefficient if the address space of the running process could not be contained in a hardware map because the lookup in the page table and then further lookup in the hash table could be expensive of time unless special hardware to aid the hashing process were available. If the page table were organized as a hash table also, then two levels of lookup in hash tables would be required. It is important to recognize that the motivation for use of hashing in the case of the page table and the table relating real and logical memory are different. In the former case, it allows a smaller table size to result if all the logical space is not in use. In the latter case, it allows one copy of changing information to be shared by many page tables and simplifies updating when the information changes.

This concludes our discussion on methods for relating virtual-memory, auxiliary-storage, and main-memory addresses. The use of hash tables is a common mechanism as a means for organizing tables of changing information for rapid retrieval.

CLEAN AND DIRTY PAGES To make the swapping process more efficient, use can be made of the fact that some pages of processes are *read-only* and that not all pages contain locations which are modified when a process is run. Pages which have not been modified are said to be *clean;* pages which have been modified are said to be *dirty.* Read-only and unmodified (clean) pages do not need to be returned to auxiliary storage during a swap because correct copies of these pages already exist there. On the XDS-940, this concept is implemented by use of software and the hardware memory-protection system. When the real relabeling registers (map) for a process are set up, all pages have the read-only bit set. A software code exists in the PMT indicating whether the page is truly read-only or not. Then when the process attempts to write into the page, a memory-fault trap is generated. The system checks to see whether or not the page is truly read-only. If the page is not, a bit in the PMT is set to indicate that this page has been written into, the read-only bit in the relabeling register for this page is cleared, and the write instruction allowed to proceed. Other systems automatically set a bit associated with each physical block when it has been modified. This bit can be tested with an instruction to determine whether the page is dirty.

SUMMARY To review, we see that physical memory can be accounted for by mechanisms such as the real-memory and real-memory count tables, which have one entry for each page of physical memory. Each entry of the RMT indicates in effect the job and which page of the job is using this physical block. The RMC is used to indicate which physical blocks are being shared. The virtual memory of a XDS-940 process is determined by the pseudo relabeling registers used in conjunction with the program memory table and the shared memory table. The RMT, PMT, SMT, pseudo-relabeling-register mechanism is one technique for relating virtual memory and real memory. Another approach using page tables and a hash table was discussed. This approach is more straightforward conceptually but does require more storage.

Within Multics, tables similar to those described in this section exist to keep track of physical memory. The virtual memory of a process is kept track of in a series of tables starting with file directories (to be discussed in Sec. 6.1), an active-segment table, which is used for keeping track of segments known to the system; known-segment tables, segment-descriptor tables, and page tables, which are used for keeping track of segments known to a process. These tables and their use were discussed in some detail in Sec. 2.5.

5.3.3 Swapping

INTRODUCTION Let us now look in more detail at the problems encountered with swapping in general and demand paging in particular. If there were enough main memory, swapping would be unnecessary or at least might have to be performed less frequently. The prime limitation on the present capacity of main memories is cost, although signal-propagation time is also a factor. Hardware technology is changing rapidly, however, and the cost and physical size of main memory can be expected to decrease.

Even with this main-memory cost reduction, main memory is still likely to be an order of magnitude more expensive than auxiliary storage such as drums, and designers will therefore try to take advantage of this cost differential by designing systems which utilize swapping. There are two important parameters of an auxiliary-storage device: (1) the average length of time required to access the required block of information and (2) the time required to transfer the block to or from main memory. The former is called the *average access time*, and the latter is inversely proportional to the *transfer rate*. The average access time for most drums used for swapping is between 15 and 40 milliseconds, although UNIVAC has a small 1.5×10^6 character drum with an average access time of 4.25 milliseconds. Transfer rates can vary on drums from a few hundred thousand 6-bit characters per second to several million 6-bit characters per second. Besides the times mentioned above associated with the hardware characteristics, additional time is required to locate the required information.

One solution to problems associated with swapping is to use auxiliary storage devices with smaller average access times and higher transfer rates. Solutions in this area using bulk core are discussed in this section. At this point, it is useful to review some basic decision-making problems which must be solved by the scheduler and memory-allocation system.

Early systems used very simple allocation and swapping strategies. No attempt was made to overlap the execution of one process with the swapping of another. Only one complete process resided in memory at once. When the processor was to be switched, the previously running process was removed entirely to auxiliary storage and the next process was loaded into main memory. All processes were loaded relative to a constant fixed location, say location O. That is, no dynamic relocation was used. The MIT CTSS system used such a scheme with the slight modification that only as much of the previously running process was removed as was required to make room for the second incoming process. Memory protection was used. The idea here was that if the first process should regain control of the processor, some time might be saved if a part of its virtual memory were still in physical memory. The concept, based on the CTSS technical notes, is illustrated in Fig. 5.4. If a third process larger than the second were loaded, more of the first would be swapped out.

The next refinement was to introduce dynamic relocation, in order to make it easier for several processes to reside in memory concurrently.

The dynamic-relocation approach was then followed by strategies for overlapping the execution of one process with the swapping of another. Also introduced was the concept of *demand paging*, which attempts to bring into main memory only those pages currently required by the process and at the time required. While a page is being brought in, execution of another process is attempted. We discuss this concept in some detail later in this section.

OVERLAPPING EXECUTION AND SWAPPING Let us consider now some general problems involved in overlapping execution and swapping. We assume for the following discussion that several processes or parts of processes reside in main memory concurrently and that a process is run only when it is completely loaded into main memory. A simple strategy for dispatching a process to run, when it is desired to overlap execution and

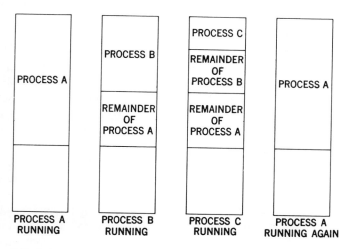

FIG. 5.4 Memory contents in time when processes A, B, C, D are run using the CTSS memory-allocation algorithm.

swapping, is the following. Go to the ready list and find the highest-priority process. If it is in main memory, run it; if it is partially in main memory or entirely on auxiliary storage, set up the swap commands and turn execution over to the highest-priority process residing in main memory while swapping takes place.

Immediately, the reader can see some of the problems facing the designer of an overlapped swap and execution scheduling and allocation strategy. If a process is to be swapped in, which process or parts of processes should be swapped out to make room in memory for the incoming process? One answer is to mark the pages of the in-memory process to be run during swapping and then choose the pages to be removed according to some simple strategy. A commonly used strategy is to remove the pages of the most recently run process.[27] But what if the process to be run blocks soon after it is started and swapping is still in progress? It may be that the next highest priority process in main memory is losing some pages in the swap. One can begin to think of strategies for choosing processes or pages of processes to be swapped out to make room for an incoming process which get around the above problem but which introduce further possible complications. The memory-allocation computation could become quite elaborate and constitute a serious system drain.

A strategy that tends to guarantee that some useful computation can be overlapped with swapping is to maintain in memory at all times one or more compute-oriented processes which are not likely to block soon after they are started.[21,23] These compute-oriented processes can usually be recognized by the system if a multilevel scheduling strategy is used such as that discussed in Sec. 5.2.6. We place a process in main memory which has been computing for a long time under the reasonable assumption that it will continue to compute.

When a process blocks and then another is chosen from the ready list to be swapped in, we assign the incoming process to unused pages or to the pages of the lowest-priority process in main memory which is not the compute-oriented process. Additional efficiencies can probably be gained if one swaps out pages being shared by several processes as a last resort, because removing shared pages immediately removes several processes from the status of residing entirely in main memory. After the pages have been chosen to be swapped to make room for the incoming process, the highest-priority process residing in main memory is run while the swap is going on. If the running process blocks, control is switched to the next highest priority process in main memory. If this process blocks, control is switched to the next highest priority process in main memory, and so on, until finally control may be switched to the compute-oriented process. When the swap is finished, control is switched to the new process brought into memory.

The compute-oriented process is allowed to remain in main memory until it blocks.   At this point it is replaced with another compute-oriented process and is placed at an appropriate place in the ready list.   Such a conceptual approach, as outlined above, seems to ensure effective processor utilization even with swapping and shows that scheduling and memory allocation are closely interrelated.   These ideas can also be applied to systems without paging but having dynamic relocation aids such as base registers.

DEMAND-PAGING PROBLEMS   Let us now examine additional complications introduced by the demand-paging concept.   The choice of a swapping algorithm and the success or failure of a total demand-paged system are related to:

1   The page-demand characteristics of programs
2   The software time required to locate pages on auxiliary memory
3   The accessing and transfer characteristics of the auxiliary storage devices used as backing stores

A number of studies have been made of the page-access characteristics of programs,[5-8] and they all tend to show that after a process begins execution, the page-access characteristic of the process is that given in Fig. 5.5.   It shows that very early in a time slice a process has accessed most of its pages.   This implies that within a short time after beginning execution, a demand-paging scheme requires a high page traffic.   In the Fine study[5] five rather large programs were examined.   Program size varied from 14K to 44K words and averaged 30K words.   Each program was considered divided into 1K word pages.   None of the programs were in any way designed for a paged machine.   Fine found that very early in a time slice (at 30 milliseconds) 18 to 20 pages on the average had been accessed. In fact, Fine found that if a program required 20 pages, 25 percent of the time the program required these pages within 7 milliseconds.   This

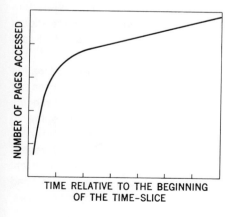

TIME RELATIVE TO THE BEGINNING
OF THE TIME-SLICE   FIG. 5.5   Page-access characteristic.

high page demand seems to imply that very frequently, using a demand-paging swapping algorithm, the process is going to be halted waiting for a page. These results tend to be pessimistic about achieving efficient operation using a demand-paging strategy. Even though the data gathered in the studies to date were not obtained from programs written for paged machines, Coffman argues that programs designed for a paged machine will yield similar results.[6] Denning, on the other hand, is not convinced of this.[9] In our view a reasonable assumption for designers, until more data may indicate otherwise, is to assume that programs will exhibit the characteristic shown in Fig. 5.5.

When a page of a process is brought into memory and execution is begun, the process will show brief periods of activity until a page not in memory is accessed, followed by periods of inactivity while the required page is fetched to main memory. As more pages are brought into main memory, the periods of activity will lengthen. The attempt to overlap the periods of inactivity by running other processes is going to be successful only if some of the other processes have most of their pages in main memory or if the access time and transfer rate for required pages are very short. Using demand paging there seems to be a critical relationship between size of main memory required and speed of access to auxiliary storage. Otherwise the system is soon going to be spending most of its time swapping and little time executing user processes. Fine found that the first 10 active periods would have a total average active time of 0.8 millisecond (on the SDC-Q32 computer). If we used a drum with an average access time of 17 milliseconds and an infinite transfer rate, the total inactive time, waiting for pages required to achieve the 0.8 millisecond of execution, would be 170 milliseconds. Because all other processes in the system are going to behave with similar statistics and be halted for I/O services, demand paging from even a fast drum may soon result in a system performing information transfers but no computation. Nielson's simulation of an early version of the IBM 360/67[10,11] system showed similar results. With this introduction to problems of demand paging, let us examine resource-allocation problems more generally and then discuss solutions to the demand-paging problems which have been implemented or proposed.

One can consider two bounding approaches to resource allocation as suggested by Randell and Kuehner:[13] (1) preallocate to a process all resources a process may need during its execution period and (2) allocate resources to a process only at the point it requires them. Swapping in the entire address space, or a large part of the address space, of a process before starting it in execution represents the first approach with regard to the memory resource. Demand paging represents the second approach. Use of paging allows processes to be handled in convenient units, and one can develop strategies which are tradeoffs of these two approaches.

Neither of the bounding strategies mentioned above is good or bad in itself. There is a tendency to assume without careful analysis that strategy 1 is not as good as strategy 2. The choice of a resource-allocation strategy should take into consideration the following:[13]

1 The cost of nonproductive resource utilization

2 The cost of waiting for a resource requirement to be satisfied

3 The frequency with which demands for a resource are made

4 The effect of a strategy for allocating one resource on utilization of other resources

5 The cost in time and memory space of storing and executing the resource-allocation strategy itself

Understanding how all these factors interrelate requires considerable study in the context of any particular system. With this introduction we can go on to study demand paging further because as a bounding and frequently discussed strategy it helps bring out a number of useful ideas.[9,12–14]

APPROACHES TO SOLVING PROBLEMS OF DEMAND PAGING Several approaches have been suggested to solving the problems of demand paging, the more important being:[9]

1 To improve program structure by user or compiler optimization to decrease the page-demand rate or obtain user advice for the system about the structure of the processes

2 To improve the strategy for scheduling processes and allocating main memory

3 To minimize the average access time for the swapping medium

There has been some practical success in accomplishing suggestion 1 above, an example being Bobrow's work with a paged version of the list-processing language LISP,[30] but much more work is required.

Denning[9] points out that users probably cannot be expected to be able to supply useful advice because:

1 A user may build his work on that of others and not know how the shared processes are structured, or the accessing structure may be data-dependent.

2 It is not clear what advice one would want to solicit from users.

3 Any advice a user would give would tend to try to optimize the system for his job, but the system must consider all jobs.

Denning further points out that compilers cannot be expected to supply information on the structure for two reasons: (1) Programs will be modular in construction and the structure of various modules may not be available at compile time. There will be data dependencies of structure which can be determined only at run time. (2) Compilers which have the machinery to carefully trace out structure will be very slow and large. Thus users requiring rapid compilations during program development will be dissatisfied, and these compilers will be a drain on resources.   Denning therefore argues that only by making allocation decisions based on currently observed process-behavior characteristics, suggestion 2 above, or by using more rapid access devices, suggestion 3 above, can the demand-paging concept be made practical.

The prospects of improving the structure of the operating system to decrease its page-demand rate are better.   Statistics can be gathered on the operating system's page-access characteristics, as discussed in Chap. 7, and the operating system's modules can be reloaded in an order that minimizes the page-demand rate.

INTRODUCTION TO MEMORY-ALLOCATION STRATEGIES   There are two main points at which memory-allocation and scheduling decisions can be made: (1) at the point a page is required and (2) at the point pages must be removed to make room for the ones coming in.   Let us assume for the moment the first point is to be handled by using a strategy of bringing in a page only when it is required.   We come back to this point below.

The process of removing pages is often called *page turning* or *replacement*.   An algorithm for choosing pages to remove would be a replacement strategy.   Some of the problems involved in choosing such a strategy were introduced in Sec. 5.3.3.   The goal of replacement strategies is generally to try to remove the page least likely to be referenced in the immediate future.   We assume that all of memory is filled with pages of one process or another.   Two straightforward strategies suggest themselves.   In the first strategy, called *first in, first out* (FIFO), whenever a new page is required, the page least recently brought in is removed.   In the second strategy, called *least recently used* (LRU), whenever a new page is required, the page unreferenced for the longest time is removed.   A third more involved strategy illustrates a number of important concepts.   It is called the *working-set strategy* and is related to the LRU strategy, but chooses to replace pages only from the currently executing process.

FIFO AND LRU STRATEGIES   The FIFO strategy has the advantage of being easy to implement.   It can be implemented by placing page identification on a first in, first out list as pages are brought into memory.   The LRU strategy is more difficult to implement but has seemed attractive on the assumption that the least recently used page in the past is the least likely to be used in the future.

A number of approaches to implementing an LRU strategy—all very similar—have been used or suggested.   The basic idea is the following. Associate a counter with each block of main memory.   When a page is referenced, set the counter to a predetermined value. Periodically decrement the counters for all pages. The least recently used page is the page with the lowest counter value. The counters are often called *aging registers.* Decrementing the counter ages a page.

For practical systems, the counters must be of some finite length. Therefore, all pages having a counter with value zero are considered to be of the same age and the first candidates for replacement. One way to implement this idea might be to add extra hardware to the physical memory. For example, when a memory block is referenced, a counter could be set or a capacitor charged. Then as time goes on, the counter would be counted down at a fixed rate or the capacitor would discharge. Whenever the digital or analog timer runs down, a flag is set marking the page as a candidate for removal.[9]

A similar mechanism can be implemented in software by associating a set of bits, called an aging register, with each block of physical memory. Conceptually the approach is the following. When the page is referenced, the leftmost bit of the aging register is set. Then periodically all the age registers are shifted one position to the right. A zero is entered from the left on a shift, and bits shifted out on the right are dropped. With this scheme, all pages which have been referenced in a given interval will have at least one bit set in their age register. Figure 5.6 illustrates an aging register for a page before page reference, after page reference, and after aging (shifting).

A number of problems arise in implementing the aging-register idea in software. (1) The system must detect the first reference to each page in between each shifting point. The memory-protection system can be used in conjunction with the memory tables to give such an indication, but an extra system load is created. The discussion of clean and dirty pages (Sec. 5.3.2) indicates the basis for such a mechanism. The GE-645 has hardware to detect a page reference. There is a reference bit associated with each physical block of main memory. When a page is referenced, the corresponding physical-block reference bit is set. This bit can be tested with an instruction. At the sampling interval used to age the pages in main memory, the hardware reference bits can be entered into the age register and then the reference bits can be reset. (2) Shifting all aging registers may be a significant load if the aging interval is too short. (3) Searching the aging registers to find the least recently used page may be

| 0 | 0 | 1 | 0 | 0 | 0 | 0 | 0 |

| 1 | 0 | 1 | 0 | 0 | 0 | 0 | 0 |

| 0 | 1 | 0 | 1 | 0 | 0 | 0 | 0 |

FIG. 5.6   Aging register: (*a*) before page reference; (*b*) after page reference; and (*c*) after the shift.

time-consuming.   Careful choice of the shift interval and the length of the aging register can minimize these problems.

Corbato used a modification of the above idea to study the effect of age-register length on system efficiency, as follows:[16]

> **1**   The candidate pages for removal are kept on a circular list (a circular list is one in which the last entry points to the first entry).
>
> **2**   Each block of memory has an age register associated with it the leftmost bit of which is set to a 1 when the page residing in the block is referenced.
>
> **3**   Only one page on the list at a time has the age register associated with it aged (shifted right 1 bit), and the age register is checked for zero.
>
> **4**   Aging takes place only when a new page not in main memory is required.
>
> **5**   The first page found wth a zero-value age register is replaced.   An age register of length zero gives a FIFO strategy.

Corbato found that a significant improvement in system performance resulted between using a counter of length zero and using a counter of length 1.   Increasing the counter length beyond length 1 gave no significant improvement in performance.   The actual memory-allocation algorithm used by Corbato contains more refinements than mentioned above, but the presentation here illustrates the aging concept and the design problem of picking aging-counter length and a method of determining an aging interval.

The problem with the FIFO and LRU strategies is that they are global to all processes residing in memory.   That is, the pages of all processes residing in memory are considered candidates for removal.   Such strategies can cause undesirable interactions among processes by causing the removal of a process's own pages and those of other processes which may be required if processing is to be executed overlapped with swapping. The situation can result in which no process can keep enough pages in main memory to execute for a reasonable length of time before requiring another page.   While the required page is being brought in, other pages of the process may be lost, due to aging (LRU) or position on the FIFO page list, to make room for a page required by another process executing in the meantime.   This situation has been aptly called *thrashing*.[9,14]

THE WORKING-SET STRATEGY   In our earlier discussion we suggested when pages are removed from main memory to make room for those of another process, that we choose pages for removal with some strategy which will leave at least one or more processes intact.   The processes which are intact can probably be executed overlapped with swapping.   Denning has suggested a version of this idea for a demand-paging situation which he calls the *working-set* strategy.[9]   The working-set strategy has, as seen below, a number of practical implementation difficulties, but it does appear to be a goal which practical demand-paging strategies should try to reach. The observation on which the working-set idea is based is shown in Fig. 5.5. Here it is noted that after some subset of pages is in main memory, the page-demand rate decreases sharply. This situation seems to result because programs work in subsets of pages over periods of time and that this subset, once established, varies at a reasonable rate.

Denning has called the subset required at a given point the *working set*. He has suggested methods for determining a working set, which are similar to those used in LRU strategies, and has given suggestions on how to use this information in processor and memory allocation. In fact the working-set strategy can be thought of as a form of LRU strategy in which only the pages of the currently executing process are considered for removal. He defines the working set of information $W(t,\tau)$ of a process at time t to be the collection of data items referenced by the process during the process time interval $(t - \tau, t)$. The parameter τ must be selected to reflect other parameters such as main-memory size, auxiliary-storage transfer rates, and access time. The number of pages in the working set is $w(t,\tau)$. The first problem is to determine $W(t,\tau)$ and $w(t,\tau)$. The working set of a process is determined by using the aging techniques described in the last section. Only pages of the currently executing process are considered, however.

Assuming that at some expense we know the working set and its size, how do we use this information in scheduling and allocation? Denning's suggestions are that (1) no process be loaded into memory for execution unless there is room for as many pages as are in the current working set and (2) as a replacement strategy, pages from the process executing, but not in its current working set, are to be removed first. The goal of this strategy is to keep in core only those processes which contain their working sets of pages and on replacement to minimize processes' removing pages from each other's working set. This strategy increases the probability of overlapping processing and swapping. To make room for the working set of an incoming process, the working set of some process presently in memory must be removed. If more processes are in memory than there is room for their working sets, a *space-squeezed* situation results. The thrashing described in the last section can result in a space-squeezed memory. Denning's suggestions intuitively seem to offer a solution to the problem but at the cost of keeping track of the working set, which could be a burden to the system; therefore, the idea has yet to be demonstrated in practice. But the idea of trying to minimize the interaction of the memory demands of the processes residing in main memory is important and may be the goal which strategies easier to implement should aim toward.

One could further suggest that in light of Fig. 5.5 no process start executing until the previous working set of pages actually is returned to main memory, rather than, as Denning suggests, until there is room for the working set. This concept is called *affinity paging* or *preloading* of pages. Denning argues that when a process blocks or completes an interaction, the working set next required may be very different from the previous one and extra pages not required may be brought in thus expending unneeded resources. The argument for prefetching seems to be that a process may run for more than one quantum period before it blocks or completes its service of a user request. Therefore, the working set at the start of an execution may often be the same as the one which finished the last execution. This would suggest that before the start of execution, the last working set be returned and then demand paging be used from this point. If one has adjusted the quantum size so that most processes complete in one quantum period, as discussed in Sec. 5.2.3, this argument may be invalid.

In summary, Denning has made the important point that the scheduling process and memory management are interrelated for a system using a swapping algorithm based on a working set. The important point here is that main-memory and auxiliary-memory parameters will indicate what the nature of the basic swapping philosophy will be. This latter choice will in turn influence the other important resource-allocation algorithms.

USE OF BULK CORE   Let us now consider the third approach to improving swapping performance, mentioned above, use of fast-access auxiliary storage. Faster swapping media, such as bulk core, are being used. Bulk core is random-access storage but with a longer access time than main memory and less expensive. Decreasing the average access time of rotating devices below the UNIVAC drums' 4 milliseconds will probably require making drums even smaller, which will require breakthroughs in increasing information-packing densities. Otherwise, large numbers of such drums will be required, thus decreasing the cost advantage of drums over bulk core. Some improvements can be expected, but a factor of 2 seems optimistic. Bulk core is still expensive relative to rotating devices, but total system performance may make it economical. Disk storage with its longer average access time due to read/write head positioning and generally slower transfer rates would seem a poor choice for a swapping medium, although fixed-head-per-track disks having drum characteristics are available.

Let us now briefly consider the use of bulk core, as its use is expected to be more common, particularly as its cost drops. There are presently two basic types of bulk core, one represented by IBM large-capacity storage (LCS) and the other by CDC extended-core storage (ECS). These two types of storage have different properties as backing stores and would probably lead to the implementation of very different swapping systems. At Carnegie-Mellon Institute they have experimented with LCS as a swapping medium for their IBM 360/67.[17,27] LCS has an 8-microsecond cycle time and a 4-microsecond access time and can be directly accessed by the CPU. In addition, transfer can be made in blocks via a storage channel, making the LCS appear as a drum with an 8-microsecond average access time and a transfer rate of 400,000 32-bit words per second. In an LCS system there are, in effect, two different page sizes, a 1,024-word page size, which is swapped via the channel, and an LCS double word, which can be directly accessed. If the monitor "knew" that only a few words in a page were to be referenced, it would be cheaper to access the words directly in LCS rather than performing the swap. How the monitor is to know such a fact is an unsolved problem, but the opportunity is there. Fikes et al. discuss this problem[27] and point out that there is a system cost to move a page from LCS to main memory and there is a system cost to execute directly in LCS. There is some number of accesses to a page during a time slice such that the system costs either to move the page from LCS to main memory or to execute directly in LCS are equal. If one could define the costs precisely, this crossover number of accesses could be calculated.

Given this crossover number of accesses and the ability to measure what Fikes et al. call the *access density* of each page, the system could make the appropriate decision as to whether or not to move the page to main memory for execution. The access density of a page is the average number of accesses to the page per time slice, where only those time slices where the page is accessed at least once are considered in computing the average. The other factor entering into the decision is whether there is room for the page in main memory or whether some other process must lose a page from its working set.

Fikes et al. give no method for determining the access density but do discuss some intuitive criteria for deciding whether to execute in LCS or swap. They argue that as a first approximation, all system pages and sharable pages should be swapped. User private-procedure pages and data pages can be executed directly in LCS. Further study of this problem is required before more sensitive decision rules can be developed.

It takes 2.5 milliseconds to swap a 1K word page from LCS, and, assuming some time to process the page demand, this means latency for LCS is about 3 to 4 milliseconds. This is an improvement over a drum, and if the cost can be reduced by a factor of 5 or so, LCS will probably be economically competitive with drums as a swapping medium. Experience at Carnegie-Mellon using LCS has shown a significant performance improvement, as would be expected.

The use of bulk-core storage still does not solve the swapping problem completely because, without placing restrictions on program size, it may not be economically possible to keep all user's programs and data in bulk storage and thus the swapping problem is pushed back one level in the storage hierarchy between bulk core and drums or disks. Fikes et al. discuss the problem of allocating bulk core in some detail. The problems are conceptually similar to those found for allocating main memory. When pages in LCS must be replaced, one wants to replace the pages least likely to be used next. Fikes et al. order the processes according to priority on the ready list followed by ordering based on length of time processes have been blocked. That is, the highest-priority process is the highest-priority process on the ready list, and the lowest-priority process is the one that has been blocked for the longest time. Pages of the low-priority processes are recommended for removal first, with the refinement that pages in the memory space of a process not being referenced or pages which are read-only or have not been written can be removed ahead of any others.

Another philosophy of LCS use is represented by systems which do no swapping at all but leave all user processes and infrequently used system processes in bulk core and execute directly from bulk core.[18,19] Measurements on the University of Pittsburgh IBM 360/50 system, which uses this method, with an interactive language interpreter in fast memory and user programs in bulk core, showed a 20 percent degradation in speed of program execution over what it would have been had both interpreter and user program been in fast memory. If a faster CPU had been used, the degradation would have been even greater. If the speed of the hardware processing units is reasonably balanced with the speed of bulk core, the inefficiencies which result from executing directly from bulk core may be less than or equal to those introduced by swapping. Executing directly from bulk core seems to simplify system design.

CDC's extended core storage cannot be directly addressed by the CPU and requires 3 microseconds to access the first 60-bit word. Once the first word is located, a transfer rate of 10 million 60-bit words per second can be maintained. Thus a 1K word block can be transferred in 100 microseconds. This high speed has two implications: (1) swapping and computation cannot be overlapped because the transfer requires all the memory cycles, and (2) processing necessary to locate the required block in ECS constitutes the major delay in accessing the block.

Because of the high speed of transfer in an ECS system, a process or segment rather than a page would be more suitable as the main unit of information transfer. Thus a machine designed around ECS can probably be designed with a simpler storage-management system than one designed around a drum or LCS.[35]

SUMMARY   The memory-allocation problem results because economic and physical constraints limit the size of main memory available to the system. Memory allocation is a technological problem. The algorithms which schedule the processors are closely interrelated to the memory-allocation strategies as well. One can recognize two basic problems in memory allocation: (1) maintaining records of physical-memory use and of where in physical storage a process's logical space is stored and (2) developing decision-making rules to allocate available main memory to contending processes. The latter we called the swapping problem. A range of allocation strategies exist from (1) allocating enough physical memory for all of a process's logical space or some sizable fraction of it and then fetching the logical space to main memory before beginning execution to (2) allocating an initial amount of memory equal to a page size and then increasing the allocation as needed. The latter concept is called demand paging.

A reasonable goal in all allocation strategies is to attempt to overlap execution of one process with swapping required for another process. To make overlapping possible, the replacement strategy used to determine which processes or pieces of processes to remove from main memory to make room for an incoming process or piece of a process should probably be chosen so that memory requirements of several processes do not seriously interact.

Besides examining operating system strategies as methods to improve swapping, the use of high-speed auxiliary storage was discussed, as was the technique of improving program structure. Use of high-speed auxiliary storage, particularly bulk core, seems to minimize many of the problems examined and simplify system design. We can expect present economic and technological trends to lead to developments which will ease many of the problems considered in this section.

5.4 SYSTEM PROTECTION

5.4.1 Introduction In our view, the design of the protection system is one of the most important aspects of a timesharing system. System protection exists at many levels, both in hardware and software.[2,20,34] Protection problems are of two kinds, intrinsic and technological. The intrinsic problems are primarily involved in the file system and involve privacy and sharing of information. This area is discussed further in Chap. 6. The technological problems exist because a large number of virtual processors are sharing a limited physical configuration, in order to achieve necessary economies by balanced utilization of this equipment. We are primarily concerned with the technological problems in this section. The basic problem is to provide protection of the system processes from the user processes and the user processes from each other. It would probably be useful at this point for the reader to review Sec. 4.1, where protection was first introduced primarily with respect to hardware aids for protection.

Two ways of looking at protection are (1) protection of resources themselves (software and hardware) and (2) protection of access paths to the resources. A well-designed system will probably have an integrated approach to both points of view, uniformly and clearly implemented throughout the system. Also, a well-designed system will probably offer many levels and types of access rights to its facilities with the minimum level of control required.

5.4.2   Need for Levels of Protection   The protection scheme of Multics is conceptually important because protection throughout the system has been treated in a very general and uniform manner. On the 940 system, in contrast, protection exists at many points but is handled in a nonintegrated way. The Multics ring approach (to be described below) offers many levels of protection, whereas the 940 offers only two. The ability to have many levels of protection is a desirable feature as seen from experience on the XDS-940. The two basic levels of protection available in the XDS-940 system are executive status and nonexecutive status. A user with executive status has access to all system routines and has great power to modify various tables and other parameters. For this reason, users are not given this status, and yet some users could usefully employ some of the system facilities not presently available. The risks involved, however, are very great because the executive-status user has uncontrolled access to the system, and this risk generally prevents giving any user executive status. The system processes can also usefully run with various levels of protection. Such an approach should increase system reliability by limiting the area of damage caused by hardware and software errors. User processes can also use multiple layers of protection to increase their reliability.

5.4.3   Protection by Tables   Within the software system, protection information for specific resources is maintained in various tables associated with these resources. For example, as is discussed in Chap. 6, the files are protected with information stored in the table called a file directory. In the case of Multics, protection information for a segment (in Multics, the terms file and segment are identical) is transferred to the segment-descriptor table when a segment is activated. Access to subsystems can be similarly restricted with information stored in user's account tables and the tables used to initialize the subsystems, as on the XDS-940. Users of the XDS-940 have a subsystem status which defines the subsystems they have access to. I/O devices are protected by information stored in device- and file-control blocks, as discussed in Sec. 6.2. A user's account table can indicate whether the user has access to magnetic-tape drives or graphical displays, or similar information can be kept in tables associated with the devices. The most general problem is defining access privileges of processes with respect to each other.

5.4.4 Protection in Multics

A general, integrated, and clearly defined approach to defining access privileges of processes with respect to each other is found on the Multics system.[20] The Multics hardware, as discussed in Chap. 4, protects segments rather than the access paths to segments. Therefore, the software system must provide mechanisms for controlling access paths. Rather than controlling each access path from one segment to another, segments are grouped into classes. What is controlled is the access path between classes. The protection scheme is based on the idea of concentric rings of protection, with the inner rings having the highest protection. Segments are assigned to these rings. The most critical system segments (those interfacing to the hardware) are in ring 0, and less critical system segments are in ring 1, and so forth. User segments are assigned to rings further out in the series. In outline, the system works as follows (the concept is illustrated in Fig. 5.7). A segment can directly access any other segment in the same ring. If a ring boundary is crossed, a call to the system is made. Access is freely granted from a segment to segments in higher ring numbers but is restricted for access to segments in lower ring numbers. To call an inner ring only certain entry points, called *gates*, are allowed. The system checks the target address against the entries on a valid entry list for the target segment. If the process is allowed access and the target entry point is valid, further checking takes place. Because addresses can be passed as arguments, they must be checked to see that the calling segment has access to the segments they refer to. This is necessary because the inner ring has greater access privileges and these addresses might not be checked when used. The addresses passed as arguments, if improper, could cause the inner segment to perform

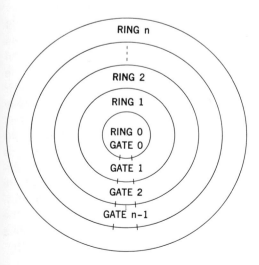

FIG. 5.7   Multics ring-structure protection concept.

erroneous action and thus cause considerable damage to itself or other system segments.

Other complexities with the ring system exist because two processes can share segments and after validation one process may be blocked and another process started which can modify the validated addresses.[20] Graham points out that it is not sufficient just to inhibit interrupts until the called procedure in an inner ring is finished using the validated addresses, even if the long inhibition of interrupts could be tolerated. The reason is that another process may be executing on another physical processor, and if it shares a segment with the process containing the argument addresses, it may modify them during the time the inner procedure segment is executing. Graham then goes on to indicate that a solution to the problem is to copy the addresses in the argument list into a data area in the same ring as the called procedure segment and then validate the addresses. In this way, only a procedure in another process with the same access privileges as the called procedure can modify the argument addresses.

Another argument-passing problem may exist. When a procedure segment in an inner ring calls a procedure in an outer ring, the inner procedure may want to pass arguments located within itself which the outer segment cannot access. This problem is solved by copying the arguments into an area accessible to the outer procedure.

The ring system uses the protection available in the hardware fully but still requires software manipulation for validation and for remembering which ring is presently in control and in which ring to return control after a routine in a particular ring is completed. Simple additions to the hardware could decrease the bookkeeping required for the latter. Such additions are suggested by Graham.[20] The simple additions would be to add additional bits to the procedure base register described in Sec. 2.5 to indicate the ring number of the segment in execution and to add a ring number to the information stored as a segment descriptor. This information would ease the problem of knowing which ring the executing segment is in and speed the crossing of ring boundaries. Presently this information is maintained in the file directory.

A version of the mechanism suggested by Graham has been implemented in hardware on a Japanese computer having segmentation hardware similar to the GE-645. In this machine, the HITAC 5020,[33] there is a 2-bit access control and a 4-bit lock in each segment descriptor. There is a 4-bit key in the descriptor base register. These pieces of information are used to provide protection as follows. In terms of the previous discussion one can think of the key and lock as ring numbers. The key is associated with the executing segment and governs, in relation to the locks, access to the other segments of the process. If the key is O (the inner ring), full access is granted to all other segments. If the key value is less than or equal to a lock value, an access matching the access control (read-only, read/execute, read/write, all) is allowed.   If the key value is greater than a lock value, read-only access is allowed and write access is never allowed. An attempted transfer between segments having an unequal key and lock causes an interrupt.   This is an example of the type of hardware aids one can expect when further experience is gained with a total system.

5.4.5   Capabilities   One can think of a timesharing system as containing different types of objects for which protection is desired.   Example objects are files, processes, pages or segments of memory, software channels for communication between processes, and system operations or calls.   Each object, depending on its type, can be allocated in varying quantity and can be accessed or operated upon in alternate ways.   For example, one may only be allowed to create files of a certain length or less, or access a file as read only, execute as procedure only, write only or some combination.   The nature and number of these *options* for each object will be different for each type of object.   What is desired in a protection system is to treat the various types of objects in a uniform manner and to allow a process access to only those objects required and with the minimum set of options required.   A scheme which allows this ability can serve as a framework for creating multiple layers or levels of protection.   It is also desirable that the protection scheme minimize the system overhead required during execution.

As we have indicated, one can think of protection as being placed on an object or on the access path to the object.   Protection placed on the access path to an object will generally require less overhead than protection placed on the object, although both types of protection will probably be required.   For example, a process referencing some object repeatedly may require the system to check for each reference if the referencing process is entitled to make the reference.   Certain system calls in the XDS-940 system can only be made by the processes of certain users.   Each such call requires searching a list of authorized users to see if the process making the request should be allowed to proceed.   Protection in this case is on the object (system call).   If references to each object were made through elements of a linear array, for example, each entry of which was initialized when the process was created or on the first reference, to allow access to those objects legal to the process, then checking would be minimized while yet giving full protection.   Such a scheme we would call protection placed on the access path to an object, although tables associated with different objects might have to be referenced during the initial checks.

A way to think about protection of hardware and software objects meeting the requirements for protecting different types of objects in a uniform manner, for allowing many levels of protection, and for allowing protection to be placed on the access path to objects was introduced in an important paper by Dennis and Van Horn[31] and given further extension and refinement in a valuable contribution of Lampson.[34,35]   In this scheme all objects in the system are named by *capabilities*.   Capabilities are kept in *capability lists* or *C-lists*.   Capabilities have two functions, (1) to name objects, that is, to tell what type of object is being referenced and its location, and (2) to establish the options for access to the object available to processes using this capability.   A C-list defines a sphere of protection or what Lampson calls a domain.   A C-list can be considered an object and can be protected with a capability.   Because a capability is the protected name of an object, only the system can create or modify a capability.   A user process could be given the capability to examine a C-list for which it has the capability, copy a capability between C-lists possibly decreasing the number of options associated with the named object.   For example, when a process creates another process it can associate it with a C-list made up of a subset of its own capabilities.

If the inferior process tries to access an object not in the C-list or in a manner not specified in the options, then the process can be blocked and an error signal can be passed back to the superior process.   The superior process can then take appropriate action such as destroy the inferior process or increase the capabilities or options of the inferior process.

Errors can be handled more generally in a hierarchy of processes by associating two numbers with an error,[35] an error class and an error number. Each process in the hierarchy has associated with it an error selection mask. A process accepts an error if an error class has its associated error selection mask bit on.   When an error occurs a search up of the hierarchy is made until a process is found with the appropriate error selection mask bit set. This process is called with the error class and number as arguments.   The called process can then perform the required action.   There are several ways to implement the capability idea.[31,34]

Each capability has a name, that is, location.   If a hardware mechanism exists to tag individual memory words as read only except to the system, then the name of a capability can be a memory location.   Such a mechanism allows the names of capabilities to be protected also.   Most systems do not have such hardware and so software mechanisms must be used.   The mechanism suggested by Dennis and Van Horn and used in the CAL system by Lampson is to organize the C-lists as linear arrays and use the index in the array as the name of the capability.   Thus, if a process names a capability which exists in its current working C-list, this is taken as proof of its right to access the object specified.

In the CAL implementation capabilities are represented by two 60-bit words.   One word contains an object type and option bits.   The second word contains a unique name for the capability and a pointer into a master object table (MOT).   The MOT in turn contains a unique name and a pointer to the object. This implementation has these advantages: (1) if damage is done to the capability the unique names in the capability and MOT probably will not match; and (2) one can delete or move objects and only need to change the entry in the MOT and does not have to search all the C-lists to perform modification.

Another implementation alternative suggested by Lampson is to set up a bit table where capabilities are represented by bit rows and domains or C-lists are represented by bit columns. Thus a domain contains a capability if the bit in its column and in the proper row is on. Further mapping to the actual object is of course required.

One further topic needs clarification—with what are C-lists associated? Many possibilities exist. For example, each process could have its own C-list and thus each operate in its own domain, or many processes might operate in the same domain, or procedures in a single process might each operate in the same or different domains. The choice here will of course depend on other design and implementation decisions taken. What is of interest in all cases is what must happen when transfers are made between different spheres of protection. A process cannot be allowed to arbitrarily move from one domain to another without the potential for damage existing. The example given by Dennis and Van Horn illustrates this potential for damage.[31] Consider two processes A and B operating in different spheres of protection using routine S in yet another sphere of protection. We want to be certain that malfunction of A or B cannot cause improper execution of the other or damage a common data base used by S. It's the latter point that is of immediate interest. If A and B could enter S at an arbitrary instruction, then S might erroneously modify the common data base. Therefore, entry to a domain must be controlled. The control is accomplished by creating a *protected entry point* or *gate* through which entry is accomplished.[31,34] These gates are objects which can be protected by capabilities. A process A operating in a particular domain can create a capability for a gate which can be copied by processes in other domains authorized access to A. Entry at the gate will allow proper execution of A and the sphere of protection to be changed.

Transfers between domains are usually made by subroutine calls and therefore some method of return must be used. Lampson points out that it is not satisfactory to create another gate through which the called process can return because the called process could use this gate at some other inappropriate time. The use of a push down stack for storing returns accessible only to the superviser solves this problem (see Sec. 2.5.6). On entry one saves the return location and a pointer to the C-list of the calling process or domain.

The above discussion has introduced the basic idea of the capability concept. Additional extensions and ramifications of the idea are discussed by Dennis and Van Horn[31] and Lampson.[34,35] The important points about the idea are that capabilities allow many types of objects to be protected in a uniform manner, many levels of protection to exist, and protection to be placed on the access path to the object rather than requiring each object to maintain and search a list of processes allowed access and degree of access allowed.

5.4.6 Summary This section pointed out the need for several levels of protection. Protection information exists in the hardware and in many of the system tables used for resource allocation. The flexible and general ring-structure protection scheme of the Multics system was outlined. The capability system is a software scheme to place protection on the access paths between segments or other resources. Protection is discussed further in the next chapter.

REFERENCES

1 Saltzer, J. H.: Traffic Control in a Multiplexed Computer System, MAC-TR-30, (thesis), Massachusetts Institute of Technology, Cambridge, Mass., July, 1966.
2 Lampson, B. W.: A Scheduling Philosophy for Multi-processing Systems, *Commun. ACM*, vol. 11, no. 5, May, 1968.
3 Coffman, E. G., and L. Kleinrock: Computer Scheduling Methods and Their Counter Measures, *AFIPS Conf. Proc., Spring Joint Computer Conf.*, vol. 32, p. 11, 1968.
4 Schwartz, J. I., and C. Weissman: The SDC Time-sharing System Revisited, *Proc. ACM Natl. Conf. 1967*, pp. 262–271.
5 Fine, G. H., et al.: Dynamic Program Behavior under Paging, *Proc. ACM Natl. Conf. 1966*, p. 223.
6 Coffman, E. G., and L. C. Varian: Further Experimental Data on the Behavior of Programs in a Paging Environment, *Commun. ACM*, vol. 11, no. 7, p. 471, July, 1968.
7 Varian, L. C., and E. G. Coffman: An Empirical Study of the Behavior of Programs in a Paging Environment, *Proc. ACM Symp. Operating System Principles*, October, 1967.
8 Freibergs, I. F.: The Dynamic Behavior of Programs, *AFIPS Conf. Proc., Fall Joint Computer Conf.*, vol. 33, pt. 2, pp. 1163–1168, 1968.
9 Denning, Peter J.: The Working Set Model for Program Behavior, *Commun. ACM*, vol. 11, no. 5, May, 1968.
10 Nielson, N. R.: Computer Simulation of Computer System Performance, *Proc. ACM Natl. Conf. 1967*, pp. 581–590.
11 Nielson, N. R.: The Simulation of Time-sharing Systems, *Commun. ACM*, vol. 10, no. 7, pp. 397–412, July, 1967.
12 Randell, B., and C. J. Kuehner: Dynamic Storage Allocation Systems, *Commun. ACM*, vol. 11, no. 5, p. 297, May, 1968.
13 Randell, B., and C. Kuehner: Demand Paging in Perspective, *AFIPS Conf. Proc., Fall Joint Computer Conf.*, vol. 33, pt. 2, pp. 1011–1018, 1968.

14 **Denning, Peter J.:** Thrashing: Its Causes and Prevention, *AFIPS Conf. Proc., Fall Joint Computer Conf.,* vol. 33, pt. 1, pp. 915–922, 1968.

15 **Dijkstra, E. W.:** Structure of The Multiprogramming System, *Commun. ACM,* vol. 11, no. 5, May, 1968.

16 **Corbato, F. J.:** A Paging Experiment with the Multics System, *MIT Project MAC Mem.* MAC-M-384, July 8, 1968.

17 **Lauer, H. C.:** Bulk Core in a 360/67 Time-sharing System, *AFIPS Conf. Proc., Fall Joint Computer Conf.,* vol. 31, pp. 601–611, 1967.

18 **Babcock, J. D.:** A Brief Description of Privacy Measures in the RUSH Time-sharing System, *AFIPS Conf. Proc., Spring Joint Computer Conf.,* vol. 30, pp. 301–302, 1967.

19 **Badger, G. F., Jr., and E. A. Johnson:** The Pitt Time-sharing System for the IBM Systems 360, *AFIPS Conf. Proc., Fall Joint Computer Conf.,* vol. 33, pt. 1, pp. 1–6, 1968.

20 **Graham, R. M.:** Protection in an Information Processing Utility, *Commun. ACM,* vol. 11, no. 5, p. 365, May, 1968.

21 **Rehmann, Sandra L., and Sherbie G. Gangwere, Jr.:** A Simulation Study of Resource Management in a Time-sharing System, *AFIPS Conf. Proc., Fall Joint Computer Conf.,* vol. 33, pt. 2, pp. 1411–1430, 1968.

22 **Lampson, B. W., et al.:** A User Machine in a Time-sharing System, *Proc. IEEE,* December, 1966.

23 **Oppenheimer, G., and N. Weizer:** Resource Management for a Medium Scale Time Sharing Operating System, *Commun. ACM,* vol. 11, no. 5, p. 313, May, 1968.

24 **Reiter, Allen:** A Resource-allocation Scheme for Multi-user Online Operation of a Small Computer, *AFIPS Conf. Proc., Spring Joint Computer Conf.,* vol. 30, pp. 1–7, 1967.

25 **Corbato, F. J., et al.:** An Experimental Time-sharing System, *AFIPS Conf. Proc., Spring Joint Computer Conf.,* vol. 21, pp. 335–344, 1962.

26 **Anderson, G. B., et al.:** Design of a Time-sharing System Allowing Interactive Graphics, *Proc. ACM Natl. Conf. 1968,* pp. 1–6.

27 **Fikes, Richard E., et al.:** Steps toward a General-purpose Time-Sharing System Using Large Capacity Core Storage and TSS/360, *Proc. ACM Natl. Conf. 1968,* pp. 7–18.

28 **Maurer, W. D.:** An Improved Hash Code for Scatter Storage, *Commun. ACM,* vol. 11, no. 1, pp. 35–38, January, 1968.

29 **Morris, Robert:** Scatter Storage Techniques, *Commun. ACM,* vol. 11, no. 1, pp. 38–44, January, 1968.

30 **Bobrow, D. G., and D. L. Murphy:** Structure of a LISP System Using Two-level Storage, *Commun. ACM,* vol. 10, no. 3, pp. 155–159, March, 1967.

31 **Dennis J. B., and E. C. Van Horn:** Programming Semantics for Multiprogrammed Computation, *Commun. ACM,* vol. 9, no. 3, pp. 143–155, March, 1966.

32 **Van Horn, E. C.:** Computer Design for Asynchronously Reproducible Multiprocessing, *MIT Project MAC Tech. Rept.* MAC-TR-34, Ph.D. thesis, November, 1966.

33 **Motobayashi, S., et al.:** The HITAC 5020 Time Sharing System, *Proc. ACM Natl. Conf. 1969,* pp. 419–429.

34 **Lampson, B. W.:** Dynamic Protection Structures, *AFIPS Conf. Proc.,* vol. 35, *Fall Joint Computer Conf.,* 1969, pp. 27–38.

35 **Lampson, B. W.:** An Overview of the CAL Timesharing System, Computer Center, Univ. of Calif., Berkeley, 1969.

36 **Spier, M. J., and E. I. Organick:** The Multics Interprocess Communication Facility, *Second ACM Symposium on Operating Systems Principles,* Princeton Univ., Oct. 1969.

chapter SIX

The file system and general input/output

6.1 THE FILE SYSTEM

6.1.1 Introduction What is a file? A file is a collection of related information with a name. Files are stored in a computer system as a string of elements: bits, characters, computer words, and so forth. Examples of files are procedures, strings of text, and arrays of numbers. A file has all the characteristics given in the definition of a segment. And in fact, the words file and segment are interchangeable in the Multics system. The Multics system is designed to treat files in a very general and uniform manner. The XDS-940 system does not treat all files in a uniform manner but in the end offers the user many of the main functions he desires in a file system, although at a cost to the user of more explicit interaction with the system.

The need for a file system arises because of the limitations on the size of main memory. Because of these limitations auxiliary storage is required in the form of disks, drums, tape strip, paper tape, magnetic tape, cards, photostores, and so forth.

The file system is that portion of the total memory management system dealing primarily with auxiliary storage. The file system must interface smoothly with the schemes used for addressing and allocation of main memory. In systems such as Multics, where the logical-address space is very large, the total memory-management system is the file system. That is, Multics is designed so that the programmer thinks that he is using a very large main memory (his logical-address space) and all movements of information between auxiliary storage devices and main memory are invisible to him. The Multics user can also deal explicitly with the file system. In the XDS-940 system, on the other hand, the user must deal explicitly with the file system.

A general purpose timesharing file system should satisfy the following intrinsic requirements:

1 The user should be able to create, change, and delete files.

2 Users should be able to access each other's files in a controlled manner in order to build on each other's work.

3 The user should be able to control who has access to his files and the type of access allowed, such as read, write, and execute.

4 The user should be able to structure his files in a form appropriate to his problem.

5 The user must be able to communicate information between files.

6 The user should be provided with file backup in case a file is accidently deleted or damaged.

7 The user should be able to access files by symbolic name, i.e., the file system should be hardware-independent as far as the user is concerned.

The common technological problems for a general purpose file system are (1) to achieve adequate capacity, access speed, and economic storage with available auxiliary storage devices and (2) to achieve adequate file protection of one user from another and protection against system hardware or software malfunctions. We consider each of these requirements in the sections to follow and then move on to discuss other types of I/O.

The design of the I/O system in general can be conceptually integrated with the file system. This integration can be achieved by considering all I/O devices as files with fixed system-specified names. The system can check for these names and channel the information accordingly. The only conceptual difference to the user between I/O devices as files and more general files is that many of these devices can transmit information only in one direction. The user can use the same system calls, file commands, and language output statements to handle all information-moving operations. At the implementation level, a number of differences arise between auxiliary storage and other I/O devices which are brought out in the discussion.

The design of the software for handling remote devices should be easily adapted to handle a wide variety of devices and to interface remote-terminal I/O with the rest of the system. Finally we outline briefly the functions of the command-language interpreter which communicates with the user.

The file and I/O system constitute a large fraction of the total programming in the system. In order to make the task understandable and manageable, the design should probably be split into function modules.[6] The sections of this chapter give such a functional breakdown. The subjects of file-system and data management are very broad. This chapter covers only the basic facilities which present timesharing systems offer as a base for creating specialized application-oriented systems. Before going into the file-system software concepts it is useful to discuss some of the hardware characteristics of auxiliary storage devices which directly affect the design of the file system.

6.1.2 Auxiliary-storage-device Characteristics Auxiliary storage devices for use with a timesharing system can be subdivided into two main categories, *online* and *backup stores*. The online devices are also called *direct-access* or *random-access devices*. Online storage devices are large-capacity core memory, magnetic drums, and magnetic disks. Backup storage devices are devices with removable media, such as disk packs, data cells, and magnetic tape. Very large capacity devices use photographic and laser techniques and are nonerasable. The important characteristics of any device are its access mode, access time, transfer rate, capacity, and cost. All the devices listed above have random access except tape, which has a sequential mode of access. Large-capacity core was discussed in Sec. 5.3.3 and is not considered further here as it does not appear that it will have either the capacity or low cost required as a primary file-storage device. The other random-access devices are not random access to the word or smaller information unit but are random access to a block of word or character information. Magnetic tape with its sequential access and long tape-moving times does not seem to be a suitable online file device and should probably be restricted to backup or special applications.

Access time or latency (the average length of time one must wait before the addressed information can be transferred) is a function of the rotation speed or other mechanical characteristics of the device, the mechanism used to position read and write sensors, and the size of the device. Access time varies from around 4 milliseconds for small fast drums (capacity around 10^6 characters) to 1 second or more for the laser and photostores (capacity upward of 10^{10} characters). These figures are for online capacity. Removable media devices have effectively an infinite capacity. In between these access times and capacity limits are a range of devices with corresponding cost differentials. The most popular file-storage device is the large disk unit, with a capacity of several hundred million characters and an access time of around 100 to 200 milliseconds.

Transfer rates and costs are functions of the storage density of information on the recording surface and the number of read/write sensors and associated addressing and control electronics. Packing densities are increasing, and electronics cost are decreasing. At present the disk units mentioned above can store information for around 10 cents or less per 1,000 characters stored. Transfer rates are presently 100 to 200 $\times 10^3$ characters per second for disks and can be increased up to main-memory speeds by parallel reading and writing of data on the devices. To achieve the capacities necessary for large timesharing systems may require a hierarchy of devices. Given this general background, we can turn our attention to the important problem of space allocation on direct-access devices.

6.1.3 Access and Allocation of Direct-access Devices

INTRODUCTION One of the goals of the file-system design is to make the user independent of system hardware. The user works with *logical records*. The auxiliary storage and I/O devices of the system are more naturally organized around *physical records*. A file is made up of one or more logical records. Logical records may be of arbitrary length and structure and are process-dependent. Physical records are of a fixed length appropriate to the particular device. Logical records can be made up of one or more physical records. If the logical records are smaller than the physical records, more than one logical record will usually be packed in a physical record to increase I/O transfer and storage efficiency. On a magnetic-tape system, the physical records are arranged sequentially on the tape. Tape files have the disadvantage of being difficult to change by addition or deletion without rewriting the entire file. The characteristics of direct-access devices make it easy to modify parts of a file without changing the remainder. Besides this flexibility available for use in file updating, direct-access devices can also give rapid access to the required information. The organization of the storage space on these devices to yield these advantages can be handled in many ways. We discuss one set of techniques here to give a feeling for the concepts involved. Our discussion applies to disk units, but the concepts extend easily to other devices as well, such as drums or data cells. An example of using a special microprogrammed processor for automatically performing allocation and access-request optimization for a swapping drum or disk system is discussed in Sec. 6.1.3.

PHYSICAL ORGANIZATION OF A DIRECT-ACCESS DEVICE A disk unit is made up of a stack of plates coated with a magnetic material. The plates are constantly rotating and are organized into concentric circles called *tracks*, on which information is stored. The tracks are also commonly broken up into sections called *sectors*. In most systems, the minimum quantity of information which can be transferred is a sector. The organization is shown in Fig. 6.1.

There are two common types of disk unit. One type has a read/

write head associated with each track so that access to a particular track can be gained at electronic speeds. The other has one or more head/arm assemblies which must be mechanically positioned to the required track. This positioning operation is called a *seek*. The time required to perform a seek ranges upward from about 75 milliseconds, depending on the number of head/arm assemblies and on disk size. To address information on the disk, the unit must be sent a plate, track, and sector address. Files of information are organized on the disk in physical records equal in size to a sector or group of sectors. The physical records can be stored any-where on the disk, although for transfer and seek efficiency many systems try to store the physical records in contiguous sectors or on parallel plates in the same track if the read/write sensors are mounted on a comblike assembly of arms, one arm per plate, as shown in Fig. 6.1. The comb unit moves as a single positioner.

Two main problems have to be solved: (1) to keep track of the locations and proper sequencing of physical records on the disk and (2) to keep track of free space which can be used for new files and the expansion

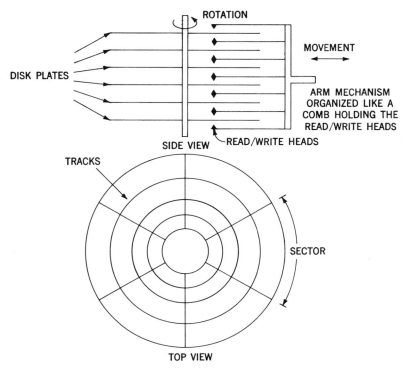

FIG. 6.1 Organization of a typical disk unit.

of old files.   In order to prevent a few users from using all available space, restrictions on the space individual users can take may also be required unless additional devices are available.

The basic file system has no way of knowing how a file is organized internally.   To the file system, the file is just a string of information units. The internal structuring of a file is the responsibility of the applications program or special system data-management routines.[15]   Different applications require different types of file access.   A properly designed basic file system can provide the required access flexibility to the user.   It is useful to outline the two common access requirements before discussing the actual allocation of the direct-access device.

SEQUENTIAL AND RANDOM ACCESS   The simplest type of access is *sequential*.   In sequential access the file is accessed in contiguous blocks equal to the logical-record size.   Most program I/O is from sequential files.   A sequential file is like a magnetic tape.   One cannot access or write logical records randomly; the next record to be accessed or written must immediately follow the one previously accessed or written.   The system handles the fetching of physical blocks and the transmission of the logical records requested to the requesting process.   On output, the system assembles logical records into physical records for writing on the device.   A sequential file does not utilize the full capabilities of random-access storage but can be implemented on such devices.   The XDS-940 system offers commands to read or write the next character, word, or a given block of words from or to the sequential file.[10]   Packing or unpacking characters into words for transmission between process and file is handled by the system. In the XDS-940, the user process must maintain information on logical-record length.

The random-access storage can be effectively used by a *random-access* method.   With random files, the user can access any logical record within the file, either by specifying a location relative to the start of the file and the number of words, characters, or bits to be transferred or by naming the record or other information in the record.   A further refinement can allow the user to access the file sequentially from the initial random point.   Various other access methods can be created using variations of these techniques.

SPACE ALLOCATION   There are many tradeoffs available with regard to storage space used to keep track of where files are stored, the free space available, and the time (measured in number of disk accesses) required to access a file.   If files are to be variable in length, the physical records containing the file must be *chained* together.   Chaining is a basic concept in random-access auxiliary-storage organization.   The technique used on the XDS-940 for chaining the physical records of a file uses what are called *index blocks*.[10]   An index block is nothing more than a table of contiguous words, the *i*th of which has the address of the *i*th physical record in the file sequence.   A file may be of such size that several index blocks are required.   The blocks can be chained together by using one word in the index block to contain the address of the next index block in sequence, or one can use several levels of index blocks.   The index blocks are kept on the disk and are usually a sector in length.   The address of the first index block is maintained in a table called a *file directory* (Sec. 6.1.5).   This concept is illustrated in Fig. 6.2.

   A physical record can contain a symbol indicating the end point of valid information.   The technique above is used with minor variations on many systems.   Another method of chaining the physical blocks together is to put pointers in the physical blocks themselves pointing from one to another rather than have the pointers grouped together in a table.   The index-block method has the advantage that with one or a small number

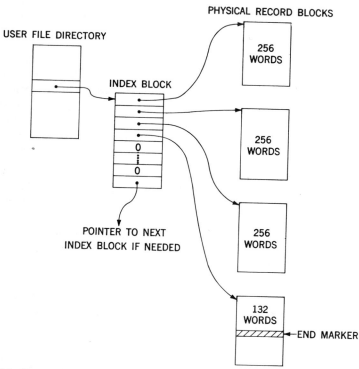

FIG. 6.2   Data organization for a file.

of accesses the system can obtain the information about where a file is stored for administrative purposes rather than having to fetch each physical record. Administrative tasks include adding physical blocks to the middle of the file if the file should have material inserted into it, returning blocks no longer needed to free space, locating blocks for random access in a multiblock file, and checking the consistency of the file system after some malfunction. A file organized as described above can be accessed either sequentially or randomly. For the sequential case the system keeps track of the next physical record to be read or written.

As an example illustrating these concepts, assume that the physical blocks are 256 words long and that the file being accessed contains 900 words, as shown in Fig. 6.2. Assume further that the user wants to access 30 words starting from location 500 relative to the start of the file and have them stored in particular cells in his address space. The system checks the user's file directory for the address of the index block for this file and makes an access to the disk to fetch the index block. The system can determine that relative file addresses 500 to 529 are on the second and third physical records. The system can read the addresses of these physical records from the index block. The system then reads the second physical record into a buffer and passes the contents of file words 500 to 511 to the appropriate place in the user's memory space. The system then accesses the third block into the buffer and passes file words 512 to 529 to the appropriate place in the user's space. The user need know only the name of the file to be accessed and the relative locations within the file of the desired information. The user knows nothing about the kind of device his file is stored on or how or where it is stored on that device.

If the user wants to change 25 words of information after relative location 212, the system overwrites the information contained in relative locations 212 to 236.

To create a file system which allows records to be inserted at random rather than overwritten requires an access method which addresses the file not by relative location but by record name. This access method requires an index table containing the logical-record name or number and the address of the physical block in which the record begins and the length of the logical record. If the logical record crosses physical-block boundaries, a pointer in the physical block can indicate the address of the next physical block, or this information could be contained in the index table. A file system using random addressing to relative locations such as illustrated above can be converted into the latter type of system or a wide variety of other structures with the use of additional tables.

A very large random or sequential file can be declared, but physical space needs to be allocated only to those physical blocks which contain that part of the file's address space with stored information. That is, when information is written, the system can allocate a physical record and update the index block.

Gaps, which may develop in physical blocks of a file during deletion, can be removed during the file backup and reloading operations to be discussed later. During reloading the system may also attempt to place physical blocks next to each other for more efficient block transfer. The file system can then make an appropriate allocation in order to speed block transfers by decreasing the number of disk accesses. In this way, the user may achieve faster response, and the system can utilize the disk more effectively.

KEEPING TRACK OF FREE SPACE The discussion above introduced the important concept of chaining physical records together to create the space required for a file. The problem of keeping track of *free space* has yet to be discussed. To keep track of free space many methods can be used, depending on the size of the disk file, acceptable time to find a free sector, and so forth. One method is to chain free sectors together. This method is simply done and takes little main-storage space but does require access time if the system is to obtain more than one sector. Another method is to use a *bit map* (table). In the bit map a sequence of words large enough for one bit to be available for each sector is set aside.[10] The bits are set if the corresponding sectors are free and cleared if they are in use. The bit table for a disk plate with 32 tracks and 8 sectors per track is shown in Fig. 6.3.

For a disk unit with more tracks per plate and several plates, organization of the bit table with a particular computer word length is somewhat more involved. Given the bit position in the map (word index and bit position in word), simple calculations can determine the corresponding physical address of the sector on the disk. This procedure works well for devices with limited capacity but requires excessive main storage for the map if used with large capacity devices. One solution to this problem is to only keep part of the bit map in main storage. The remainder is kept

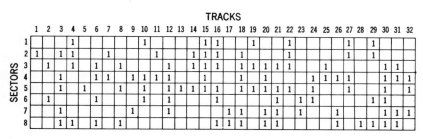

FIG. 6.3 Free-space bit map for a disk plate with 32 tracks and 8 sectors.

on auxiliary storage.   Obtaining storage for the map is simple and inexpensive with this method.   When the storage represented by the part
of the map in main memory has been allocated (all words equal zero),
a different section of the map can be brought into main storage.   To return
storage requires bringing in the part of the map representing the area of
the device being freed so that the appropriate bit can be changed.   This
traffic with the bit map can be reduced by keeping a list of returned sectors
and then when a portion of the map is brought into main storage, it can
be updated.

Another technique of free-space management is to preallocate contiguous blocks of physical records of the device for each user.   Each reloading of the device after a backup operation is assumed to repack a user's
file into contiguous blocks.   With this method, one word can be used to
keep track of the position of the next free physical record and the count
of how many records have been allocated.   Returned blocks are marked
as free but are essentially lost to the system until the next repacking, unless
extra words are used to keep track of the holes.   When a user's block
of physical records has been used up, he can be assigned space in the
same fashion on overflow areas.   This method of allocation still uses chaining.   Recording free space with this method is fast and requires little main-
memory space.   The method is dependent on periodic dumping and repacking of the file storage.   If this repacking can be handled as part of the
normal backup procedures, little extra time is required for the repacking
operation.

A MICROPROGRAMMED STORAGE CONTROLLER AND ALLOCATOR
In Sec. 4.3.3 we saw that those system areas which meet the criteria of
frequent use and real-time demands and about which we have a clear understanding of the problems involved are candidates for integration into a microprogrammed controller..   One such area is that of the control and allocation
of auxiliary storage.   This is particularly the case for auxiliary memory used
for swapping, such as fast drums and disks.   To indicate the type of concepts involved here, we outline some features of the allocation and accessing
of a fast swapping drum system which could be implemented with the help
of a microprogrammed controller.   Assume a drum with a head per track
and a sector size equal to a page.   Free space on such drums is usually
kept track of with a bit table.   To optimize the transfer rate to and from
such devices, present systems queue requests according to sector order
so as to maintain as constant a stream of information between drum and
main memory as possible.   Maintenance of the bit table and queues can
be a large enough drain on system resources to make it useful to consider
placing these functions in a small microprogrammed processor.   We call
this the *drum processor.*

The drum processor would probably require the following characteristics. It would have to have fast registers to maintain the current sector number under or next to come under the read/write sensors. These registers would be counters driven by a timing pulse from the drum. A request to write a page on the drum would be sent to the drum processor along with the main-memory block number to be transferred. The drum processor would place this request on a write queue. The drum processor would keep in its local memory (or have access to main memory) a bit table of free space, as discussed in the previous section.

The bit table would be so organized that the microorders used to search for available space would address the bit table via the registers used to hold the number of the next available sector under the heads. These microorders would return the address of the first free sector to come under a write head. The bit used to indicate the availability of that sector would be set to indicate it was unavailable, and then the transfer would be initiated. The address of the drum on which the page is written would be returned to the central processor to be used later when this page is again read into main memory. In other words, the time spent by the central processor in preparing for a page write operation would be only the time to issue the write request and the time to store the drum address on which the page is actually written. Because the drum processor can utilize the next available block on the drum, due to its constant awareness of drum position, drum writes can proceed with very little waiting time. One could even build the drum processor to handle blocks larger than a page. The drum processor would perform the allocation and chaining of drum physical records, returning the address of the starting record to the CPU.

On reads, the CPU would send a read request, the main-memory address where the page or block was to be transferred, and the drum address to the drum processor. The drum processor would then queue the request in its local memory according to drum sector. The drum processor would perform transfer in an order that keeps the information flow between main memory and drum as constant as possible, based on its awareness of drum position. After a read, the space on the drum could then be marked in the bit table as available. However, this would not allow techniques such as the "clean-dirty logic" discussed in Sec. 5.3.2 to be used. The idea could be elaborated to make room for such techniques.

These concepts are introduced to indicate only the type of systems which are candidates for use with microprogrammed processors and the type of considerations which might go into the design of a specialized microprogrammed processor.

SUMMARY   In this section we have seen that users work with logical records but that online auxiliary storage devices are most naturally allocated in physical records. Physical records are either convenient-sized blocks of information for buffering or are related to the smallest addressable units on the devices. Online devices can be accessed sequentially or randomly.

To allow flexibility in storage allocation, physical records are chained together to form logical records and files. The pointers for the chaining can be kept in the physical records or in tables of such pointers called index blocks. Index blocks are usually the length of a physical record and are stored on auxiliary storage. The pointer to the index block is kept in a table called a file directory.

Keeping track of free space must also be considered. Use of bit tables for this purpose was suggested. For large-capacity devices, the bit tables can become very large. The bit tables must then be kept on auxiliary storage and partially in main memory. Another approach to allocating large devices is to preallocate large contiguous blocks to each user. Keeping track of free space is simplified using such an approach. When files are deleted, holes are created. One can choose to allow the free space represented by holes to be lost to the system until the next repacking of the device, or one can use chaining or other techniques to keep track of the holes. These concepts were illustrated by outlining the design of a microprogrammed processor to automatically allocate space and schedule access on auxiliary storage devices.

6.1.4   File Sharing and Accessing

INTRODUCTION   A number of important concepts related to the file sharing and accessing are best brought out by examining how these functions are achieved in the XDS-940 and Multics systems. The two systems approach the problem of sharing files and allowing users to access each other's files in different ways because of their differing design goals. Multics, as we have seen in Chap. 2, treats all files as segments, and all segments are treated in a uniform manner. All segments can be shared with complete generality, with only one copy of each residing in the system. In the XDS-940 system, the designers realized that, based on frequency and type of usage, there are different classes of files and that system economies can be achieved if these classes are treated differently.

SHARING AND ACCESSING IN MULTICS   Many of the mechanisms for accessing and sharing files (segments) in Multics were discussed in Chap. 2. Additional material is given in Sec. 6.1.5. In this section we briefly review some of the characteristics as seen by the user.

In the Multics system, a file is a segment, and therefore any file in the system can be directly addressed by name and location. The system locates the file by use of tables called *file directories*, to be discussed in

Sec. 6.1.5.   If the user addressing the segment is allowed access, the segment is made known to him, as discussed in Chap. 2.   Files in Multics
can be addressed either explicitly or implicitly.   All the instructions of the
machine which address operands can access any file (segment) in the system
implicitly.   The user of Multics can create a file explicitly by performing
output to a new segment which he names.   The user deletes a file by
explicit command to the system.   All procedures in Multics are written
as reentrant and therefore can be fully shared, with only one copy existing
in the system.   All compilers or other subsystems are segments in Multics
and treated in a uniform manner with all other system and user segments.
Data segments can be fully shared even if they contain address pointers
for structuring purposes.[3]   Only one copy of such common data bases
is required in the system, and no position conflicts result in the logical
space of the users.

Given the overall design goal of Multics[3] to serve the diverse computing needs of a large community of users by providing a large machine-
independent virtual memory, by allowing a high degree of programming
generality (the ability to use a procedure by knowing only its name and
without knowledge of its storage requirements or other procedures which
it may call), and by permitting sharing of single copies of procedures and
data subject only to proper authorization, the design goals of the Multics
file system seem to follow naturally.

In achieving these very valuable intrinsic goals at any point in a
developing software and hardware technology, the solutions to the technological problems encountered will exact payment in such areas as hardware
cost, system complexity, possible overhead, and development time.   These
costs must be weighed against such gains as the possibility of attacking
new problems requiring large memory space, simplified and more economic
development of application programs and systems, more effective cooperation
and use of past efforts by fuller sharing of procedures and data, and generally
greater ease of use.   It is our experience and that of others[17] that a large
fraction of the investment and operating expense in a computer installation
is in the development and maintenance of application programs and systems.   One of the goals of the Multics file system design is to help decrease
these significant costs.

SHARING AND ACCESSING IN THE XDS-940   The designers of the
XDS-940 had much more limited goals for their system than those of Multics,
and therefore they sacrificed generality wherever frequency of use and associated cost in terms of increased system complexity and development time
did not seem to merit it within their context.   One of their goals was to
develop a system which would support in a highly interactive manner a
limited number of terminals.[16]   Each process is usually less than 16K

in size. The designers wanted to experiment with system design concepts for such a system and therefore did want flexibility. It should be understood that all the tradeoffs discussed below were made in the context of such a medium-scale system.

There are three classes of files in the XDS-940 system:

1 Files which can be shared by multiple users with only one copy existing in the system. These files are all procedures, such as compilers, text editors, debugging routines, and assemblers, and are called *subsystems*. At present there is no provision for sharing single copies of data files.

2 Files which all users can access by acquiring a separate copy. These files are called *system library files*.

3 Files which are semiprivate to each user.

Each of the above classes of file is accessed in a slightly different manner.

Subsystems are reentrant procedures which are accessed by command from the terminal to the XDS-940 system. The system fetches the subsystem, assigns it space in the user's program memory table, sets up pseudo relabeling registers for the subsystem, and finally transfers control to the subsystem. The subsystem may then ask for the names of additional files it may require. An example is a compiler requesting the name of the file containing symbolic source-code input and the name of the file in which to output the compiled binary code. Only one subsystem at a time can be running for a given user. This restriction on generality, which does not seem to be serious, considering the nature of the procedures running as subsystems, is one of the cost-generality tradeoffs available.

The library-file mechanism allows users to build on each other's work and concurrently use multiple procedures developed by others. The price paid is the possibility that multiple copies of a given procedure will be introduced into main memory. The designers felt that the frequency was low with which a given 940 library file would be used concurrently by several processes and therefore introducing mechanisms to allow sharing of one copy with full generality did not seem worth the possible associated costs. If, because of the nature of the work at a particular installation, a given set of library routines should frequently be used concurrently by several processes, these routines could be made into a subsystem. The amount of effort required to make such a conversion would depend on whether or not the procedures were originally written with such a possibility in mind. No conflicts in positioning in logical space result through use of multiple library routines by a single process because each process using a given library routine has its own copy; thus, the library routine can be loaded anywhere in the process's logical space.

A user can access another user's semiprivate files, if he has permission, by commanding the system to copy the desired file into his file space either from the terminal or through a subroutine. The result is that two copies of the file exist in the system. Again ease of system development was traded for a slight extra effort on the user's part and some waste of secondary storage space. There is also some potential danger associated with use of multiple copies of information in the system. If there are multiple copies of a file, then updating one copy, such as removing an error from a procedure, may require locating all other copies. If there are multiple copies of a file and it is possible for any of these copies to replace the original, a modified copy could become the new original, unknown to other users.

The 940 designers considered these factors and felt that sharing of multiple copies within a small community of users could be adequately controlled. If use became widespread, the file could be made into a subsystem or library file. The latter case still could leave multiple binary copies in the system. Again, a cost-generality tradeoff decision was made.

The case of sharing one copy of data files needs to be discussed. The XDS-940 system contains no mechanism for this purpose. Data files can be accessed by multiple users only through the library or semiprivate-file mechanism. Paging, as we saw in Chap. 2, places no restrictions on sharing of single copies of data if the data do not contain addresses. If the data contain address pointers for structuring purposes, then such shared data would have to be placed in the same position in each processes map which accesses it.

We have discussed problems related to sharing of files and now indicate briefly how a user communicates between files. The user of Multics can communicate directly between files just by addressing data files with the normal machine load and store instructions, by use of I/O instructions, or by transferring between procedure files by normal machine-transfer instructions. The linkage process was discussed in Sec. 2.5.6. The user of the XDS-940 system must explicitly *open* the required data files with system calls, as discussed in Sec. 6.2.4 and then input and output to the files with special system-programmed operators, which to the programmer are about as easy to use as load and store instructions but are more expensive of system time. The system handles the buffering and the actual transfers between main memory and secondary storage.

Two types of file-access methods are available in the XDS-940 system, sequential and random. The system calls available for sequential access allow the user to read or write a character, word, or block of words between his memory space and the next sequential position on the file. The system calls available for random access allow a user to read or write a word or block of words to any position in the file. The sequential-access methods are the normal ones used by higher-level language statements. The random-access methods require a subroutine package to be used in higher-level languages.

To communicate between procedure files, the XDS-940 user must create intermediate data files, transfer control to the system, and then explicitly request that control be given to a new procedure file by command from the terminal or use a subroutine package based on the system calls discussed above. Thus, a price paid in the XDS-940 system is that the user must have more knowledge of what is going on and may have to interact more frequently with the system from his terminal.

For a large number of applications, the XDS-940 file-system approach is quite adequate as judged by extensive experience with the system; however, there are many applications requiring structured data files which call for a more general system.

This discussion has pointed out the differences in two possible design approaches. A few words on their similarities will also be instructive. A file in Multics and a file in the XDS-940 are both a string of information units with a name. Both systems leave internal structure of the file to the user. Both systems allow the user to address randomly within the file by specifying a position relative to the beginning of the file. Both systems offer solutions to the intrinsic problem of allowing procedure and data files to be shared.

SUMMARY   This discussion and that of Chap. 2 have brought out a number of important concepts on sharing and indicated the similarities and differences between a file system for a large-scale system treated as an integral part of the address space of the virtual processors and a file system for a medium-scale system treated as having an address space outside the address space of the virtual processors. The former approach is very general conceptually and easy for the user. The latter approach requires the user to interact with the system more frequently and work in two address spaces, that of the virtual processor and that of the file. We now turn our attention to the nature of file-system structure and the concept of a file directory.

6.1.5   File-system Structure

FILE DIRECTORIES   It was pointed out in Sec. 6.1.1 that files are commonly considered a single block of information to the system. Individual files have no structure as seen by the system. However, it is possible and useful to create a structure in which the files are taken as the basic units. This concept is discussed below. Before looking at this problem in its more general form as seen in the Multics system it is useful to introduce some basic concepts using as an example a system like that found on the XDS-940.

The first topic is keeping track of a user's files and maintaining access control and administrative information about each file. The basic concept is that of the *file directory*. Each user has a file directory which is maintained permanently on disk or other storage medium between sessions. During a session, a given user's directory can be brought into main memory by the system. The system must maintain a *master*, or *root*, directory containing the location of each user's directory. The directory can be considered as a file.

The directory contains the following types of information for each file, usually stored as a table of contiguous computer words:

1 The file name as a character string or a pointer to such a character string

2 Type of file, i.e., binary, character, or other type as defined in a particular system

3 Access protection (possibly a pointer to a list of other users who have access to the file and the kind of access which they are allowed such as read-only, write-only, read/write, or execute-only)

4 Information indicating directly where the file is stored or a pointer to further tables containing such information, i.e., a pointer to the index block discussed in Sec. 6.1.3.

5 Other information such as date of definition, frequency of use, or additional facts felt to be useful by an installation or system designer

A user can gain access to his directory to change file names, have his file names listed on his terminal, add, modify, or delete access rights for other users to his files, delete files, check file type for a specific file, and so forth. Remember that a user is an abstract concept defined by an account number and other identification as discussed in Sec. 1.5.5. A user may be a person or group of people such as a project using the same account number. For example, if the user is defined by two components, an account number and programmer number, all users with the same account number constitute a class of users. The question of file protection is discussed further in Sec. 6.1.6.

FILE TYPE Two common *file types* are *permanent* and *temporary* files. Permanent files exist within the system until explicitly deleted by their owner. Temporary files, on the other hand, exist only during a particular terminal session. When the user logs out, these files are deleted unless the user converts them to permanent files by command to the system.

Two other common types of files are *character* files and *binary* files. A character file contains a string of symbols which are encodings of the characters on the terminal keyboard. Character files pack several characters per computer word depending on word size. This packing and unpacking process was discussed in Sec. 6.1.3. A binary file contains data or is information directly loadable into main memory for execution.   Whether the file is binary or character should be immaterial to the system.   The indication placed in the file directory should serve only as a reminder to the user.   The file system should consider a file as a string of bits.

A SIMPLE FILE-SYSTEM STRUCTURE   The simple file-system structure to be discussed is that of a tree with two levels, as shown in Fig. 6.4.   The file system of the XDS-940 is of this type.   Circles represent directory files, and squares represent information files.   The numbers are for identification in the discussion.   Each entry in the file directory has a name and is represented by a branch.   For example, the name of the entry labeled 1 is USER 1, the name of the entry labeled 2 might be any string of characters depending on the file-naming conventions of a particular system, for example, ABC.   The name of the entry labeled 4 might also be ABC.   The ony restriction on file names is that they be unique within the directory which points to them.   The *system name* of a file is the concatenation of entry names reaching from the root directory to the file.   For example, the system names of the files pointed to by branches 2 and 4 are USER1:ABC and USER3:ABC, respectively.   The system name (called a *tree name* because it traces a path through the tree to the file) is unique for each file.

A given user need only use his file name when referring to his own files because the entry name of his directory file in the master directory is implicitly understood by the system, which knows whose process is running.   If the user wishes to access any other user's files, he must state the full tree name.   For example, if user 1 wishes to copy user 3's file

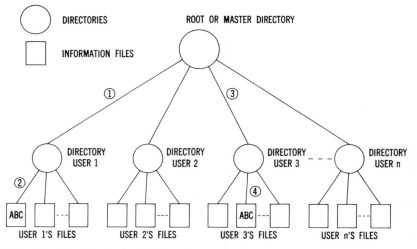

FIG. 6.4   Simple two-level file-system structure.

named ABC into one of his files named X, he must issue a command of the form

COPY USER3:ABC TO X

The system retrieves user 3's file directory and checks to see whether user 1 is allowed to copy file ABC. If so, the transaction is allowed to proceed.

A MORE GENERAL FILE-SYSTEM STRUCTURE The two-level tree structure is very useful, but one can visualize information-storage situations where a more general structure would simplify the information-system design or administration. For example, instead of file directories belonging to users, one might like to group files by projects and subprojects to any depth, or one might be storing information having a treelike classification structure such as a document-retrieval system.

The two-level structure can be generalized, as is accomplished in the Multics system, allowing directories to point to other directory files as well as information files to any depth, as shown in Fig. 6.5. The material on Multics that follows is based on the paper by Daley and Neumann.[1]

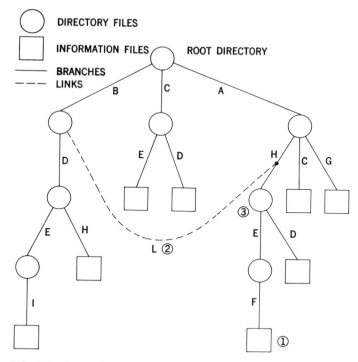

FIG. 6.5   General tree-structured file system.

As before, circles are directory files and squares are information files.   All the naming conventions discussed earlier are also used in this more general case.   For example, the file labeled 1 has the tree name A:H:E:F.   Unless explicitly stated, the tree name is given relative to the root.   A user is considered to be using one directory at a particular point in time called the *working directory*.   The working directory can be assigned by convention by the system, or the user can explicitly indicate which directory is to be considered his working directory by command to the system, giving the tree name to the directory as an argument.   For example, one way of organizing a file system having this generality is shown in Fig. 6.6.   The system contains three major subtrees of files, a library subtree,

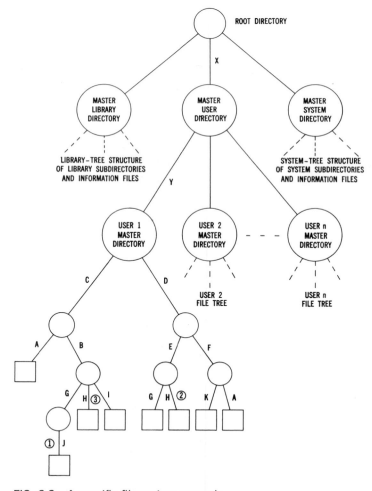

FIG. 6.6   A specific file-system example.

a user subtree, and a system subtree. The library subtree might have a subdirectory listing mathematical files, which in turn might have subdirectories for statistical files, matrix-manipulation files, differential-equation-solving files, and so forth. Further structure might be used for other classifications of library functions. The system subtree might have subtrees for various classifications of routines based on function, protection rights, or some other scheme.

The user subtree would contain entries for directories for each user, each of which had its own subtree of information files and directory files. The system might assign each user his master directory as the working directory unless explicitly commanded to do otherwise. All the statements about access control also apply to this more general case, including access control to directories. The Multics system allows tree names to be specified relative to the current working directory.[1]

When a segment in Multics refers to an external segment not known to the process currently executing, the system must search the file-storage hierarchy to find the external-segment name in a directory entry and make it known to the process, as described in Sec. 2.5. Because a file name is unique only relative to a directory and there may be several files in the system with the given name, the user must depend on the conventions of the search pattern to find the correct one or he must supply the system with his own search procedures. For example, referring to Fig. 6.6, assume a user 1 process is executing in segment J, which has path name X:Y:C:B:G:J, and makes an external reference to a segment named H, which is at the moment unknown to the process. Depending on the search strategy of the file structure, the system might assign segment H labeled 3 or segment H labeled 2 to the process. If the following search strategy was used, the file H labeled 3 would be found:

1 Start at the immediately superior directory of the file creating the reference.

2 First search the subtree below the directory before proceeding up the tree.

3 Then search each subtree defined by the next superior directory.

A search starting at the user's master directory and proceeding on a tree search from right to left would find segment H labeled 2. Or the user might have given a path name as a search guide. The system would start its search at the lowest directory indicated by this path name and search the subtree of which it is the root. If the named segment were not found, the system would move to the next highest directory in the suggested search path and search the subtree defined by it, and so on. If the search moved up to the master user directory, it might continue into each of the other user's trees to which access was granted or by convention might proceed to search the library structure. The point of this discussion is that intersegment references to segments in a complicated tree may require some awareness on the part of the user of searching strategy.

One additional concept in Multics needing brief mention is that of the *link*. A link is an entry in a file directory which points not to a file but to an entry in another directory, as shown by the dotted line in Fig. 6.5. Links can have a name, there is no access control associated with a link because access control exists on the branch to which a link points. A link serves as a shortcut to a branch somewhere else in the hierarchy and has the effect of a branch pointing directly to the file specified by the entry pointed to by the link. For example, in Fig. 6.5, link L has the effect of creating an entry in directory B pointing directly to the directory labeled 3. The concept of tree name can now be generalized to *path* name. A path name is either a tree name or the concatenation of all branch names and link names from the root or working directory to the designated file. For example, the file labeled 3 has the path names A:H or B:L.

SUMMARY We have seen that basic information about a file, its name, location, access control, and other administrative information is kept in a table called a file directory. The location of a file kept in the file directory is commonly a pointer to the index block(s). File directories are stored in auxiliary storage.

A simple file-system structure consists of a root directory which contains the location of the file directory of each user. In order to allow users and the system greater flexibility to structure information systems, more general file-system structure is useful. A general file-system structure can be achieved by treating directories as files, which results in a tree structure. File names are unique relative to the file directory in which they are defined. A unique system name is obtained by concatenating to the file name the names of the directories passed through in going from the root of the tree to the defining directory. If files are referenced by their local name and not system name, conventions must be established for searching the file system.

6.1.6 File Access Control The ability to share files among communities of users is an important intrinsic goal of a timesharing system. The easy access afforded by online storage gives extra incentive for people to build on each other's work. Sharing files creates the need for a file access-control system offering a variety of access modes.[1,13] As information becomes increasingly centralized in central computer facilities accessible from anonymous remote terminals, great social responsibility rests with the system designer to provide foolproof methods to assure privacy and protection of the stored information.[14] In this section we discuss protection ideas developed to date. Further research and development are needed in this important subject.   The ideal access-control system is probably one which cannot be compromised even by persons understanding its implementation.

Access rights which a user may be able to define, depending on system design, are *free access,* meaning that anyone can access the file, and *restricted access,* meaning that certain users are permitted access or no access.   Users given access may have power only to read, power to write or modify, power to append, power to delete, and power to load only for execution.   These modes are referred to as *usage attributes.*   Different users may be allowed different access rights and different usage attributes. For example, a user may have several coworkers on his project who are granted access with the usage attributes of full power to delete or modify, but other users may be able to access the file only with the usage attributes to read or execute.   Instead of taking space to list each of these coworkers explicitly, the account number can be the basis for defining access privileges for a class of users.   Usually only the owner, i.e., any person with the specific identification used to log in when the file was first created, can add, delete, or modify access privileges and usage attributes.

A powerful access attribute has been suggested for implementation in the Multics system called TRAP.[1]   If the TRAP attribute is on for a given user, a transfer (trap) would occur to a procedure specified in the access-control table for the file when any reference is made by that user to the file.   This mechanism allows a file owner to keep track of who is using his files and with what frequency.   Access privileges and usage attributes are most easily implemented with lists of users granted access and bit encodings of the various access attributes.   Logically the access-control information can be considered to reside in the branch (access path) leading to the file.

In addition to these types of control another mode of protection is worth mentioning.   To ensure that one user is not modifying a file while another is reading it, if concurrent access is allowed, interlocks are required. When one or more users are reading the file, the read interlock is set, preventing any other user from writing on it.   Similarly, if any user is writing on the file, the write interlock is set, preventing other users from reading or writing on the file.

It is useful to summarize and comment further on the file-protection concepts introduced.   Protection facilities commonly required are the following:[1,18]

1   Protection against one user posing as another.   Protection against this problem is handled at log-in time, when the user supplies his identification to the system.   The identification may include nonprinting characters in order to attain an extra measure of security.

2   Protection against file access by users not authorized to share them.   This problem is commonly solved by associating access-control

attributes, indicating which users or classes of users can access the file. There are three main ways of restricting access:

a Keeping the name of the file secret. This is difficult in many situations, and systems employing this mode may require frequent file name changes. One can improve on this method by assigning a non-printing password as part of the file name.

b Restricting access to classes of users such as the file owner, all users of the system, or classes based on common identification components such as account numbers. The user can specify for each of his files the classes of users which can access it. The disadvantage of this method is that a user cannot allow a single user to access the file without also allowing all members of that user's class to access. Restriction by classes has the advantage of being easy to implement.

c Specifying individual users who have access. To provide this general capability requires more extensive software. This method is usually implemented with a list which can be modified by the file owner through system commands. In Multics each branch has such a list called the access-control list.

3 Protection against authorized users accessing the file in unauthorized ways. This problem is solved by defining usage attributes for each authorized user or class of users indicating the kind of access they are granted. Examples are read, read/write, append, execute. Not all systems have all modes. Read and write attributes exist in most systems. Where access is by class, the access mode is the same for all members of the class.

4 Protection against the file owner's mistakes in manipulating the file. The access-mode attributes above can be used by the owner to give himself protection from his own possible mistakes. The backup mechanisms to be described in the next section also give protection in case of accidental deletion or other self-inflicted damage, as well as protection against hardware and software errors.

6.1.7   File Backup and Recovery

INTRODUCTION   The system designer must assume that hardware and software malfunctions will occur, and he should probably give reliability, backup, and recovery procedures consideration from the earliest design stages. In this section, we discuss protection mechanisms for the file system, and in Chap. 7 we discuss the problem from the point of view of the rest of the system.

The files in the system represent a large investment of time and energy and are therefore critical. Loss of central files could have such effects as the bankruptcy of a firm or several months' delay in a research project. Types of malfunction range from transient CPU and main-memory malfunctions, to unreadable tracks of data on a device, to total device destruction if the read/write sensors hit and destroy the recording surface.

PERIODIC DUMP   The most common kind of backup procedure is to *dump* all files and file directories periodically onto a removable medium such as disk packs or magnetic tape.   If a failure should occur, the file can be reloaded from the dump tape.   This mechanism of protection in its simplest form has a number of disadvantages:

1   The system usually needs to be shut down during the dump operation.

2   The dumping operation can be very lengthy for large file systems, running from sizable fractions of an hour to possibly hours.

3   Recovery is from the last dump.   Therefore, users can lose several hours of work because dumping usually takes place only once a day.

The dumping operation can allow certain other operations to be performed simultaneously such as collecting user's files into blocks for reloading onto contiguous areas of the storage device.   Such a reloading can speed access and increase system efficiency.

INCREMENTAL DUMP   A more elaborate dumping procedure which avoids the problems mentioned above is called *incremental dumping*.[1,13] With incremental dumping, copies of files modified during a session are copied onto a dump tape when the user logs out.   The system can set a bit in the file-directory entry of each file modified during a session.   At log-out time a routine can add the names of the files which were modified and add a pointer to the file directory to a queue of work to be dumped by a low-priority system process.

This mechanism still leaves users endangered who may have a long terminal session, but the approach can be modified by allowing the low-priority dumping process to scan all the file directories continuously, looking for files which have been modified.   When such a file is found, it can be dumped along with the current file-directory entry for the file.   The code indicating that the file has been modified is then reset.   Certain modifications to the directory entries, such as changing the file name or access rights of individuals, are also important and therefore worth saving.   In this case, the entire file does not need saving, but the file-directory entry can be saved.   By properly adjusting the priority of the dumping process the average length of time each directory is scanned can be adjusted.   This incremental-dump approach is used on Multics and of course creates large quantities of data.

RECOVERY USING DUMP INFORMATION   Recovering from a system failure could require a long time to search all the incremental-dump tapes for the latest version of each file.   Therefore, to enable the system to recover faster from catastrophic failures, Multics periodically performs what is called a *system checkpoint* dump,[1] which copies system files and the file direc-

tories.   Then to recover, the most recent system checkpoint dump is reloaded along with the most recent incremental-file dump.   This process
allows the system to go back into operation faster and service many users
while the incremental-dump reload proceeds as a low-priority process.   *User
checkpoint dumps,* dumping all user files, can be performed every few weeks
and can also help speed up restart for those users who have stable older
files, because the most recent user checkpoint dump can be reloaded before
the older incremental-dump tapes are searched.   The process of recovery
using this procedure is shown in Fig. 6.7, which is based on a similar
figure in the Multics system programmer's manual.   A user checkpoint dump
was taken at time TU, the last system checkpoint dump was taken at time
TS, and a serious failure occurred at time TF.   To get the system recovery
to the point where it can serve users, the incremental-dump tapes back
to time TS are reloaded, placing the most recent files of each user in the
system (1); then the last system checkpoint dump is reloaded (2).   At
this point the system is usable to those wanting to create new files as
well as to many other users.   The incremental dumps back to time TU
can now be loaded as a background task (3), followed by the last user
checkpoint dump (4).   At this point the file directories are up to date,
and all but a very small fraction of the files have been restored.   The
effort to search back into further dump tapes is probably not worthwhile.
The directory entries of files not restored can indicate that if they are requested, the system should search further back in the incremental-dump
tapes.

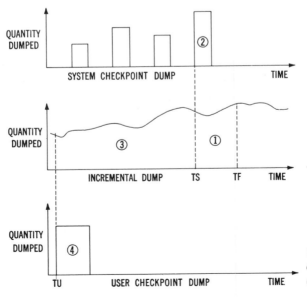

FIG. 6.7   Recovery pro-
cedure   using   various
dumps.

RECOVERY FROM PROCESSOR OR MEMORY ERRORS   The discussion of the last section covers catastrophic failures and the case where the user, having accidently deleted a file, requests the system to reload the corresponding file from the most recent incremental or other dump.   Most failures are not catastrophic and may affect only files being modified at the time of failure or those represented by file directories in main memory.   When such failures occur, the entries in the file directories in main memory may point to incorrect addresses or be inconsistent in some way.   Recovery from such failures can be made without requiring a total reload.[5,13]   This recovery is made by checking the file directories in main memory for consistency.   The details of the checking procedures are very system-dependent.   Most systems are full of implicit or explicit redundant information useful in checking.   The system programmer must use his knowledge of the system in defining these consistency checks.   This checking and recovery process can at least straighten things out to the point where damage will not be propagated when the system is restarted.   The few files found to be (or suspected of being) damaged can either be reloaded from the recent incremental-dump tapes and flagged in the file directory so that the user can be notified or just flagged for user notification.   The user can check to see whether the files were in fact damaged and then specifically request a reloading.

Another type of error is damage to the tables used to keep track of available space on auxiliary storage.   About all that can be done here is to make the information consistent so that no further damage will occur and then at points such as the checkpoint dumps redetermine which physical records are in use and which are free by examining all the index-block structures as the files are saved.

SUMMARY   Error protection and recovery are possible, but detailed design of such procedures is not easy and requires some inventiveness on the part of the designer.   At least two levels of protection are required, file dumps on a periodic basis and consistency checks of system tables, file directories, and index-block structures.   The designer must be able to visualize the different malfunctions which might occur and their effect on the system.   The earlier in the design process these problems are considered, the simpler it probably is to organize table structures and storage allocation to ease the problem.   Recovery procedures should be automatic wherever possible and require minimum intervention by the operator or user.   Complete reload should be avoided unless absolutely necessary.   When a file directory is reloaded, all files to which it is pointing must be reloaded since the old pointers may be to areas which have been freed and reassigned since the dump.   If a failure should occur during incremental dumping, the current incremental-dump tape may be improperly terminated.   Recovery procedures should be able to handle such a situation.

6.1.8 Handling a Hierarchy of Auxiliary Storage Devices   The basic problem here results because physical and economic considerations make it impossible to provide unlimited storage on a single device.   Therefore, several levels of online devices with different access speed and storage capacity may be required.   The online devices may also be backed up by archival storage on removable media such as disk packs or magnetic tape.   Such a hierarchy is represented by the triangle of levels shown in Fig. 6.8, where the slower, less expensive, larger-capacity devices are at the bottom of the triangle and the faster, more expensive, smaller-capacity devices are at the top.   The goal is to devise algorithms which allow information to settle to the level its activity rate indicates is appropriate or which reflects a user's desired access performance.

Let us consider first a system with just a disk and tape.   Files can be moved from disk to tape explicitly by request from the user or under system control.   The type of information the system can use to determine which files are to be placed on tape includes such statistics as the last time the file was accessed, its frequency of access over some given period of time, or assigned priorities.   When the disk reaches a certain capacity, a system routine can be activated to search the file directories for files which can be moved to tape.   Files moved to tape should still have entries kept in the file directory with the appropriate information to permit the file to be automatically retrieved when the user next requests access.   The file system should keep track of all files until explicitly deleted by the user.[13]   Because there is a finite amount of online storage, each user is usually restricted to some fixed amount of such storage.

When these ideas are generalized to a hierarchy of devices, the

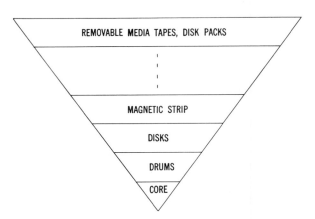

FIG. 6.8 Hierarchy of storage devices.

same concepts apply.   Some algorithm based on usage must be developed to indicate on which device a file is to reside.   The *occupancy factor* (percent of capacity kept filled) of each device is an important parameter in the design of such systems and must be studied with simulation or system experiment and measurement.[12]   When a file is referenced, its access-rate count can be incremented and then as time goes on this count can be decayed.   When the access rate of a file falls below the setting for the device, the file becomes a candidate for removal.   Removal may take place immediately, be dependent on the capacity of the device and lower-level devices, or be dependent upon a user's overriding indication that he wants the file stored on no devices of lower level.   Higher storage rates are usually charged for the override privilege as a means of limiting its use.

When a device reaches a capacity limit or residency criteria set as a software parameter, the files it contains can be ordered by activity rate and some of them can be removed to a lower-level device.   In Multics the moves, when implemented, are to be accomplished dynamically as part of the normal page and segment accessing processes.   Thus, a segment which has an activity rate indicating it is to be moved to a lower-level device can be moved in pieces as each page is brought from main memory back into the auxiliary-memory hierarchy.

The goal of a hierarchical system is to keep the most frequently accessed information on the higher-speed devices.   Problems arise when a file requiring fast access is infrequently accessed.   To handle such cases requires setting up careful accounting and administration procedures which can override the dynamic-allocation algorithm.   Some information may normally reside on slower devices but temporarily move to higher-speed devices during a user session.

This discussion completes our introduction to basic file-system concepts, and we can now examine more detailed concepts involved in actual I/O operations.

6.2   GENERAL I/O

6.2.1   Introduction   The I/O system must cope with a wide variety of devices and therefore is quite complicated at detailed levels of design.   This complication arises because of the large number of special situations which can arise in handling communication with each type of device.   To create a design which is as conceptually simple as possible, the designer should probably isolate as many device-dependent characteristics as possible in separate routines (often called *device drivers*) and then interface these routines with more general routines which are device-independent.[11]   One approach to this problem is whenever possible to place device-dependent characteristics in tables which have been designed to be used by general routines.

One can recognize four major functions in handling I/O devices:

1 Buffering of information transmitted between I/O devices, auxiliary storage, and memory

2 Proper handling of interrupts or other device to processor signals and their interface to the rest of the system

3 Reserving and allocating I/O resources

4 Protection of the resources dedicated to one user or process from interference by another

The sections to follow discuss concepts and mechanisms useful in performing these functions. Most of the mechanisms to be described are common in various forms on many systems, but we are most familiar with them as they exist on the XDS-940 as programmed by L. P. Deutsch, B. W. Lampson, and others.

6.2.2 Buffering A major I/O concept is that of *buffering*. A buffer is a storage area used to give a better match between central-processor speeds and I/O-device speeds. During the accessing of a file by a process, the system tries to maintain a buffer full of information so that when a process requests information from the file, the system has anticipated the request and the required information is in main storage. Thus, the process can immediately access the required information and can keep executing. Without the buffering, the process would have been blocked, and the system might have to swap in another process while the required information was brought into main storage. On output, the process fills a buffer, and the system automatically outputs it to the required device when it is full. When the buffer is full, the process is blocked until it is emptied.

Two types of records are maintained by the system: (1) logical records and (2) physical records, as mentioned in Sec. 6.1.3. The buffer size maintained by the system is usually equal to the size of a physical record, which varies according to the device. For example, as discussed earlier, physical records on disks are commonly a sector size or some multiple of a sector size; a physical record for a line printer would be a line of text; and so forth.

With *double* or *multiple buffering*, also frequently used, the user process works from one buffer area while the system empties or fills the other buffer areas. When the buffer area currently in use by a process is empty, the system switches a pointer so that the process can access from a second buffer while the system fills the first. On output, a process fills a buffer area and then is switched to a free area to fill while the system empties the first. The technique of double or multiple buffering is useful with sequential file access but yields little or no benefit when files are accessed randomly. The concept of a double buffer is illustrated in Fig. 6.9.

The question where these buffer areas are kept must be answered. Each process or job in the system usually has some memory associated with it which is considered a part of that job or process but is not directly accessible by the job or process. This area is normally swapped with the process and is used by the system for temporary storage, constants, tables, and other system functions in support of the process or job. It was mentioned in Sec. 5.2.5, for example, that one page of memory is associated with each job in the XDS-940 system for this function. It is within this memory that the system maintains its buffers. Because this space is limited, only a few transfers can be going on through these buffers at once. A job has three single buffers in the XDS-940 system. One of the functions discussed below associated with initiating a data transfer is reserving one of these buffers.

For transfers requiring double or multiple buffering or buffers larger than the standard physical-record size, the process must define these buffers in its address space, and the addresses of these buffers must be communicated to the system. In the XDS-940 system, the process can transfer blocks of information to the disk which are larger than the standard physical record. When the process requests such a transfer, it gives the system a starting memory address, the length of the block to be transferred, the file name, and starting address within the file.

If a process requests a word of data from an I/O device which is not available in a buffer, the process is blocked but the page or area containing the buffer is locked in memory (not assigned to another process) until a buffer has been filled. At this point the buffer area can be stored on drum or kept in memory until the process regains control of a processor. Similarly, if the process attempts to output to a buffer which is full, the

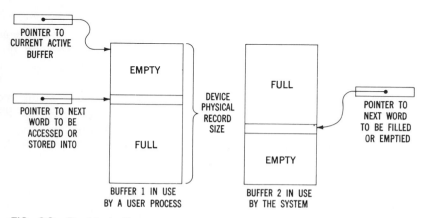

FIG. 6.9 Double buffer.

process is blocked until the buffer is emptied. The area containing the buffer is kept in main memory even through the rest of the process is swapped out. Identical actions are taken if the buffer is maintained by the process in its accessible memory.

Associated with buffer handling are a number of administrative tasks, e.g., manipulating pointers to indicate the next word to be transferred to the process from a buffer on a read or to the buffer from the process on a write, checking to see when a buffer is empty or filled, keeping track of which physical file block to transfer to or from next, or keeping track of buffer size and location.

6.2.3   Interrupt Handlers

DESIGN OF INTERRUPT HANDLERS   Interrupts or functionally equivalent mechanisms are considered at a number of places in this book because of their central role in the system design.   In this section we review and expand on a number of concepts introduced in Sec. 5.2.4.   The discussion is in terms of interrupts, but the concepts also apply to other communication mechanisms.   Interrupts are of three basic types: (1) indications of completion of the currently assigned task, (2) requests for service, and (3) indications of error or malfunction conditions.   The third type requires special handling unique to each type of device and therefore is outside the scope of our discussion here, except to indicate that a common approach to many types of errors is to try the operation several times before reporting failure to the system.   An example is a parity error on a data transmission.   When such an error condition arises, the operation is repeated.   Repeated trial is based on the experience that many errors arise from transient causes.

Interrupts of the first two types are major inputs to the scheduling process and generally indicate that a process should be awakened.   Classes of interrupts, such as those generated by data channels or other general I/O processors which have several types of devices attached, have a meaning specific to the service function being performed.   Interrupts from these devices can usually be properly interpreted only by the routine which requested the service.   Therefore, a common design approach is to write one general routine to intercept the interrupts, retrieve whatever status information may be available from the channel or interrupting device, and then pass this information to the specific device driver which initiated the service or which is designed for handling the specific device requesting service.   To perform this function means that the channel-driving routines must keep track in some manner of the services they have initiated.   The channel-driving routines must also keep the address to transfer to, in the requesting routine, when an interrupt from a specific device arrives.   These device-oriented interrupt routines can interpret the status information, try to recover if there is an error condition, or initiate the next action if a sequence of actions is required, as, for example, in a disk where an address seek request must be followed at a later point by a data transmission. The device-oriented routines must keep track of the process which requested service or the location of communication cells to be used for communicating with the requesting process. The interrupt-handling routine must keep track of this return information in order to communicate completion or other conditions to the requesting process.

A DETAILED I/O EXAMPLE   These ideas, along with a number of additional concepts, can be illustrated with an example. Consider a process P inputting from a sequential file F. The file is on a disk unit connected to the system through a channel. The channel has one interrupt line. The system maintains a single buffer. A possible communication path is shown in Fig. 6.10. When the buffer is empty and the process P requests input, the routine, which we call B, handling the buffer blocks process P. Routine B then requests input from the file system. The request is made by placing an entry on a queue of disk service requests. Routine B maintains a record of the process it is presently serving. The queue entry contains the location of the buffer and the location on the disk of the next physical record of file F. This latter information was obtained by routine B from appropriate

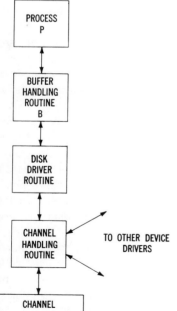

FIG. 6.10   Communication path for an I/O operation.

tables (to be discussed in the next section). The routine used to drive the disk takes entries from the disk queue and issues appropriate I/O commands to the channel handler.

When the request to access file F reaches the head of the queue, the disk driver first gives the channel handler a seek command to position the read sensor over the desired sector. The disk driver notifies the channel handler to return control to it at a specified location, when an interrupt from the disk arrives. When the seek is completed, an interrupt is generated. The channel-handling routine services the interrupt by obtaining status information from the channel. Examination of the status information indicates that the interrupt came from the disk controller. The channel-interrupt routine, using the previously supplied information, returns control to the disk driver.

The disk driver then issues the I/O commands to read a physical block from file F into the buffer for process P. The disk driver also notifies the channel to return control to it on the next block-transfer-completed interrupt. When the physical record has been transferred, the channel word-count register goes to zero and the channel generates a block-transfer-completed interrupt. The channel-interrupt handler services the interrupt by obtaining status information from the channel. When it is determined that the interrupt was a block-transfer-completed signal, control is returned to the disk driver. When the disk driver regains control, it checks its information indicating which routine it was servicing and finds it to be routine B. Control is returned to routine B along with the information that the transfer was correctly completed.

Routine B would have had to be informed if a transmission error had occurred so that it could inform process P. The error indication would have gone from the channel interrupt-handling routine to the disk driver. The disk driver would have tried the I/O request several times before reporting failure to routine B.

Routine B, on a correct transmission, would awaken process P. Process P would again issue its request for information from the file F. On an incorrect transmission P might also be awakened but have begun executing at some error-handling point. Or routine B might awaken an entirely different process to type a message to the user informing him of the error condition or perform some other action. This example has indicated the type of communication mechanisms needed between various levels of I/O and interrupt-handling routines.

Related to the problem of interrupts is the problem of how to handle status checking for those situations which do not signal their completion or condition by an interrupt. An example on the XDS-940 system is that of requesting a tape to rewind. When the tape has rewound, no interrupt is generated. This condition can be tested for with a special type of test instruction which skips if the I/O condition indicated in its operand code is satisfied. It would be unsatisfactory to tie up the operating system continually testing for this condition. The technique used is to have the tape routine which started the rewind call other system routines to create a system process. The system process is assigned the task of checking for the rewind-completed condition. The tape-handling process is then blocked until awakened by this system process. The system process is placed in the normal queue of processes and is awakened every few seconds by the clock-handling routines to perform its checks of the tape-rewind condition. This approach is used throughout the Multics and XDS-940 systems.

SUMMARY   A uniform interrupt-handling procedure should be designed to interface cleanly with the scheduling function as well as the specific devices. To achieve this uniformity requires the design of standard types of service requests for all devices, with appropriate caller identification to permit return communication.

6.2.4   Allocating I/O Devices

DEDICATED AND SHARABLE DEVICES   One can recognize two types of devices: (1) dedicated devices and (2) sharable devices. *Dedicated* devices are those which are most effectively assigned to one user for a given time period, even though the user may not be able to utilize the device continuously. In this category are tape drives and reels, line or other printers, card equipment, and optical scanning equipment. *Sharable devices* are those which, while allowing access to only one process at a time, can rapidly complete their service for individual processes and be quickly switched to service requests of other processes. In this category are such online auxiliary storage units as drums, disks, and data cells.

Dedicated devices may require advance reservation for their use by specifically reserving them for a given time and a given duration. Reservation can be handled through a noncomputer administrative procedure, or the user can log in and through commands to the system discover when the desired device is to be free, place a reservation with the system, and then log out. At the scheduled time, the user can log in and request, for example, that his reserved tape drives be made available to his processes. The system can check its reservation schedule and assign the resources. Such a scheme is available in the Multics system.

On the 940 system, the reservation has to be performed outside the computer system because the system handles requests for devices on a first come, first served basis. If a user requests transferring a file to the printer, for example, and the printer is in use, a message indicating "printer in use" is sent back to the user's terminal. The user must place his request again later. One could design a service-request queue for the printer, and if the printer were busy, it would inform the user of this fact and then later when the request was honored supply this information to the user also.

Sharable devices can be allocated among different processes at a rate such that the sharing is invisible to the user. No special reservation is required. We now discuss a number of concepts applicable to both dedicated and sharable devices.

DEVICE OPENING AND CLOSING Allocation of devices takes place through a process called *opening a device* or *opening a file*. When a process is finished with the device, the device is *closed*. These functions are handled by system routines invisible to the user processes. When a dedicated device is opened for a process, it cannot be used by another process until it is closed. This is not true of sharable devices. When the system attempts to open a dedicated or sharable device for a process, it checks a table containing information about the particular device.

The name *device-control blocks* or *device-control tables* is often given to this type of table, which might contain such information as the channel number to which the device is attached, the device number, an indication whether the device is character- or word-oriented, an indication whether the device requires a buffer, the buffer size if required, the number of subunits attached to the device, whether the device is random or sequential, the address of the device driver routine, and so forth.

If the device is presently in use, the device table will indicate this fact. When the device is in use, two courses of action can follow depending on the system design: (1) the process can be removed from running, placed on the ready list, and required to place its request when its turn in the ready list arrives, or (2) a request for this device can be placed on a queue and the process blocked until the device can be assigned to this process. The record in the table which indicates that the device is in use is the protection mechanism to ensure that no other process can interfere with the information transfer going on. In other words, protection is achieved by channeling all requests for access through a single routine and table.

All the information logically associated with an entity—device, file, process, and so forth—can be considered a logical record or entry. The records in turn can be chained together using list processing or located in contiguous areas of memory. A related set of records is referred to as a table, queue, or list. Use of list processing was illustrated in Sec. 5.2.6. For this discussion we assume that logical records or entries are in contiguous areas of main memory. There are two common ways to organize such records in main memory. One method places the fields for a

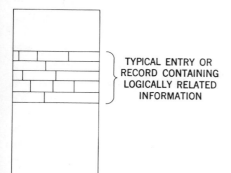

TYPICAL ENTRY OR
RECORD CONTAINING
LOGICALLY RELATED
INFORMATION

FIG. 6.11   Fields for a record organized in contiguous words.

record in contiguous memory locations, as shown in Fig. 6.11. Such a
table is commonly accessed by placing a pointer to the first word of a
record in an index register and placing in the address field the relative
location within a record of the word containing the desired field. This
approach is used because the particular field of information desired is usually
known at the time of coding but the record desired varies at run time.

The second method of organization places words for a record in
the same relative location in several one-dimensional arrays, as shown in
Fig. 6.12.   All words in a given array have the same structure.   This table
is usually accessed by placing a relative pointer to the needed record in
an index register and the address of the desired array in the address field.

Dedicated devices cannot be opened for a process unless they are
free.   Requests for opening these devices can be queued.   Sharable devices
can be opened for a process even if they are presently busy, but specific
access requests are queued.   Handling queues for I/O devices is conceptually similar to handling the queue for the CPU.   Queues for I/O devices

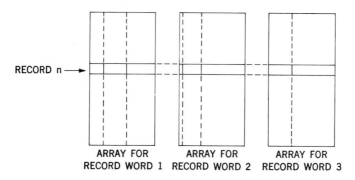

RECORD n ⟶

ARRAY FOR   ARRAY FOR   ARRAY FOR
RECORD WORD 1 RECORD WORD 2 RECORD WORD 3

FIG. 6.12   Fields for a record organized in words of several
arrays.

can be simple first come, first served queues, or they can be based on the priority of the process requesting service.

Queues for access requests to sharable devices such as disks may have a more elaborate queue-scheduling algorithm to take into account not only process priorities but also characteristics of the device.[8] For example, the scheduling of access to the disk may take into account present read/write sensor-arm position in an effort to optimize the total use of the disk.

The information required on the queue entry is that required to specify the service required adequately, the process requesting service and its priority, and the type of awakening signal or indication to be sent when the service is completed.   This latter function, as discussed in Sec. 5.2.4, can be as simple as passing the address of a memory location to be set greater than zero when service is completed.

The process of opening a device or file is often confused with the idea of defining a file.   A file is defined when an entry in the file directory is created.   The file remains defined until explicitly deleted.   The concept of *opening* is related to a specific data transfer or sequence of transfers and requires allocation of resources for the transfer, such as buffer areas and access to the required device.   As mentioned in Sec. 6.1.1, the words device and file are often used interchangeably because specific devices other than online auxiliary storage can be treated as files with special names. During a given terminal session a user's process may open and close a given file several times.

Assuming that the required device is free or sharable, it is assigned to the requesting process and is opened for the process.   The device-control table associated with the device is consulted to determine the size of buffer required, as well as other device-dependent information.   The file directory is consulted to locate the file index block and other file-dependent information.   A *file-control block* is set up associated with this particular transfer, which contains all device, file, and process-dependent information required for the generalized I/O and interrupt-handling routines actually to perform the required I/O.

The type of information in this block of several words would give the address of the buffer or buffers to be used in the transfer, the address of the index block for the file if the device is a disk or other online auxiliary store, an indication whether the file is read-only, random, or sequential, the device number of the actual device assigned, an indication whether the information-transfer direction is reading or writing, the transfer-status information, the channel number, and so forth.   Each time a transfer for this device or file takes place, either explicitly by process request or by the system in filling or emptying a buffer, the information in the file-control block is used to set up the I/O request.

The user refers to a file by a symbolic name.   The system refers to a file by number. This file number is usually just the index into a table of file-control blocks. The file number for a given file varies from file opening to file opening. The symbolic name remains fixed until changed by the user. The total number of files which can be opened concurrently depends on the devices requested, number of available buffers, and number of available file-control blocks. The number of devices is fixed by the hardware configuration. The number of buffers is a design parameter dependent on how buffer space is allocated, and the number of file-control blocks is a variable parameter. When an access transaction is completed, the device or file is *closed*. Closing the device frees the resources allocated.

SUMMARY The important concepts introduced above were dedicated and sharable devices, opening and closing a device or file, tables of device-dependent information, file-control blocks, and file number. These concepts are the center around which a unified device-independent I/O system can be built. Many of these concepts can also be integrated with the handling of remote devices as well.

6.2.5 Terminal I/O

INTRODUCTION We consider only character-oriented remote terminals because of their importance, although the basic concepts discussed here carry over to many other types of terminals. Terminals such as general purpose graphic terminals or terminals attached to small remote computers are special areas of study.[7] There are two main approaches to terminal communication: (1) transmitting a single character and (2) transmitting a block of characters at a time. The former approach would seem to give the user greater flexibility than the latter in designing interactive systems, but it requires more system time in character handling. The XDS-940 system uses the single-character approach for teletype I/O. Many of the character-oriented graphic terminals require block transfers. The IBM Quiktran system transmitted on a line-at-a-time basis. The software handling of either approach has much in common, and only the single-character approach is discussed here.

On the XDS-940, the communications interface is connected to the CPU's direct I/O lines, and each character input or output requires about 300 microseconds of processing by the system. An alternative approach commonly used, and the one used on the GE-645, is to input characters directly into memory through a multiplexor channel. For a system such as the 940, which usually has 16 to 32 teletypes attached, the overhead involved in handling the terminal I/O is not excessive. For large systems, using 50 to 200 terminals, this approach is too inefficient. Designers of large systems are beginning to use separate small processors to handle the terminal communications.   These communications processors have their own memory and access to the system main memory.   Efficient instructions for packing and unpacking characters from machine words are also important in decreasing the system effort expended in character handling.

The wide range of available character-oriented terminal devices and range of data rates associated with these devices make it essential for terminal-interface hardware and software to be modular in design.   Devices are available with varying character sets which must be recognized by software routines.   Each device may have special control codes for its operation. Data rates of available devices range between 10 and 240 characters per second.   Systems such as the XDS-940, which were designed for teletypes as the main terminal, have required extensive modifications to the software routines to add other terminals and modifications to the hardware interface equipment to accommodate the higher data rates of character-oriented graphics terminals.   The design goal is to make the system modular so that a variety of terminals can be used with few if any system modifications.

BUFFERING   An important concept about I/O in general, as well as with terminal I/O, is that the user process rarely communicates directly with the I/O device but rather communicates with a buffer.[10]   In the case of terminal I/O, when the user process issues an instruction which is to send a character to a terminal, the system interpretively executes this instruction (a system call is actually generated) and places the character to be sent to the terminal in an output buffer associated with this process.   Later, other system routines, which are "aware" of the I/O activity of all terminals, can remove the characters from the buffers and send them to the terminals. If a process has a great deal of output to the terminal, it may overflow the buffer.   The system watches the load level of the output buffer, and if it is about to be filled, the process is blocked until the buffer has been emptied.

On input, the characters from the terminal are automatically loaded by the system into an input buffer.   When a process is executing and issues an input-character instruction, it is interpretively executed by the system. The system takes a character from the input buffer and places it in a register assigned by convention or in a user-designated memory location.   If no characters are in the buffer, the process is blocked until a sufficient number of characters reach the buffer.

Because the characters are arriving or leaving the computer assynchronously to the user's process, these buffers must remain in memory. Faster transfer devices require larger buffers than the slower devices.   One approach to buffer allocation is to preassign the buffer for each type of device.   Depending on the size and number of buffers, these buffers may constitute a serious drain on main-memory space.   To alleviate this problem, one can borrow list-processing techniques from other applications facing a similar problem of unknown or variable-size storage requirements. Using this approach, one can preassign a total buffer area which is subdivided into blocks of some length, say 10 to 20 words. Each active terminal is then allocated a block as required up to some maximum number, at which point the process is blocked or awakened depending on whether we are considering output or input. With list processing one can use less total storage and yet satisfy the varying buffer needs of individual terminals.

The terminal buffers are usually organized as a ring. For example, with the input buffer, one pointer I indicates which character to send to the process when it next requests input, and another pointer R indicates where to place the next character received from the terminal. The buffer is full when the pointer R points to the same place as pointer I. This condition or some advance warning of it must be checked for. The concept is shown in Fig. 6.13. A similar structure is used for the output buffer.

TERMINAL NUMBER Associated with each terminal is a terminal number. The terminal number, like the job number and the file number, is a number used by the system for indexing tables associated with terminal I/O and for accessing the correct buffer. This number is assigned when the terminal makes contact with the system. Each terminal has a table associated with it containing various types of status information used for control purposes: indications of whether the terminal is linked to another terminal (see below), whether another terminal is linked to this one and the terminal number of the linked terminal, the status of the data set, the break character set (see below), the type of character-code conversion desired, and other status information.

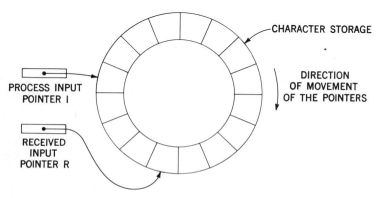

FIG. 6.13 Input-character buffer organized logically as a ring.

CALLING THE SYSTEM Another important concept associated with terminal I/O is a mechanism for returning to the system or next higher level process, no matter what a process is doing.[10] Situations in which the user may want to exit from the current process are getting stuck in a loop, having started printing out a long table all the output of which is not desired, or having finished with a phase of the problem solution controlled by the current process.

In the XDS-940 system, this function is provided by one of the character codes. The input-character routines test for this special character. Control can be directed to the system or a particular process depending on settings of software interrupts. By hitting this special character enough times or by having two such characters follow each other in very close succession, control returns to the root process of the system. Other systems use a special switch or button for the same function.

COMMUNICATION-LINE MALFUNCTIONS Also requiring careful terminal programming is the handling of the several different situations that can occur during transient communication-line malfunctions. If the line should be disconnected, it is important that the system be able to detect this situation. If the system cannot detect it, the user will still be logged in and using resources. The files in use at the time are also endangered. The system should wait some time to ensure that the malfunction is not transient before automatically logging out the user.

BREAK CHARACTERS The user may have written his process to accept single-character commands. In this case setting some limit on the number of characters which must be in the buffer before the process is awakened would be unworkable. The XDS-940 and other systems use a concept of *break characters* to get around this problem. Certain characters or possibly all characters (the number and extent of the break-character set is established by commands which the user can give the system) have the significance that when they are received, the process is awakened so that it can obtain the character from the buffer.

ECHOING Another concept associated with terminal I/O is called *echoing*.[10] Echoing exists in the 940 system and other systems as well. This mechanism makes use of the fact that terminal send and receive units are usually logically separate from one another, although they may exist in the same physical frame. In the echoing approach, when the user presses a key, the character code goes into the central computer and is not printed on the terminal by the user's action. The system accepts the character and then puts it in a buffer separate from the other output (so as not to mix it with the process-generated output). The system then outputs

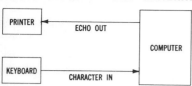

FIG. 6.14 Echo communications.

the echo buffer. The echoing concept is illustrated in Fig. 6.14. Since teletypes have a switch which can directly connect the input and output mechanisms together so that when a key is pressed the character is printed, why go through the more expensive echo procedure? There are two main advantages: (1) The echoing process gives an error-detection ability. If the correct characters come back, the user knows that the characters were correctly received. The usefulness of this type of assurance for data input is clear. (2) The echoing process gives a code-conversion or translation capability by which a user can send in one character and receive the same, a different, or no character back.

For communications systems which use store and forward techniques, as discussed in Sec. 3.4.3, the delay time to send and echo a character may be sufficient to make echoing confusing because the user's input and output get so far out of phase. In this situation a half-duplex mode of transmission with the keyboard and printer mechanisms directly connected together may be better. Therefore, it is useful to design the system to accept both modes of operation, half duplex and full duplex with echoing. These modes can be switched by command to the system.

LINKING Another feature available on many systems allows terminals to be *linked* together on input or output or both.[10] Input linking is the situation where terminals are tied together by software so that keys struck on one terminal cause the same character to appear on the terminal and the one to which it is linked. Similarly output linking to a terminal causes a process output to appear on its own terminal and on the one to which it is linked. There are many uses for such a feature, for example, when instruction is taking place or two or more people are working together on a problem.

SIMPLE EDITING System response can be significantly speeded up if the teletype routines handle simple editing chores, rather than requiring the various subsystems to have separate editing routines. When a user hits the wrong key, he can send an editing character to cancel the last character or entire line. This frequently required editing task can be performed immediately without the expense of swapping in a subsystem if the terminal input routines can perform the task. A very large number of requests for service are of this simple editing type and require only a few instructions to perform. If these simple editing functions are performed within text editors, interactive compilers, and application routines, the system can be more easily overloaded due to the amount of traffic in and out of main memory to satisfy these simple requests. By using a small computer to interface to the communication lines, more involved editing functions, as well as file manipulation, can be performed without interference with the CPU. Use of a small communications computer also facilitates handling a wider variety of terminals and transmission speeds.

SUMMARY The system designer must pay particular attention to the design of the terminal communication system. A flexible and powerful system can be a great help to the user in his applications design and simplify the addition of new terminals as they appear on the market. Related to system functions are the concepts of buffering, simple editing, and suggestions for handling communication-line malfunctions. Techniques useful to the user include the ability to call the system no matter what his process is doing, use of break characters, the ability to link with other terminals, and the ability to communicate in half or full duplex (echoing). Using a small communications computer to handle terminal I/O seems to offer a number of advantages.

6.3 THE USER INTERFACE

Many routines associated with serving the interface between the user at a terminal and the system, are generally nonresident. The interface with the user and other nonresident routines are lumped together in the XDS-940 system in a reentrant procedure called the *executive*. The Multics system consists of segments, some of which are locked in core, *resident segments*, and others of which are available on call, *nonresident segments*. The particular segment interfacing with the user is called the *command system*.

Timesharing commands are available:

1   To log in and out of the system
2   To create, destroy, and manipulate files
3   To gain access to subsystems (subsystems may also have a command language of their own)
4   To determine system status

Privileged commands are usually available to the operator:

5   To define new users, delete users, change user privileges, access accounting information, and access more detailed system status information than is available to the general user

When a user logs in to the system, various tables are set up for him and the command system is made available to him. The command system is written with reentrant code, and logically each user thinks he has a private copy of the command system. The user can gain access to the command system at any time, even though he may be communicating with a subsystem or one of his own programs, by pressing a character conventionally assigned by the system for this task. When the teletype-handling routines "see" this character, transfer is made to the routines required to bring the command system into memory if it is not already there.

The command system collects a string of characters forming a command, decodes the command, and transfers to the routine for handling the decoded command. Any arguments for the command are passed to the routine also. The routine to handle the command may handle the command directly or create a process to perform the function.

For example, if the command is a call for a subsystem, the subsystem is assigned to the user by setting up the appropriate memory tables of the calling user, and if the subsystem is not in core, it is then read into core by calls to the appropriate I/O routines. Information required to set up a subsystem is stored in special tables.

The command system is most naturally looked at as an interpreter for a special programming language, the command language. If this point of view is adopted, as in Multics, the notion of a command-language program follows. There are many situations where a user may require a sequence of commands interspersed with interactions to accomplish some task. An example is loading into main memory, assembly, and loading onto a drum the files necessary to create a system. If a command-language program can be written and stored as a file and then the command-language interpreter instructed to execute this file, effort can be saved. This approach also allows simplified procedures to be developed for accessing special purpose programs to be used by people who do not need to know the details of the command language. Design of a command language, both syntax and features, should be given considerable care, because the command language is one of the user's main points of contact with the system. All aspects of the user interface to the system should be considered carefully from the point of view of ease of use and ease of learning.[9]

REFERENCES

1   **Daley, R. C., and P. G. Neumann:** A General Purpose File System for Secondary Storage, *AFIPS Conf. Proc., Fall Joint Computer Conf.,* vol. 27, 1965.
2   **Organick, E. I.:** A Guide to Multics for Subsystem Writers, *Project MAC Doc.,* March, 1967.

3   **Daley, R. C., and J. B. Dennis:** Virtual Memory Processes, and Sharing in MULTICS, *Commun. ACM*, vol. 11, no. 5, p. 306, May, 1968.

4   **Corbato, F. J., and J. H. Saltzer:** Some Considerations of Supervisor Program Design for Multiplexed Computer Systems, *IFIP Conf. Proc., Edinburgh*, August, 1968.

5   **Oppenheimer, G., and K. P. Clancy:** Considerations for Software Protection and Recovery from Hardware Failures in a Multiaccess, Multiprogramming, Single Processor System, *AFIPS Conf. Proc., Fall Joint Computer Conf.*, vol. 33, pt. 1, pp. 29–37, 1968.

6   **Madnick, S. E.:** A Modular Approach in File System Design, *AFIPS Conf. Proc., Spring Joint Computer Conf.*, vol. 34, pp. 1–13, 1969.

7   **Sutherland, W. R., and J. W. Forgie:** Graphics in Time-sharing: a Summary of the TX-2 Experience, *AFIPS Conf. Proc., Spring Joint Computer Conf.*, vol. 34, pp. 629–635, 1969.

8   **Denning, Peter J.:** Effects of Scheduling on File Memory Operations, *AFIPS Conf. Proc., Spring Joint Computer Conf.*, vol. 30, pp. 9–21, 1967.

9   **Hargraves, R. F., Jr., and A. G. Stephenson:** Design Considerations for an Educational Time-sharing System, *AFIPS Conf. Proc., Spring Joint Computer Conf.*, vol. 34, pp. 657–664, 1969.

10   **Lampson, B. W., et al.:** A User Machine in a Time-sharing System, *Proc. IEEE*, December, 1966.

11   **Ossana, J. F., et al.:** "Communication and Input/Output Switching in a Multiplex Computing System, *AFIPS Conf. Proc., Fall Joint Computer Conf.*, vol. 27, pp. 231–242, 1965.

12   **Ver Hoef, Edward W.:** Design of a Multi-level File Management System, *Proc. ACM Natl. Conf. 1966*, p. 75.

13   **Wilkes, M. V.:** "Time-sharing Computer Systems," American Elsevier Publishing Company, Inc., New York, 1968.

14   **Hoffman, L. J.:** Computers and Privacy: A Survey, *ACM Computing Surv.* vol. 1, no. 2, pp. 85–103, June, 1969.

15   **Dodd, G. G.:** Elements of Data Management Systems, *ACM Computing Surv.* vol. 1, no. 2, pp. 117–133, June, 1969.

16   **Lichtenberger, W. W., and M. W. Pirtle:** A Facility for Experimentation in Man-Machine Interaction, *AFIPS Conf. Proc., Fall Joint Computer Conf.*, vol. 27, pp. 589–598, 1965.

17   **Smith, M. G., and W. A. Notz:** Large-scale Integration from the User's Point of View, *AFIPS Conf. Proc., Fall Joint Computer Conf.*, vol. 31, pp. 87–94, 1967.

18   **Ha, E. P. L.:** Unpublished notes on time-sharing file systems, Shell Development Co., 1968.

chapter SEVEN

Measurement, reliability, and recovery

7.1 SYSTEM MEASUREMENT AND EVALUATION

7.1.1 Introduction The design process requires a continuous series of decisions. The design of a timesharing system requires deciding which functions to implement in hardware and which to implement in software. After these decisions are made, many more are required in determining how the hardware and software goals are to be met. All along the way the designer is faced with cost, generality, speed, and other tradeoffs.

When the design is completed and implementation is under way, the components, modules, and final system must be tested and evaluated. In general, the multiple interactions of the modules, in such complicated systems as we are studying here, cannot be fully anticipated at design time. Therefore, even after the system is logically correct, there will probably be room for performance improvement. Since each installation has a different environment, tuning to that installation, in terms of choosing the configuration and resource-allocation algorithm parameters, may take place. When the workload at the installation grows or varies, further decisions about reconfiguration may be called for. Configuring a system is a difficult design problem not generally well understood. Finally, the original designers may want to analyze the results of their efforts and start the process over again for the next generation of systems.

How are the required decisions and evaluations to be made?   The answer is with measurement and evaluation at each step along the way.[1-3] The comments to follow are based on the experience documented in the three references just cited.   One can view the design process as consisting of a theoretical or conceptual component and an experimental component with a constant iteration between them.   The theoretical component consists of the designer's hypothesis or concept of how the system or module under consideration is to work.   The experimental component consists of measuring how the system actually does work.   These measurements may alter his understanding and create the need for further measurement.

Measurement, and the interpretation of the numbers which result, is a difficult task which may lead only to erroneous conclusions if the person doing the measuring does not have a clear understanding of how he *thinks* the system works.   The generation of numbers by one means or another is easy; gaining insight from these numbers requires careful thought and planning.   One cannot emphasize strongly enough that theoretical or conceptual understanding or measurement alone is not sufficient.   Theoretical analysis may solve a nonexistent or minor problem while overlooking the important one.[3]   Measurement without an understanding of what is being measured and the expected results might overlook important parameters or result in meaningless numbers.

The complexity of timesharing and other multiprogramming systems has created a need for great efforts in developing measurement and evaluation tools.   Designers in the past, we feel, have relied too often on primitive component-oriented tools in the design process; rarely could they justify or fully evaluate the correctness of many of their decisions.   Only since the middle 1960s have papers been published describing measurement and evaluation techniques meeting the needs of system designers.   Much further effort is required because the design and application of systems seem to have outpaced their full understanding and evaluation.   In this chapter, we outline some of the concepts and experience emerging in this important field.

The first principle is that measurement and evaluation are to take place throughout the life of the system, from early design phases to sale, configuration, installation, and reconfiguration.   The proper measurement "hooks" required at each stage must be designed into the system from the earliest stages, so that measurement and evaluation are natural parts of the life cycle of the system.   In order to place these measurement hooks in the system, the designer will have to be very clear about his design goals and his understanding of how he expects his design to achieve these goals.   This process leads to a major indirect benefit of designing measurement and evaluation techniques into the system from the beginning, namely, better understanding. It results because of the extra effort it requires toward clear and rigorous thinking to define what is to be measured. It means that the designers must understand how their modules or system *actually* works at each step. The direct benefit will be a better performing system.

Measurement techniques can usefully be grouped into two classes, hardware techniques and software techniques. Hardware techniques are further classed into standard features which can be used for measurement and special hardware-instrumentation techniques. Software techniques can be classed as simulation and analytical models or measurement processes within the system.

7.1.2 Hardware Measurement Standard hardware features were incorporated in early systems to simplify program debugging. The IBM-650 allowed one to set an address breakpoint by switches at the console. The machine ran until it reached this address and then stopped. The programmer could then examine the registers or dump memory for analysis. The IBM-704 and later systems had a *trapping-transfer* mode, in which the computer interrupted itself each time a transfer instruction was reached and transferred to a fixed location where the user program recorded the event. Similar features exist on current machines but usually are operable only from the maintenance panel. Similar software features exist in online debugging systems in timesharing systems.

These features are not very useful for system measurement. The first feature above is a manual process, and the second multiplies running times significantly. Even if one were willing to pay the price of time, this increase may alter the system timing so much that the measurements become meaningless. This result is very probable in the highly time-dependent timesharing systems because of the interaction of CPU timing, peripheral-unit timing, remote-terminal timing, and auxiliary-storage timing. To slow down one component, such as the CPU, may seriously distort the system. The concept to be understood here is that one's measurement technique must not seriously disturb the system if the numbers produced are to be meaningful. What "seriously disturb" means is not rigorously definable, but the designer must be aware of the potential dangers.

Since standard features have not proved very useful for measurement, designers have turned to special equipment, which is quite simple in concept but seems to require skill in application and in evaluating the results. A representative hardware measuring device is IBM's systems performance activity recorder (SPAR)[5] which consists of 256 high-impedance probes, like those used on an oscilloscope, which can be connected to circuit points to obtain logic pulses or levels; several counters; clocks; basic logic elements such as AND gates, OR gates, complement gates, flip-flops, and comparators; a plugboard; and the ability to store the counter contents on magnetic tape.

The probes can be connected to address lines, the instruction counter, mode flip-flops, or other control and information points. The probe signals, possibly in combination with a clock signal, are then routed through the logic elements by plugboard programming to create an event measure. The signal representing the event is plugged into a counter. The counters can be dumped to tape periodically or dumped to tape under event control. The SNUPER system at UCLA carries the above approach one step further by connecting the event signals and counters directly to a general purpose digital computer.[4] The computer can affect the logic by outputting to the collection device.

To see how we would measure some events of possible interest, consider the following examples. Assume we want to know the percent of time a unit like a CPU, channel or disk, is utilized. There is usually a flip-flop which outputs a *true* logic level when the unit is operating and a *false* logic level when the device is idle. Therefore, by attaching a probe to the output of this flip-flop and then to the input of an AND gate, with a clock signal on the other AND-gate input, we obtain a source of clock pulses only when the unit is operating. Now by attaching the output of the AND gate to a counter, we can count the number of pulses which occur during the unit operation. Attaching the clock lead directly to another counter gives a time base. By dividing the event counter by the time-base counter we know the fraction of utilization during the measuring period. Figure 7.1 illustrates this example.

Let us consider another example. Suppose we want to know what

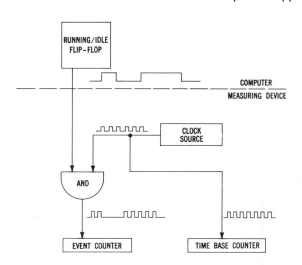

FIG. 7.1 Use of a measuring device to measure CPU utilization.

percent of time the system spends in a particular routine. We know the starting and ending addresses of the routine. We attach some probes to the memory-address lines. These signals are routed through the logic elements to produce one signal indicating that the process has entered the routine and another signal indicating that the process has left the routine. The first signal can be used to start a free-running counter and the second to stop the counter. Another counter can be used to record a time base. With this arrangement, we have obtained the desired measurement. More sophisticated measurements can be made, but these examples illustrate the basic principles.

The data collected on the output tape for any given experiment or experiments can later be processed by computer, and output-analysis reports can be printed. Since the principles of data reduction and interrelation of theory and measurement are the same for both the hardware and software techniques, we defer these subjects until Sec. 7.1.3.

The apparent advantages of this hardware-measurement technique are that it (1) effectively creates no system interference, (2) allows very fine measurements at the microsecond or submicrosecond level, as well as grosser measurements, such as percent CPU utilization, and (3) allows access to all parts of the system. The technique can be used to measure both hardware and software performance.

The apparent disadvantages of the hardware measurement technique are that (1) the experiments must be carefully planned with a knowledge of the hardware, (2) only a limited number of experiments can be undertaken at one time because the number of probes, counters, and logic elements is limited, (3) the plugboard program must be carefully debugged, (4) a person who knows the hardware is required to perform the measurement, (5) it may be difficult to obtain cause-and-effect relationships, and (6) a considerable amount of time is required to set up each experiment. In the next section we consider software techniques which are adequate for many measurements. They appear particularly easy to use when built into the system from the start. The hardware techniques may be easier to use on a limited basis for systems in which measurement hooks were not placed in the software during design. The hardware techniques are also more useful for very fine-grain sampling at the microsecond level or for measuring events which are not program-accessible.

7.1.3 Software Techniques

SIMULATION   The usefulness of simulation in timesharing system design is a matter of controversy because experience in this area is still limited. A number of misunderstandings seem to exist, particularly because of some bad initial experiences, perhaps resulting from simulations which tried to model the entire system at a uniformly fine level of detail, with the result that it usually took longer to write and debug these large simulation models than to write the skeleton system. Therefore, questions one would like the similator to help answer could not be answered at the time they occurred.

Designers have to have confidence in the validity of the simulation model in order to accept the data produced. Usually the writers of the simulation and the designers have been different people. This fact and the fact that the designers had no way of knowing for sure whether the simulator reflected the current state of the system created a lack of confidence in the model. The designers preferred to use the skeleton system as the simulator.

Simulation models can be produced at many levels of detail depending on the questions under consideration. One can produce a useful model by using gross levels of detail for many system components and the level of fine detail required on only one or more components in order to answer a specific class of questions. Scherr, for example, produced useful results with a rather coarse model.[6] Experience at General Electric, where the system designers could themselves sit down at a timesharing terminal and produce simple simulations to make specific decisions, found simulation a very useful approach.[2] Results from simulation did get used because they were timely and were performed by the designers themselves, thus generating confidence. Nielson's model at Stanford was quite useful in configuring Stanford's IBM 360/67 and in isolating potential bottlenecks.[7,8] Oppenheimer and Weizer used simple simulation models to evaluate alternate scheduling and paging algorithms.[9] Fine and McIsaac also used a simulation model to evaluate scheduling-algorithm and parameter choices. Their results were used in the design of the SDC system.[12,13] Pirtle successfully used simulation to study the design of memory and memory-bus organizations.[10] Other successful uses of simulation are being reported as experience in this field grows.[27]

The conclusion to be reached is that simulation can be a useful tool both during design and configuration planning but that like any other tool it must be used with discrimination. It is beyond the scope of this text to go into detail on how to design a simulation of a computer system, although a few comments can be made. One needs data to drive the simulator. If the system already exists, measurements can be taken of various parameters and these data used to study variations of the current system. If the system does not yet exist, one can use data collected on other systems properly scaled to the system under design,[11] or one can use standard probability distributions. The types of data that may be useful are[6] (1) distributions of user thinking time at the console for various types of functions, (2) distribution of process memory requirements, (3) distribution of processor time required to service a request, (4) distribution of time between blocking for terminal I/O or other I/O, and (5) distributions of shared-memory requirements. The exact data required depend on the system and simulation design. The simulator can pick parameters from these distributions for processes and use these data as input to the model. The output of the model will be information about response time, equipment utilization, and so forth. The important finding to date seems to be that relatively simple models are quickly developed and give useful answers to specific questions. Each question may require a separate model.

ANALYTIC MODELS There is increasing interest in developing analytic techniques to study various aspects of computer system design.[6,15-21,28] The mathematics involved may be as simple as determining the algebraic relationships of the variables under study, or it may require sophisticated techniques for studying random processes, such as queuing theory, mathematical programming, or the theory of Markov processes, techniques which are beyond the scope of this text.

The remaining discussion applies to random-process models. Analytic models of random processes generally use average values as their data input. They usually require many simplifying assumptions about the system under study in order to be mathematically tractable. The shape of real data distribution is often such that the use of average values may introduce serious distortions in the results. Similarly the many simplifying assumptions required may make it impossible to study many questions of interest. Analytical models seem primarily useful in studying gross phenomena and general effects.

The use of analytical modeling techniques in actual computer system design has not yet had the type of successes reported with simulation modeling. One reason may be the number of simplifying assumptions required, which reduce confidence in the model, and another reason may be lack of widespread knowledge of the mathematical techniques involved. The use of analytical techniques in actual design situations will probably increase as further experience is gained in their use.

INTERNAL-SYSTEM MEASUREMENT Internal-system measurement techniques can be classified into three main types, event counting, trace techniques, and sampling techniques. Events counting simply counts the number of times an event occurs in a given time. Trace techniques record data about events in the sequence in which they occur. Sampling techniques periodically interrupt the system and record the status of registers, cells, tables, other data structures, hardware units, and so forth. Before going on to discuss these techniques in more detail let us give an example of the interaction of theory and measurement in a problem analysis.

The question of interest in most analyses is: Where did the time go?   Once one has the answer, one can apply a judgment, based on one's theoretical understanding of the system, whether the answer is reasonable or not.   If the answer does not seem reasonable, one can then probe further to determine causes for the time allocation found.   For example, Cantrell and Ellison mention how they examined account data which gave the starting and terminating time for each program.[3]   The question asked was: Where did the remaining time go?

They hypothesized that the time went into overhead.   They had statistics available on CPU and I/O utilization of all system modules of the same type as those kept for user programs.   They could have written a program to produce polished reports from these data but instead followed a useful principle which says that *initial polished reports may be a waste of time* until the working of the system is more fully understood.   Therefore, they simply took a core dump of the tables containing system-utilization statistics and gave them a quick scan.   They found that overhead did not seem excessive, but, much to their surprise, they found the system to have a high idle time even though it was supposed to be heavily loaded.   Thus, the polished report was unnecessary.

Since the accounting-type data were not sufficient to determine why the high idle time was being obtained, the operating system was run in TRACE mode, in which major events, such as entering the scheduling algorithm allocating main memory, were captured by a trace collection program and each event was *stamped* with the time of day.   These data were buffered and eventually written onto tape.   Data for a 5-minute run totaled 350,000 entries, and 10,000 entries were printed and studied with several data-reduction methods.   At each step the theory of operation and actual measurements were compared.   Both the theory and data-reduction method were usually revised at each step.

This was hard detailed work but eventually yielded two complementary measurement methods suitable for other situations and uncovered a number of performance bottlenecks as well as the answer to the original question.

The important lessons to be drawn from the above examples are (1) the interaction of theory and measurement and (2) the usefulness in initial stages of avoiding preconceptions about how the data should be analyzed and reduced.   During the operating-system improvement cycle they found some 14 performance bottlenecks, which, when corrected, improved performance on customer sites of from 10 to 50 percent depending on the job mix.

As examples of the variety of types of analysis reports which might be of interest at different times refer to Fig. 7.2, which is modeled after a similar presentation in Estrin.[4]   These reports can be obtained from the data collected by hardware measurement or by the software measurement techniques to be discussed below.

We now return to discussing measurement techniques.   The design of measurement techniques into the system from the earliest stages is important to assure their easy availability to the developers and to assure that all parameters and statistics of interest can be easily measured.   For example, it may be important to know wait time of processes in various queues. This information may be difficult to obtain if it is not built into the system.

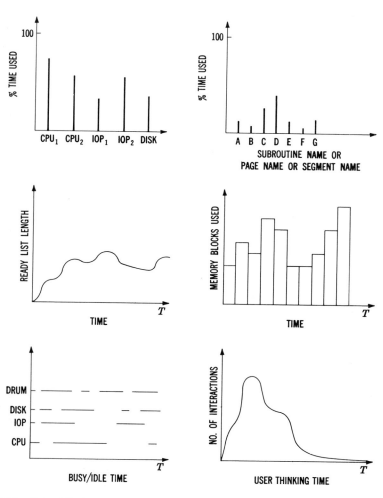

FIG. 7.2 Displays of statistics measured on computer systems.

As another example, one may want to know what processes are in main memory at a given time. This information is always available in the system, but if a method for collecting this statistic is not designed into the system initially, the implementation at a later point may take place in such a way that several tables have to be accessed to get the answer. This accessing might lead to significant interference, make collecting this information useless and the parameter in effect unmeasurable. Therefore, it seems important to design each system function so that it can be separately measured and studied without significant interference. We now consider the three types of measurements.

Event counting is a simple but useful technique. On entering a system function, a memory location is incremented. We can study the number of times a swap takes place, the number of disk accesses, or whatever event frequency is of interest. For example, Campbell and Heffner found that a system program priority had been set incorrectly and was causing too many swaps.[2] Without event counters they probably would not have discovered this, because there were no exterior symptoms, except decreased performance. Periodically these event counters can be read out onto the disk or tape and reset.

Event tracing is useful during both logical debugging and performance measurement and improvement. The basic concept is to record a code for the event and other data, such as the time when an event occurs. Campbell and Heffner list some 50 events which they trace in GE's GECOS III operating system.[2] Each event results in the recording of two words of data along with the event code. Examples of data collected, varying with the different events, are time of day, queue length, job identification, device number, and process number.

The trace of each event can be turned on or off. The trace data are collected in a large circular table which keeps a record of the last N events. Provision is also made for writing the trace events out on tape for the later analysis. The trace mechanism should be implemented in a uniform way so that new traces can be added or different data collected with a given event. Event tracing can produce large quantities of data. For analysis purposes, reports can be published counting events from trace information, giving elapsed time between consecutive events or elapsed time between similar events, sorted according to job identification or other parameters. Many other report formats are also possible depending on the question under consideration.

Sampling techniques are easy to use, powerful, and applicable to both system and user programs. The only requirement is an interval timer. The finer the timer interval possible, the more detailed the studies of system behavior can be. Theoretically, the interrupt should occur at some random or periodic time interval which is known to be statistically independent of any pattern which may exist in the program under study. In practice, synchronization between a program and the interval-timer interrupt is unlikely in a timesharing system, because of the random nature of program run times due to other programs in the environment competing for service. If synchronization occurs, the sampling interval can be modified.

At the sampling interval, one can enter the system and record hardware unit, queue, or other status information. For both system and user programs one can record the program-counter contents. Using the idea that the frequency with which the program counter is within a given instruction sequence is proportional to the total time spent in that sequence, one can isolate program bottlenecks or program areas where it is worthwhile spending extra effort in coding efficiency. Data-reduction programs are necessary to analyze the quantity of data collected and produce a histogram of time spent in various sections of the program. Because symbol tables are not usually available to the analysis programs, the histogram is in numerical addresses; the user must correlate the results with his core map given on the compile listing.

This discussion covers analysis of system or user program-time distributions. A similar analysis can be performed on hardware-unit utilization, time spent in disk seeks, queue lengths, or any other parameter collected at the sample time. Interference with the system using the sampling technique depends on the sampling interval and the amount of data collected at each point.

7.1.4 Summary The motivation for measurement and analysis has been given, and the designer has been urged to design measurement facilities into his system right from the earliest stages of the design. The importance of theoretical and measurement phases in evaluation has been emphasized. It is easy to collect data but often difficult to interpret their meaning. A useful question to be asked about a statistic to be collected is: What decision is affected by the statistic? This approach is also useful in questioning the need for a simulation. A useful discipline is to make up some mock data of the type to be produced by the simulator or measurement and then see if they can be meaningfully used. At the same time one should carefully consider the report format in which the data are to be supplied by the computer and the device on which the data should be reported. A core dump, for rough scanning, may be sufficient, or perhaps a more polished report is required. It may be appropriate to print a table as a report, or it may be more useful to print a histogram or other graphical output. An online cathode-ray tube with proper display format may enable the designer to get a better feel for the dynamic aspects of the parameters under study or may be more usable by the computer operator when the system is finally completed and delivered.

A number of hardware and software measurement concepts were discussed which seem to be desirable parts of every system designer's collection of techniques. These techniques in one version or another will appear more frequently in existing systems.

7.2 RELIABILITY, MAINTENANCE, AND RECOVERABILITY

7.2.1 Introduction To say that a timesharing system should be reliable, easy to maintain, and able to recover gracefully if a failure occurs, is clearly to state the obvious. It is useful, however, to review briefly some of the problems and approaches encountered in achieving these goals. When earlier systems used for batch processing failed, little damage was done other than that of causing a delay in returning a job to a user. In a timesharing system, on the other hand, a user may have considerable effort invested at a console which can be destroyed if a system failure occurs. The user expects the system to run when scheduled. He expects the file system to work perfectly, because his files represent his efforts at his console. If failure should occur, he expects the system to recover in such a manner that he can resume where he left off at the time of failure.

Failures can be of two types, hardware failures and software failures. Timesharing systems (particularly the larger ones, like Multics) may have considerably more hardware than comparable batch systems, and thus high reliability may be harder to achieve. Since timesharing systems may exercise auxiliary storage units and other devices more vigorously than other systems, marginal components or designs are bound to create difficulties. The very close coupling of hardware and software systems makes it difficult to determine where responsibility for trouble lies. The software systems are complex and usually designed and written by several people and are thus difficult to test under all conditions before being released for use.

These facts mean that one must design timesharing systems under the assumption that failures will occur, even after considerable development and testing. Techniques, both hardware and software, should probably be designed into the system from the earliest design stages to increase reliability in the presence of malfunctions, help isolate failure sources, and in case of failure recover smoothly with minimum interference to the user. This area of study is difficult but developing rapidly. In this section, we discuss some useful developing concepts.

7.2.2 Hardware Reliability The types of hardware failures that must be contended with include processor or memory malfunctions, power failures or transients, unreadability of data on direct-access devices, and peripheral-unit malfunctions. The best approach to reliability is clearly to design the simplest logical units which will perform the desired functions. The design should probably be a worst-case design to assure that no component, electrical or mechanical, is required to operate near its overload point. It is good practice for modules to contain proper interfaces so that failures in one module do not create electrical or mechanical conditions which can spread to other modules and so that failed modules can easily be removed from the system.

The use of error-detection and correction codes is common to check data transfers between main memory, CPU, auxiliary storage, and peripherals.[23] Codes which are preserved under arithmetic operations are also being used to check arithmetic transformations as well.[23] Error checking is useful in locating failing units and in enabling hardware and software techniques to be employed in masking or recovering from such failures. An example of masking technique is instruction retry or data-transmission retry after software or hardware analysis shows retry is feasible.[23,24]

A common approach to increasing reliability is to use hardware redundancy, which can be applied at many levels in the design, from duplicating logical gates to duplicating major functional units. The latter approach is the most common in commercial computing equipment. The Multics system shown in Fig. 3.4 is an example of such an approach. In this system, duplicate information paths exist from I/O equipment to the two processors. Either processor can handle the system functions. The increase in performance of such dual systems is not well known as yet but is not estimated to be near the theoretically possible 100 percent figure. The limitation on performance increase is caused by the hardware and software interlocks which must be set to avoid having the multiple processors interfere with each other. Performance increase is not usually the motivation for such systems, however. The idea is to enable a crippled system to continue to provide some reduced level of service in case of a failure.

Another type of duplication designed into single-processor versions of IBM 360/67 and the GE-645 is multiple data paths to auxiliary storage and some peripheral devices. For example, one could expand Fig. 3.4 to show a duplicate path from each GIOC to several devices. Thus, if one GIOC fails, another path to the device exists. Similarly, each device could have two controllers. When a system module fails, the operator or system can reconfigure the system by altering appropriate system tables and switches. The failed device can then be repaired. This idea of removing failed units also applies to memory banks.

Memory protection is as useful for protecting the system from itself as for protecting the system from user processes. Organizing the system so that much of it can be made read-only or execute-only can help in early isolation of errors and in limiting damage.

The use of special maintenance panels and circuits which allow testing of the hardware during normal operation is now becoming common.

Special checking circuits to help locate failed components are important design additions.[23]   All these techniques have their place in helping to increase hardware reliability and must be considered in the system design from its earliest stages if they are to be effective.

There is one remaining hardware element requiring mention, namely, the power supply and environmental conditions.   The reliability of the electrical power supply is easily taken for granted, but it should receive careful attention both by the original system designer and by the installation.[22] Electrical power companies employ redundant power sources and lines to achieve high reliability, but electrical faults and line switching to correct faults create power transients which can affect high-speed circuitry.   Normal regulated power supplies are not necessarily sufficient to deal with power surges, spikes, frequency variations, and cycle losses which easily can affect high-speed circuits.   Use of special motor-generator battery systems to give smooth power sources is becoming common.

Because circuit sensitivity to temperature and humidity can also create reliability problems if air-conditioning facilities malfunction, temperature- and humidity-sensing devices within system cabinets can be employed to give warning of approaching danger.

7.2.3   Software Reliability

INTRODUCTION   Software techniques for increasing reliability, for providing smooth recovery, and for easing interference during maintenance are frequently interrelated and rather system-dependent.   However, we can extract a few concepts and examples to indicate the type of techniques which have been developed.   Let us consider CPU, memory, and system program failures.   Techniques for use with auxiliary storage were discussed in Sec. 6.1.7.

Common failure modes are to get stuck in a loop and to attempt to execute in forbidden memory areas.   Small failures, which in themselves are not serious, have a tendency to grow.   The goal is to detect malfunctioning as soon as possible, in order to localize damage and allow the greatest possibility of smoothly restarting.   Failures should affect a minimum number of users.

One way to achieve this goal is to incorporate special checking programs at critical points in the system.   The increased overhead, for the techniques to be discussed, seems low, and the gains in reliability and error-location assistance make them worthy of consideration.   The critical system information is contained in tables, queues, buffers, and special cells. If smooth recovery in case of failure is to be possible, and if we want to increase our ability to mask errors entirely, then top priority must go into protecting this information.

The basic requirement behind all error-detection and correction codes or techniques is redundancy of information. The redundancy required can be implicit in the system in the conventions, structure, and interrelations of the implementation, or the redundancy can be explicitly placed in the system for checking purposes. The designer can make use of both implicit and explicit redundancy. A number of common techniques illustrating these points are discussed. In general the most effective point for checking is at the entry point to the routines which access or modify a system table. This implies that if checking is to be easily implemented, all accesses to, or modifications of, tables should take place through common routines, rather than allowing scattered system routines to manipulate the tables.

AN EXAMPLE ILLUSTRATING IMPLICIT REDUNDANCY FOR CHECK-ING Let us consider an example of the use of implicit redundancy for error detection and correction. Many systems contain tables or queues in the form of threaded lists. A specific example is the scheduling queue structure of the XDS-940 system discussed in Sec. 5.2.6. It is quite common for hardware errors or malfunctioning programs to cause these lists to become unsewn or to get sewn into tight little loops. In the first case, the scheduling algorithm which moves down the list wanders off into another code and creates chaos. In the second case, a few processes get excellent service, and the remaining processes are effectively detached from the system. The second case may also result in a more serious malfunction.

When the system has been working, and even in early debugging stages, how the lists got unsewn or sewn improperly is mystifying and to isolate the offending hardware cause or program module is difficult. The mystery results because the scheduling algorithm may slowly move down the queue, executing several processes correctly before reaching the point of failure. At the point of failure, many other tables and cells have been changed and many processes have executed, thus leaving few clues to the cause. There may be too much damage to allow smooth recovery.

A technique which can be used to reduce and isolate the problem is to place a checking routine at the point where the lists are manipulated. This routine can check initially to determine how the list was sewn together at the point of insertion or deletion and therefore can determine how it should appear after the operation. If this checking routine finds one of the list elements pointing off into space or to a wrong element, a report can be made and corrective action can be taken.

Two obvious sources of error create the problem, a hardware failure which affects an address bit in a list pointer and an incorrect pointer passed to the list-manipulating routines by the calling program.

There is redundant information which can be used to check for these error sources. In the XDS-940 system all queue entries are blocks of cells within a given memory area. Therefore, all valid list pointers must point within this area. Further, the list pointer in each block is located at the same relative location within the block. This information can also be used to check the validity of a list pointer to be used as the basis for a list modification. This type of redundant information gives a powerful error-detection ability. The exact details of the detection are clearly system-dependent, but the principle can probably be widely applied.

Assuming that an error was detected, the following XDS-940 recovery procedure can be used. The error would, of course, be logged, with appropriate information about the calling routine which passed the faulty pointer before proceeding. The queue elements are never physically moved, they are only placed in different queue positions by changing the pointers. Therefore, the system knows where every element is located. Even if the queue is unsewn, the system can run through the area containing the queue entries and sew the list back together. A correct pointer to the element originally being manipulated can be returned to the calling routine or appropriate system communication cell. At worst, the process under execution can be terminated and a message indicating this fact sent to the associated user's terminal. The remaining processes would be unaffected.

Another class of checks is possible with tables used for I/O device allocation. Instead of just checking to see whether a device is available and then proceeding, one can first issue an I/O status check to see whether in fact the device is free. Thus, one obtains redundant information. If the device is busy when the table indicates it is not busy, a malfunction has occurred at some point.

AN EXAMPLE ILLUSTRATING EXPLICIT REDUNDANCY FOR CHECKING The concept of a check sum is used in many types of data processing for checking purposes and can also be used to check system tables. The basic idea is the following. The contents of the table can be summed and this sum stored with the table. When an entry in the table is to be modified, the expected change in the check sum is computed. The table is then modified and a new check sum computed. The new check sum and the expected check sum are compared. If they differ, either there is an error in the table or an error was made in computing the check sum. If the original information has been saved, the process can be repeated under the assumption of a transient failure. If the error persists after repeated tries, it can be reported and appropriate action taken to try and avoid further damage.

The trick in using the check-sum method is to compute the expected check sum. If a bit table is being modified, one knows that the check sum is going to be increased or decreased by a power of 2, depending on bit position and whether a bit is being set to a 1 or a 0. This information can be used to compute the expected check sum. If one is replacing an entire word in a table, the value of the old contents can be subtracted from the new contents and the result can be added to the old check sum to produce the expected check sum. If one is replacing a field of a word, then one can create a copy of what the entry will be after the modification. This new entry can be logically compared against the old entry to see that all unmodified fields are the same in both words. Then the check-sum technique described for replacing an entire word can be used.

The reader may ask: Why go through this rather elaborate checking process when much less computation and referencing of memory is required just to go ahead and modify the table? The answer is that correct table contents are very important to proper system functioning and that a designer may consider the cost of checking worthwhile. The check-sum technique is particularly useful in guarding against transient hardware errors or memory-bit malfunctions. The check-sum technique can also catch gross software errors, such as storing in the wrong bit, field, or word. The check-sum technique can be used elsewhere in the system, for example, in system modules or files which are swapped. The check sum computed after the file or routine is in main memory can be compared against the sum stored with the file or routine. In this way one has a higher probability that the fresh copy or overlay is correct. To be replaceable with fresh copies modules must not modify themselves or contain data. The check-sum technique is especially useful on critical tables used for allocating auxiliary storage. Another technique used with auxiliary storage is to check the address generated to see whether it points to a legal area and/or block-starting location.

The clever designer who understands how his system is to work can think up many kinds of checks using the information redundancy implicit in the system or explicitly placed there by himself. The earlier the system can detect an error, the easier it will be to find its cause and mask it.

RECOVERY The goal in designing recovery procedures is to interfere with as few users as possible by returning to a state as close as possible to that which existed at the point of failure. A simple method of recovery is just to load a fresh copy of the system and initialize it. This approach violates the goals mentioned above because all users are affected. As mentioned above, it may be possible to detect an error early enough to make some sort of correction or recovery which does not disturb any users or possibly disturbs only one or a few. If the error is determined to be serious enough to require a fresh copy of the system, one should attempt to transplant the tables from the old system into the new system in order to try to recover smoothly.

A procedure for such a recovery used in several XDS-940 systems is to load a recovery program into memory in an empty area or areas containing read-only information which can be re-stored from auxiliary storage.   This recovery routine can move all user processes out of memory and then move the old system into the user area if the system must reside in a fixed area.   A fresh copy of the system can then be loaded.   The recovery procedure then examines the tables in the old system to see whether they can be salvaged.   This examination uses the implicit or explicit redundancy information in the system.   If the tables are determined to be undamaged or repairable, they are copied to the new system and the system restarted. Damaged table entries may affect one or a few users, but it may be possible to restart correctly for many users.   Again the details of how this is accomplished is highly system-dependent, but it can probably be applied to all systems.

When user's files are suspected or known to have been harmed by a CPU, memory, or system failure, an appropriate indicator should be placed in his file directory and a message printed out to him giving a warning when he next accesses the file.   Similarly a user whose process is terminated should be given a message.   If at all possible, users should not have their communication lines disconnected without an attempt to send them a message.

MAINTENANCE   In this section we discuss a number of concepts found useful in maintenance procedures.   The event-tracing technique discussed in Sec. 7.1.3 is also useful in system maintenance.   The trace can give the maintenance personnel helpful information about the system's recent computation path and assist in isolating the cause of failure.

When a software module is found to be in error, it may not mean that the system must be shut down.   The capability represented by the failed module may be removed from the user community, or if the failure is infrequent, the module can remain operative while a corrected version is prepared—usually from a terminal using all the system facilities.   When the module is prepared, a new copy of the system is generated for loading at a noncritical time.

One wants to apply the same philosophy whenever possible during hardware repair.   Machines are usually delivered with a set of diagnostic programs which exercise the hardware and can be used by maintenance engineers to locate trouble spots.   These routines usually require full control of the machine.   In a timesharing system, the goal is to have continuous availability of the system.   In a single-processor system, the failure of the processor usually takes the system out of use until the proper repairs are made.   However, there are many components of even a single-processor system which if they fail do not require the system to be removed from use by all users.   Failures of a memory box or noncritical I/O gear are examples of such noncatastrophic failures.

In such a situation, one desires diagnostic programs which can be run as special user programs and which enable the failure to be located and repaired without stopping the system. Many classes of failures which are not permanent but intermittent or data-dependent are difficult to isolate, but they may not require that the system be stopped if diagnostic routines can be run as special user programs. It is desirable for hardware facilities to be provided that allow maintenance engineers to place nonprogrammer-accessible circuitry in test states in a way which does not interfere with the general operation as seen by other console users.

Online test systems are conceptually straightforward.[25] They can be written as normal timesharing programs with access to special routines running in system mode and have the ability to lock sections of themselves in main memory when necessary. They can provide the maintenance engineer with a conversational language, enabling him to write diagnostic programs, as well as providing him with special library routines. They enable the engineer to remove a device from service, transmit test data to it, access its status registers, intercept interrupts generated by the device, and so forth. One of the requirements of a good diagnostic system is that it allow the maintenance engineer to place certain device functions under control of a program loop so that he can trace signals with an oscilloscope. Such a facility does not require full control of the machine. To be able to write such systems requires that the maintenance function be considered at design time. For example, execution of I/O instructions should not injure the system if the attached device is not functioning properly. The direct I/O instructions of the XDS-940 do not meet this requirement. The processor in execution of these instructions expects an acknowledgement signal from the addressed device before continuing. If this signal is not received, the machine is in effect permanently halted. Therefore, one can perform online debugging of devices only if the circuits interfacing the direct I/O lines and device are working. A better design would be to have the processor issue a direct I/O instruction, wait a fixed time, and then skip if an acknowledgement signal is not received. This should allow the interface to be exercised online without stopping the system.

7.2.4 Summary Since the designer must assume that hardware and software malfunctions will occur, he must implement mechanisms into the system from its earliest design stages. Increasing reliability is achieved through careful design, and testing, and redundancy. Redundant hardware units or subunits can be used, redundant codes can be used to check information transmission and arithmetic, explicit redundant information can be used in software routines, such as check sums, and implicit redundant information can be used by software-checking routines. Much effort has been spent on developing hardware and coding redundancy techniques, and a large body of literature and experience is available.

Only recently has similar attention been turned to developing redundancy techniques for use in the software system. It was pointed out that the system is full of implicit redundant information, which can be used by the clever designer. Protection of system tables is most important if smooth recovery is to be possible. In order to use the redundant information effectively, access to system tables must be made through a single routine.

The goal on recovery is to return to a state as close as possible to that which existed at the time of failure. Users whose processes or files are affected by a failure should be properly informed.

Maintenance procedures should be developed which allow maintenance to proceed in parallel with other uses of the system whenever possible. This should be the approach for both hardware and software maintenance.

The elements of system design discussed in this chapter require further research and development.

REFERENCES

1   **Calingaert, Peter:** System Performance Evaluation: Survey and Appraisal, *Commun. ACM*, vol. 10, no. 1, pp. 12–18, January, 1967.

2   **Campbell, D. J., and W. J. Heffner:** Measurement and Analysis of Large Operating Systems during System Development, *AFIPS Conf. Proc., Fall Joint Computer Conf.*, vol. 33, pp. 903–914, 1968.

3   **Cantrell, H. N., and A. L. Ellison:** Multiprogramming System Performance Measurements and Analysis, *AFIPS Conf. Proc., Spring Computer Conf.*, vol. 32, pp. 213–221, 1968.

4   **Estrin, G., et al.:** SNUPER COMPUTER: A Computer in Instrumentation Automation, *AFIPS Conf. Proc., Spring Joint Computer Conf.*, pp. 645–656, 1967.

5   **Schulman, Franklin D.:** Hardware Measurement Device for IBM System/360 Time Sharing Evaluation, *Proc. ACM Natl. Conf. 1967*, pp. 103–109.

6   **Sherr, A. L.:** An Analysis of Time-shared Computer Systems, *MIT Project MAC Doc.* MAC-TR-18, Ph.D. thesis, June, 1965.

7   **Nielson, N. R.:** Computer Simulation of Computer System Performance, *Proc. ACM Natl. Conf. 1967*, pp. 581–590.

8   **Nielson, N. R.:** The Simulation of Time-sharing Systems, *Commun. ACM*, vol. 10, no. 7, pp. 397–412, July, 1967.

9   **Oppenheimer, G., and N. Weizer:** Resource Management for a Medium Scale Time Sharing Operating System, *Commun. ACM*, vol. 11, no. 5, p. 313, May, 1968.

10   **Pirtle, N. W.:** Intercommunication of Processors and Memory, *AFIPS Conf. Proc., Fall Joint Computer Conf.*, vol. 31, pp. 621–633, 1967.

11   **Rehmann, Sandra L., and Sherbie G. Gangwere, Jr.:** A Simulation Study of Resource Management in a Time-sharing System, *AFIPS Conf. Proc., Fall Joint Computer Conf.*, vol. 33, pt. 2, pp. 1411–1430, 1968.

12   **Fine, G. H., and P. V. McIsaac:** Simulation of a Time-sharing System, *Management Sci.*, vol. 12, no. 6, pp. B180–B194, February, 1966.

13 **Schwartz, J. I., and C. Weissman:** The SDS Time-sharing System Revisited, *Proc. ACM Natl. Conf. 1967*, pp. 263–271.

14 **Hellerman, H.:** Some Principles of Time-sharing Scheduler Strategies, *IBM Systems J.*, vol. 8, no. 2, pp. 94–117, 1969.

15 **Belady, L. A., and C. J. Kuehner:** Dynamic Space-sharing in Computer Systems, *Commun. ACM*, vol. 12, no. 5, pp. 282–288, May, 1969.

16 **Belady, L. A.:** A Study of Replacement Algorithms for a Virtual Storage Computer, *IBM Systems J.*, vol. 5, no. 2, pp. 78–101, 1966.

17 **Babcock, J. D.:** A Brief Description of Privacy Measures in the RUSH Time-sharing System, *AFIPS Conf. Proc., Spring Joint Computer Conf.*, vol. 30, pp. 301–302, 1967.

18 **Fenichel, R. R., and A. J. Grossman:** An Analytic Model of Multiprogrammed Computing, *AFIPS Conf. Proc., Spring Joint Computer Conf.*, vol. 34, pp. 717–721, 1969.

19 **Sherr, A. L.:** Analysis of Storage Performance and Dynamic Relocation Techniques, IBM doc. Tr-000-1494, 1967.

20 **Denning, Peter J.:** Effects of Scheduling on File Memory Operations, *AFIPS Conf. Proc., Spring Joint Computer Conf.*, vol. 30, pp. 9–21, 1967.

21 **Denning, Peter J.:** The Working Set Model for Program Behavior, *Commun. ACM*, vol. 11, no. 5, May, 1968.

22 **Cheek, R. C.:** Fail-safe Power and Environmental Facilities for a Large Computer Installation, *AFIPS Conf. Proc., Fall Joint Computer Conf.*, vol. 33, pt. 1, pp. 51–56, 1968.

23 **Conti, C. J., et al.:** Structural Aspects of the System/360, Model 85, *IBM Systems J.*, vol. 7, no. 1, pp. 2–29, 1968.

24 **Higgins, Alan N.:** Error Recovery through Programming, *AFIPS Conf. Proc., Fall Joint Computer Conf.*, vol. 33, pt. 1, pp. 39–43, 1968.

25 **Nelson, G. W.:** OPTS-600: On-line Peripheral Test System, *AFIPS Conf. Proc., Fall Joint Computer Conf.*, vol. 33, pt. 1, pp. 45–50, 1968.

26 **Oppenheimer, G., and K. P. Clancy:** Considerations for Software Protection and Recovery from Hardware Failures in a Multi-access Multiprogramming, Single Processor System, *AFIPS Conf. Proc., Fall Joint Computer Conf.*, vol. 33, pt. 1, pp. 29–37, 1968.

27 **Merikallio, Reino A.:** Simulation Design of a Multiprocessing System, *AFIPS Conf. Proc., Fall Joint Computer Conf.*, vol. 33, pt. 2, 1968.

28 **McKinney, J. M.:** A Survey of Analytical Time-sharing Models, *ACM Computing Surv.*, vol. 1, no. 2, pp. 105–116, June, 1969.

Bibliography

Amdahl, G.: Unpublished simulation study, IBM Corporation, 1965.

Anderson, G. B., et al.: Design of a Time-sharing System Allowing Interactive Graphics, *Proc. ACM Natl. Conf. 1968*, pp. 1–6.

Arden, B. W.: The Role of Programming in a Ph.D. Computer Science Program, *Commun. ACM*, vol. 12, no. 1, pp. 31–37, January, 1969.

———— **et al.:** Program and Addressing Structure in a Time-sharing Environment, *J. ACM*, pp. 1–16, January, 1966.

Babcock, J. C.: A Brief Description of Privacy Measures in the RUSH Time-sharing System, *AFIPS Conf. Proc., Spring Joint Computer Conf.*, vol. 30, pp. 301–302, 1967.

Badger, G. F., Jr., and E. A. Johnson: The Pitt Time-sharing System for the IBM System 360, *AFIPS Conf. Proc., Fall Joint Computer Conf.*, vol. 33, pt. 1, pp. 1–16, 1968.

Belady, L. A.: A Study of Replacement Algorithms for a United Storage Computer, *IBM Systems J.*, vol. 5, no. 2, pp. 78–101, 1966.

———— **and C. J. Kuehner:** Dynamic Space-sharing in Computer Systems, *Commun. ACM*, vol. 12, no. 5, pp. 282–288, May, 1969.

Bell, G., and M. W. Pirtle: Time-sharing Bibliography, *Proc. IEEE*, vol. 54, no. 12, p. 1764, December, 1966.

Bobrow, D. G., and D. L. Murphy: Structure of a LISP System Using Two-level Storage, *Commun. ACM*, vol. 10, no. 3, pp. 155–159, March, 1967.

Bryan, G. E.: JOSS 20,000 Hours at the Console: A Statistical Survey, *AFIPS Conf. Proc., Fall Joint Computer Conf.*, vol. 31, pp. 769–778, 1967.

————: Joss: User Scheduling and Resource Allocation, *The RAND Corporation*, *Mem.* RM-5216-PR, Santa Monica, January, 1967.

Calingaert, Peter: System Performance Evaluation: Survey and Appraisal, *Commun. ACM*, vol. 10, no. 1, pp. 12–18, January, 1967.

Campbell, D. R., and W. J. Heffner: Measurement and Analysis of Large Operating Systems during Development, *AFIPS Conf. Proc., Fall Joint Computer Conf.*, vol. 33, pp. 903–914, 1968.

Cantrell, H. N., and A. L. Ellison: Multiprogramming System Performance Measurement and Analysis, *AFIPS Conf. Proc., Spring Joint Computer Conf.*, vol. 32, pp. 213–221, 1968.

Cheek, R. C.: Fail-safe Power and Environmental Facilities for a Large Computer Installation, *AFIPS Conf. Proc., Fall Joint Computer Conf.*, vol. 33, pt. 1, pp. 51–56, 1968.

Coffman, E. G., and L. C. Varian: Further Experimental Data on the Behavior of Programs in a Paging Environment, *Commun. ACM*, vol. 11, no. 7, p. 471, July, 1968.

—————— **and L. Kleinrock:** Computer Scheduling Methods and Their Counter Measures, *AFIPS Conf. Proc., Spring Joint Computer Conf.*, vol. 32, p. 11, 1968.

Comfort, W. T.: A Computing System Design for User Service, *AFIPS Conf. Proc., Fall Joint Computer Conf.*, vol. 27, pp. 619–626, 1965.

Conti, C. J., et al.: Structural Aspects of the System/360, Model 85, *IBM Systems J.*, vol. 7, no. 1, pp. 2-29, 1968.

Corbato, F. J.: PL/I as a Tool For System Programming, *MIT Project MAC Mem.* MAC-M-378, July 2, 1968.

——————: A Paging Experiment with the Multics System, *MIT Project MAC Mem.* MAC-M-384, July 8, 1968.

——————: Sensitive Issues in the Design of Multi-use Systems, *MIT Proj. MAC Mem.* MAC-M-383, Dec. 12, 1968.

——————: System Requirements for Multiple Access Timeshared Computers, Project MAC Document MAC-TR-3.

—————— **et al.:** An Experimental Time-sharing System, *AFIPS Conf. Proc., Spring Joint Computer Conf.*, vol. 21, pp. 335–344, 1962.

—————— **and V. A. Vyssotsky:** Introduction and Overview of the Multics System, *AFIPS Conf. Proc., Fall Joint Computer Conf.*, vol. 27, pp. 185–196, 1965.

—————— **and J. H. Saltzer:** Some Considerations of Supervisor Program Design for Multiplexed Computer Systems, *IFIP Conf. Proc. Edinburgh, August,* 1968.

"CP/CMS Program Logic Manual," IBM Cambridge Scientific Center, Cambridge, Mass., 1969.

Curriculum 68, *Commun. ACM*, vol. 11, no. 3, pp. 151–197, March, 1968.

Daley, R. C., and J. B. Dennis: Virtual Memory Processes, and Sharing in MULTICS, *Commun. ACM*, vol. 11, no. 5, p. 306, May, 1968.

—————— **and P. G. Neuman:** A General Purpose File System for Secondary Storage, *AFIPS Conf. Proc., Fall Joint Computer Conf.*, vol. 27, pp. 213–229, 1965.

Denning, Peter J.: Effects of Scheduling on File Memory Operations, *AFIPS Conf. Proc., Spring Joint Computer Conf.*, vol. 30, pp. 9–21, 1967.

——————: The Working Set Model for Program Behavior, *Commun. ACM*, vol. 11, no. 5, pp. 323–333, May, 1968.

——————: Thrashing: Its Causes and Prevention, *AFIPS Conf. Proc., Fall Joint Computer Conf.*, vol. 33, pt. 1, 1968.

Dennis, J. B.: Segmentation and the Design of Multiprogrammed Computer Systems, *J. ACM*, vol. 12, no. 4, pp. 589–602, October, 1965.

—————— **and E. C. Van Horn:** Programming Semantics for Multiprogrammed Computations, *Commun. ACM*, vol. 9, no. 3, pp. 143–155, March, 1966.

Dijkstra, E. W.: Structures of the Multiprogramming System, *Commun. ACM*, pp. 341–346, May, 1968.

Dodd, G. G.: Elements of Data Management Systems, *ACM Computing Surv.*, vol. 1, no. 2, pp. 113–117, June, 1969.

Estrin, G., et al.: SNUPER COMPUTER: A Computer in Instrumentation Automation, *AFIPS Conf. Proc., Spring Joint Computer Conf.,* pp. 645–656, 1967.

Evans, D. C., and J. Y. LeClerc: Address Mapping and the Control of Access in an Interactive Computer, *AFIPS Conf. Proc., Spring Joint Computer Conf.,* vol. 30, pp. 23–30, 1967.

Evans, G. J., Jr.: Experience Gained from the American Airline SABRE System Control Program, *Proc. ACM Natl. Conf. 1967,* pp. 77–84.

Fenichel, R. R., and A. J. Grossman: An Analytic Model of Multiprogrammed Computing, *AFIPS Conf. Proc., Spring Joint Computer Conf.,* vol. 34, pp. 717–721, 1969.

Fikes, Richard E., et al.: Steps toward a General-purpose Time-sharing System Using Large Capacity Core Storage and TSS/360, *Proc. ACM Natl. Conf. 1968,* pp. 7–18.

Fine, G. H., et al.: Dynamic Program Behavior under Paging, *Proc. ACM Natl. Conf. 1966,* p. 223.

—————— **and P. V. McIsaac:** Simulation of a Time-sharing System, *Management Sci.,* vol. 12, no. 6, pp. B180–B194, February, 1966.

Flynn, Michael J., and Donald M. MacLaren: Microprogramming Revisited, *Proc. ACM Natl. Conf. 1967,* pp. 457–463.

Freeman, David N., and Robert R. Pearson: Efficiency vs. Responsiveness in a Multiple-services Computer Facility, *Proc. ACM Natl. Conf. 1968,* pp. 25–34B.

Freibergs, I. F.: The Dynamic Behavior of Programs, *AFIPS Conf. Proc., Fall Joint Computer Conf.,* vol. 33, pt. 2, pp. 1163–1168, 1968.

Gibson, C. T.: Time-sharing in the IBM System/360: Model 67, *AFIPS Conf. Proc., Spring Joint Computer Conf.,* vol. 28, p. 61, 1966.

Glaser, E. G., et al.: System Design of a Computer for Time-sharing Applications, *AFIPS Conf. Proc., Fall Joint Computer Conf.,* vol. 27, pp. 197–202, 1965.

Gold, M. M.: Time-sharing and Batch Processing: An Experimental Comparison of Their Values in a Problem Solving Situation, *Commun. ACM,* vol. 12, no. 5, pp. 249–259, May, 1969.

Graham, R. M.: Protection in an Information Processing Utility, *Commun. ACM,* vol. 11, no. 5, p. 365, May, 1968.

Hargraves, R. F., Jr., and A. G. Stephenson: Design Considerations for an Educational Time-sharing System, *AFIPS Conf. Proc., Spring Joint Computer Conf.,* vol. 34, pp. 657–664, 1969.

Hellerman, H.: Some Principles of Time-sharing Scheduler Strategies, *IBM Systems J.* vol. 8, no. 2, pp. 94–117, 1969.

Higgins, Alan N.: Error Recovery through Programming, *AFIPS Conf. Proc., Fall Joint Computer Conf.,* vol. 33, pt. 1, pp. 39–43, 1968.

Hobbs, W., et al.: The Baylor Medical School Teleprocessing System, *AFIPS Conf. Proc., Spring Joint Computer Conf.,* vol. 32, p. 31, 1968.

Hoffman, L. J.: Computers and Privacy: A Survey, *ACM Computing Surv.,* vol. 1, no. 2, pp. 85–103, June, 1969.

IBM Systems J. vol. 5, no. 1, 1966 (devoted to a description of OS/360).

Jackson, P. E., and C. D. Stubbs: A Study of Multi-access Computer Communications, *AFIPS Conf. Proc., Spring Joint Computer Conf.,* vol. 34, pp. 491–504, 1969.

Kay, R. H.: Management and Organization of Large Scale Software Development Projects, *AFIPS Conf. Proc., Spring Joint Computer Conf.,* vol. 34, pp. 425–433, 1969.

Kilburn, T., et al.: One-Level Storage System, *IEEE Trans.*, vol. EC-11, no. 2, p. 223, 1962.

Knuth, D. E.: Fundamental Algorithms: The Art of Computer Programming, Addison-Wesley Publishing Company, Inc., Reading, Mass., 1968.

Lampson, B. W.: Scheduling and Protection on Interactive Multi-processor Systems, *Univ. Calif. Berkeley Project Genie, Doc.* 40.10.150, Jan. 20, 1967.

————: A Scheduling Philosophy for Multi-processing Systems, *Commun. ACM*, vol. 11, no. 5, pp. 347–359, May, 1968.

————: Dynamic Protection Structures, *AFIPS Conf. Proc.*, vol. 35, *Fall Joint Computer Conf.*, 1969, pp. 27–38.

————: An Overview of the CAL Timesharing System, Computer Center, Univ. of Calif., Berkeley, 1969.

———— et al.: A User Machine in a Time-sharing System, *Proc. IEEE*, December, 1966, pp. 1766–1773.

Lauer, H. C.: Bulk Core in a 360/67 Time-sharing System, *AFIPS Conf. Proc., Fall Joint Computer Conf.*, vol. 31, pp. 601–611, 1967.

Le Clerc, Jean-Yves: Memory Structures for Interactive Computers, *Univ. Calif. Berkeley, Project Genie Doc.* 40.10.110, May, 1966.

Lichtenberger, W. W., and M. W. Pirtle: A Facility for Experimentation in Man-Machine Interaction, *AFIPS Conf. Proc., Fall Joint Computer Conf.*, vol. 27, pp. 589–598, 1965.

Litt, A. S.: TSS/360: A Time-shared Operating System, *AFIPS Conf. Proc., Fall Joint Computer Conf.*, vol. 33, pt. 1, pp. 15–28, 1968.

Madnick, S. E.: A Modular Approach in File System Design, *AFIPS Conf. Proc., Spring Joint Computer Conf.*, vol. 34, pp. 1–13, 1969.

Maurer, W. D.: An Improved Hash Code for Scatter Storage, *Commun. ACM*, vol. 11, no. 1, pp. 35–38, January, 1968.

McCullough, J. D., et al.: A Design for a Multiple User Multiprocessing System, *AFIPS Conf. Proc., Fall Joint Computer Conf.*, vol. 27, p. 611, 1965.

McGeachie, J. S.: A Flexible User Validation Language for Time-sharing Systems, *AFIPS Conf. Proc., Spring Joint Computer Conf.*, vol. 34, pp. 665–671, 1969.

McGee, W. C.: On Dynamic Program Relocation, *IBM Systems J.*, vol. 4, no. 3, p. 184, 1965.

McKinney, J. M.: A Survey of Analytical Time-sharing Models, *ACM Computing Surv.*, vol. 1, no. 2, pp. 105–116, June, 1969.

Merikallio, Reino A.: Simulation Design of a Multiprocessing System, *AFIPS Conf. Proc., Fall Joint Computer Conf.*, vol. 33, pt. 2, 1968.

Morris, D., and F. H. Summer: An Appraisal of the Atlas Supervisor, *Proc. ACM Natl. Conf. 1967*, pp. 59–76.

Morris, Robert: Scatter Storage Techniques, *Commun. ACM*, vol. 11, no. 1, pp. 38–44, January, 1968.

Motobayashi, S., et al.: The HITAC 5020 Time Sharing System, *Proc. ACM Natl. Conf. 1969*, pp. 419–429.

Nelson, G. W.: OPTS-600: On-line Peripheral Test System, *AFIPS Conf. Proc., Fall Joint Computer Conf.*, vol. 33, pt. 1, pp. 45–50, 1968.

Newport, C. B.: Small Computers in Data Networks, *AFIPS Conf. Proc., Spring Joint Computer Conf.*, vol. 34, pp. 773–775, 1969.

Nielson, N. R.: Computer Simulation of Computer System Performance, *Proc. ACM Natl. Conf. 1967*, pp. 581–590.

————: The Simulation of Time-sharing Systems, *Commun. ACM*, vol. 10, no. 7, pp. 397–412, July, 1967.

Oppenheimer, G., and N. Weizer: Resource Management for a Medium Scale Time Sharing Operating System, *Commun. ACM.*, vol. 11, no. 5, p. 313, May, 1968.

———— **and K. P. Clancy:** Considerations for Software Protection and Recovery from Hardware Failures in a Multi-access, Multiprogramming, Single Processor System, *AFIPS Conf. Proc., Fall Joint Computer Conf.*, vol. 33, pt. 1, pp. 29–37, 1968.

Organick, E. I.: A Guide to Multics for Subsystem Writers, *Project MAC Doc.* March, 1967.

Ossana, J. R., et al.: Communication and Input/Output Switching in a Multiplex Computing System, *AFIPS Conf. Proc., Fall Joint Computer Conf.*, vol. 27, 1965.

O'Sullivan, T. C.: Exploring the Time-sharing Environment, *Proc. ACM Natl. Conf. 1967*, pp. 169–176.

Pirtle, M. W.: Intercommunication of Processors and Memory, *AFIPS Conf. Proc., Fall Joint Computer Conf.*, vol. 31, pp. 621–633, 1967.

————: Modifications of the SDS-930 for the Implementation of Time-sharing, *Univ. Calif. Berkeley Project Genie Doc.* M-1, April 4, 1967.

Pyke, T. N., Jr.: Time-shared Computer Systems, *Advan. Computers*, vol. 8, 1967.

Randell, B., and C. J. Kuehner: Dynamic Storage Allocation Systems, *Commun. ACM*, vol. 11, no. 5, p. 297, May, 1968.

———— and ————: "Demand Paging in Perspective," *AFIPS Conf. Proc., Fall Joint Computer Conf.*, vol. 33, pt. 2, pp. 1011–1018, 1968.

Rehmann, Sandra L., and Sherbie G. Gangwere, Jr.: A Simulation Study of Resource Management in a Time-sharing System, *AFIPS Conf. Proc., Fall Joint Computer Conf.*, vol. 33, pt. 2, pp. 1411–1430, 1968.

Reiter, Allen: A Resource-allocation Scheme for Multi-user On-line Operation of a Small Computer, *AFIPS Conf. Proc., Spring Joint Computer Conf.*, vol. 30, pp. 1–7, 1967.

Rosen, Saul: Electronic Computer: A Historical Survey, *ACM Computing Surv.*, vol. 1, no. 1, pp. 7–36, March, 1969.

Rosin, Robert F.: Supervisory and Monitor Systems, *ACM Computing Surv.*, vol. 1, no. 1, pp. 37–54, March, 1969.

Sackman, H.: Time-sharing versus Batch Processing: The Experimental Evidence, *AFIPS Conf. Proc., Spring Joint Computer Conf.*, vol. 32, pp. 1–10, 1968.

Saltzer, J. H.: Traffic Control in a Multiplexed Computer System, MAC-TR-30, thesis, Massachusetts Institute of Technology, Cambridge, Mass., July, 1966.

Schulman, Franklin D.: Hardware Measurement Devices for IBM System/360 Time-sharing Evaluation, *Proc. ACM Natl. Conf., 1967*, pp. 103–109.

Schwartz, J., E. G. Coffman, and C. Weissman: A General Purpose Time-sharing Systems, *AFIPS Conf. Proc., Spring Joint Computer Conf.*, vol. 25, pp. 397–411, 1964.

Schwartz, J. I., and C. Weissman: The SDS Time-sharing System Revisited, *Proc. ACM Natl. Conf. 1967*, pp. 263–271.

"6700 Time-sharing Computer Reference Manual," Scientific Control Corporation, Carrollten, Texas, February, 1969 (additional information was also obtained at a public presentation of the 6700).

Shaw, J. C.: Joss: A Designer's View of an Experimental On-line Computing System, *AFIPS Conf. Proc., Spring Joint Computer Conf.*, vol. 26, p. 455, 1965.

Sherr, A. L.: Analysis of Storage Performance and Dynamic Relocation Techniques, *IBM Doc.* Tr-00-1494, 1967.

————: An Analysis of Time-shared Computer Systems, Ph.D. thesis, *MIT Project MAC Doc.* MAC-TR-18, June, 1965.

Smith, Arthur A.: Input/Output in Time-shared, Segmented, Multi-processor Systems, *MIT Project MAC Doc.* (thesis) MAC-TR-28, June, 1966.

Spier, M. J., and E. I. Organick: The Multics Interprocess Communication Facility, *Second ACM Symp. on Operating Systems Principles*, Princeton Univ., October, 1969.

Sutherland, W. R., and J. W. Forgie: Graphics in Time-sharing: A Summary of the TX-2 Experience, *AFIPS Conf. Proc., Spring Joint Computer Conf.*, vol. 34, pp. 620–635, 1969.

Trapnell, F. M.: A Systematic Approach to the Development of System Programs, *AFIPS Conf. Proc., Spring Joint Computer Conf.*, vol. 34, pp. 411–418, 1969.

Tucker, S. G.: Microprogram Control for System/360, *IBM Systems J.*, vol. 6, no. 4, pp. 222–241, 1967.

Varian, L. C., and E. G. Coffman: An Empirical Study of the Behavior of Programs in a Paging Environment, *ACM Symp. Operation System Principles*, October, 1967.

Ver Hoef, Edward W.: Design of a Multi-level File Management System, *Proc. ACM Natl. Conf. 1966*, p. 75.

Van Horn, E. C.: Computer Design for Asynchronously Reproducible Multiprocessing, Ph.D. thesis, *MIT Project MAC Tech. Rept.* MAC-TR-34, November, 1966.

Wald, B.: The Descriptor: A Definition of the B5000 Information Processing System, Burroughs Corp., Detroit, Mich., 1961.

Watson, R. W., et al.: A Display Processor Design, *AFIPS Conf. Proc., Fall Joint Computer Conf.*, vol. 35, 1969.

Wegner, P.: Machine Organization for Multi-programming, *Proc. ACM Natl. Conf. 1967*, pp. 135–150.

————: "Programming Languages, Information Structures and Machine Organization," McGraw-Hill Book Company, New York, 1968.

Weizer, N., and G. Oppenheimer: Virtual Memory Management in a Paging Environment, *AFIPS Conf. Proc., Spring Joint Computer Conf.*, vol. 34, pp. 240–254, 1969.

Wilkes, M. V.: The Best Way to Design an Automatic Calculating Machine, *Manchester Univ. Computer Inaugural Conf.*, Manchester, July, 1951, pp. 16–18.

————: Microprogramming, *AFIPS Conf. Proc., Fall Joint Computer Conf.*, vol. 12, pp. 18–19, 1958.

————: "Time-sharing Computer Systems," American Elsevier Publishing Company, Inc., New York, 1968.

————: A Model for Core Space Allocation in a Time-sharing System, *AFIPS Conf. Proc., Spring Joint Computer Conf.*, vol. 34, pp. 265–271, 1969.

Wood, T. C.: A Generalized Supervisor for a Time-shared Operating System, *AFIPS Conf. Proc., Fall Joint Computer Conf.*, vol. 31, pp. 209–214, 1967.

Ziegler, James R.: "Time-sharing Data Processing Systems," Prentice-Hall, Inc., Englewood Cliffs, N.J., 1967.

Index